GOOD CHEMISTRY

ALSO BY JULIE HOLLAND, MD

Ecstasy: The Complete Guide

Weekends at Bellevue: Nine Years on the Night Shift at the Psych ER

The Pot Book: A Complete Guide to Cannabis

*Moody Bitches: The Truth About the Drugs You're Taking, the Sleep
You're Missing, the Sex You're Not Having, and What's Really
Making You Crazy*

For my parents, Richard and Clare,
connected by good chemistry for sixty years and counting

This book contains advice and information relating to health care. It should be used to supplement rather than replace the advice of your doctor or another trained health professional. If you know or suspect you have a health problem, it is recommended that you seek your physician's advice before embarking on any medical program or treatment. All efforts have been made to assure the accuracy of the information contained in this book as of the date of publication. This publisher and the author disclaim liability for any medical outcomes that may occur as a result of applying the methods suggested in this book. The names and identifying characteristics of certain individuals have been changed to protect their privacy.

FIRST EDITION

Designed by Bonni Leon-Berman

Library of Congress Cataloging-in-Publication Data has been applied for.

ISBN 978-0-06-286288-4

20 21 22 23 24   LSC   10 9 8 7 6 5 4 3 2 1

GOOD CHEMISTRY

The Science of Connection, from

Soul to Psychedelics

JULIE HOLLAND, MD

HARPER WAVE

An Imprint of HarperCollins Publishers

They are one person, they are two alone,
they are three together, they are for each other.

—STEPHEN STILLS

CONTENTS

INTRODUCTION:
A UNIFIED THEORY
OF CONNECTION

Loneliness does not come from having no people
around you, but from being unable to communicate
the things that seem important to you.

—CARL JUNG

Soul isn't something psychiatrists bring up, certainly not
in professional settings. It wasn't always that way. After all,
"psychiatry" means the medical care of the psyche, which is
the Greek word for "soul." But in the early decades of this
science, as psychiatrists struggled to professionalize and gain
broader acceptance, they focused on the scientific method
and reproducible results. Talking about a statistically unver-
ifiable concept like the soul was frowned upon. And yet I
find myself using the word with my patients more and more.
There are times when nothing else fits. I used to apologize
before I said it, but I don't anymore.

Another word that's making a comeback is "psychedelic."
Drop the tie-dye, and it means "mind-manifesting." That's
not so bad, right? These medicines were being researched in
psychiatry throughout the fifties and sixties. But in 1971,

after hundreds of published papers showed thousands of safely treated research subjects, the Controlled Substances Act set severe restrictions on a huge shopping list of psychoactive substances because of increasingly widespread popular experimentation. They placed them in Schedule I, meaning they had no accepted medical use and a high potential for abuse. Because of this scheduling, nearly all research and development was shut down immediately. For the past fifty years, scientific study of these substances by any officially sanctioned institution was practically nonexistent.

That's been changing lately, as studies by persistent researchers have achieved startling results with conditions like depression, substance dependence, and post-traumatic stress disorder. Our own federal government has taken notice, labeling both MDMA (also known as Ecstasy or Molly) and psilocybin (the psychoactive chemical in "magic" mushrooms) as breakthrough therapies, setting in motion a sequence of regulatory events that could lead to their official reclassification in the near future. Some cities are already decriminalizing personal use of these drugs.

There's a reason words like "soul" and "psychedelic" are coming back into vogue now; they're key players in fixing a hole that is growing by the day. Focusing on the soul as we do the mind, through medically supervised psychedelic use, has the potential to bring us back into alignment with our true purpose, which is connection. Our brains are wired to reward a state of unity because it's how we survive, reproduce, and nurture our young. If these actions weren't immensely pleasurable, we'd die out as a species. We are social primates. In fact, our species is categorized as "obligatorily gregarious."

This means we have to be social in order to survive, and we are hardwired for connection.

This is where good chemistry comes in.

When two people hit it off right from the start, we say they have good chemistry. They connect; they mesh; they complement each other. Perhaps they even seem to become one. In physics, chemistry, and biology, opposites attract, creating a strong, unified whole. This sort of pair-bonding occurs throughout nature: in the animal kingdom during mating, when neurotransmitters dock onto receptors, when a tree and a mycelial network share resources (think of it as a mushroom internet), and when two atoms share their electrons to align in a chemical bond. Good chemistry is everywhere, pouring the foundation for strong connections.

When they occur in humans, these acts of bonding—of reliance and interdependence—ignite pharmacological fireworks in our brains. They are referred to as "affiliative behaviors" and are designed to reward us chemically, helping to ensure our survival. The more we lock into oneness, the better we feel. Being held in a lover's arms, holding a baby, and helping a neighbor can all trigger this satisfying sense of feeling hooked in. When we belong, we feel safe; we can relax. This is why we do it.

In the modern world, most of us have discovered ways to mimic that good chemistry without actually connecting, perhaps not even realizing it's only a workaround. We stay glued to our phones and it feels good—but not quite good enough. Synthetic substitutes don't work as well as natural ones. There is a great saying in addiction medicine: you can never get enough of something that almost works. This insatiability fuels the engine of addiction. When it comes to drugs, they don't completely scratch that itch, and some drug users will opt for quantity over quality, chasing that elusive high. When it comes to human connection, when we don't get what we need, we become compulsive in our consumption of nearly everything else. And I can see, nearly everywhere I look, that we are not getting what we need. Not even close.

There's a loneliness epidemic in this country. I witnessed it most acutely in my patients at Bellevue Hospital, where I spent nine years as the doctor in charge, running the weekend night shift at the psychiatric ER. But I also see it now, in my private practice patients in New York City. They don't have enough meaningful connections in their lives. And it hurts. One definition of "patient" is "one who suffers." Using that, I feel like I can diagnose the whole city. I see this sense of isolation on the streets and subways and trains of my commute. Most frightening of all, I now notice that same terror of loneliness in the searching eyes of babies faced with the back of a cell phone.

The vicious cycle of loneliness and being glued to our screens is the elephant in the room. We don't want to talk about it because then we will have to do something about it. Most of us are already waist-deep in our addiction and deeply in love with our devices. In fact, time spent on a screen can generate brain chemistry similar to infatuation and attachment, the two stages of falling and staying in love that we'll go over in more detail in chapter two.

We're a world in denial of our own digital dependence. We see it in our kids, we see it in ourselves, yet most of us do nothing. We simply don't want to stop, even though the message from the data is clear: more time alone with your glowing screen makes you more unhappy. (Several longitudinal studies of teenagers show a direct correlation, with unhappiness rising proportionally as screen time increases. In an unrelated study, it's curious to see that in adults, screen time is rising as they are having sex less frequently.) Taking on the world's traumas is too much for any of us to bear. We're not built for it. Heavy users of social media are more likely to be depressed and lonely, and a recent study showed that decreasing your screen time by even thirty minutes a day can help reduce these feelings.

We all know our screens aren't the answer. Everywhere people are starving for human connection, physical touch, even sustained eye contact. For millennia, we lived in multigenerational communities, but now over a quarter of Americans live alone—and nearly a quarter of people surveyed in the US and the UK reported they often or always felt lonely. Nearly one-half reported they often felt left out and didn't have meaningful connections with others. We are, collectively, suffering a spiritual crisis. And it's time to face it.

As a psychiatrist, I make my living off despair. I'm sad to report that business is booming. Prescriptions for antidepressants have risen by more than 400 percent over the past twenty years. Suicide rates are at a thirty-year high. Binge drinking is on the rise, as is liver failure from alcoholism. Drug overdoses, suicides, and deaths from alcohol are labeled "diseases of despair." And in truth, despair is having a string of banner years, because loneliness is a silent killer. Social isolation has a lethality on par with being obese, or with smoking about fifteen cigarettes a day.

Another reason our birth rate is in free fall and life

expectancy is down for the third year in a row (a trend not seen since World War I) is due to the deadliest drug crisis in our nation's history. Every day more than a hundred people die from opioid overdoses, many of them marginalized, ostracized, and isolated. These casualties of loneliness, and of our nation's drug wars, eclipse the number of dead from our forever wars. For each of the past ten years, the number of overdose deaths has equaled or exceeded the total number of American casualties during the entire Vietnam War. When people feel helpless, they get depressed. When they're hopeless, they're more likely to want to die. Currently, our veterans, nearly one every hour of every day, are taking their own lives. There are more veteran suicides each year than the total number of American military deaths over the entire twenty years we spent at war in Afghanistan and Iraq.

Loneliness is clearly terrible for our mental health, but it also negatively affects our physical health. Social isolation creates tremendous stress on a body in ways we can measure. Research shows that the more incidents of loneliness a person reports—in childhood, adolescence, adulthood—the more likely they are to experience cardiovascular health risks like high blood pressure, coronary disease, or unhealthy cholesterol levels. In middle-aged adults tracked for a four-year study, chronic loneliness proved to be a reliable predictor of those who would die, of any cause. Loneliness also correlates with higher rates of cognitive decline and dementia. And these negative outcomes are not limited to elderly shut-ins or the middle-aged. Right now, those reporting the highest rates of social isolation are between the ages of eighteen and twenty-two. And that demographic is experiencing its highest suicide rates ever recorded. It's becoming clear that loneliness now qualifies as a crisis in our national health, just like the opioid epidemic.

Enter the area of psychiatry I specialize in: psychopharmacology, which means examining how brain chemistry affects behavior. I'm trained to look at a problem, even a national crisis, and see the biology. Is there something missing in the body, something we can add to the mix that can help us fix the loneliness epidemic and the overdose crisis? The truth is, as someone who writes prescriptions, I know that pills can only do so much. Pills treat symptoms. For the distracted or apathetic, I can offer stimulants like Adderall and Ritalin, which increase levels of dopamine in the brain and make it easier to pay attention and feel motivated. Dopamine can enhance the importance of something (the neurological term is "salience"), but those pills won't provide real pleasure or peace. In fact, they often backfire and make people irritable, paranoid, or obsessive.

Then there are antidepressants that increase the availability of serotonin, SSRIs like Prozac, Zoloft, and Lexapro. Because serotonin is associated with feeling calm and satisfied, SSRIs may help you feel less anxious or depressed, or perhaps they tamp down your pessimism, but too often they merely numb you to the reality of your life. Oftentimes they can also lower your dopamine levels over time, so you lose the motivation to make the hard changes to fix those things in your life that aren't working. And many of my patients on SSRIs notice they're a lot less horny or, when they actually do have sex, less likely to climax. I'm worried that these meds are actually interfering with the brain's capacity to fall in love, and to choose, pursue, or keep a mate. In other words, they're potentially interfering with the brain's capacity to make its own good chemistry. These drugs aren't intended to help people connect; they're designed to help you not mind that you're disconnected.

And then there are opiates. In primary-care settings, as many as one in five Americans receive these prescriptions, even though it's clear by now that few physicians should be prescribing them on a maintenance level. The problem is that opiates perform better than so many alternatives; they're not just physical pain relievers, they're also psychic pain relievers. What no one seems to be mentioning is that opiates act on the same receptors in the brain as the body's own naturally occurring chemicals, in fact the ones that leave you feeling loved, soothed, warm, and safe. Those opioid receptors exist in part to make bonding pleasurable. They enable social connections to relieve stress and make it possible for warm feelings between friends helping other friends. Despite our national hand-wringing over the opiate epidemic, we continue to ignore the central issue: opiates mimic the body's response to feeling cared for. In animal studies, opiates very effectively relieve separation distress. They approximate that good chemistry of connectedness and attachment. Opiates are plugging a gaping hole for millions of Americans.

Another medicine that can approximate this chemistry of connection is cannabis, a key ally in the fight against deaths of despair. States with medical marijuana programs report that the number of opiate prescriptions filled and overdoses reported is cut by 25 to 30 percent, while sales of liquor are down 15 percent. Because cannabis can help to put you in a relaxed state, it can fight the effects of stress. Many of my patients have begun to use cannabis, or just one component of it, CBD (cannabidiol), to treat their symptoms of insomnia, inattention, or anxiety, and are now in the process of tapering off their other psychiatric medicines. This may be the start of a new trend in psychiatry.

We'll cover details in the pages that follow, but now there's an even bigger revolution under way in psychiatric treatment. Thanks to pioneering studies and clinical trials in places like UCLA, Johns Hopkins, and NYU, the menu of medications in the psychiatric tool kit now includes a handful of psychedelic drugs. In carefully monitored situations with trained clinicians as guides, MDMA, LSD, and psilocybin mushrooms are driving a renaissance in our therapeutic approach. Little by little, after almost a half century of prohibitions, these powerful tools are returning to our arsenal. The results have been startling, even transformative. Used in the right setting, they seem to be lighting a path out of chronic loneliness and toward connectedness. Psychedelics can enable not just a connection with the self; they can also offer us a glimpse of the bigger picture, how we are part of the cosmos, and how we are all interconnected and reliant on one another for our survival. As any twelve-step adherent would remind you, spiritual problems often require spiritual solutions. And psychedelics can help us get in touch with our souls, and what they need, leading us back onto a truer, healthier, more meaningful path, one I sometimes refer to as "sustainable mental health."

What does this look like in practice? Take the case of a patient of mine, David K., who came to me after eight years of opiate addiction. (The names and identifying characteristics of patients and study participants in this book have been changed.) Like many of my patients who've used drugs, David was seemingly functional and prosperous, running his own talent agency in New York. But after receiving a prescription for Vicodin after a spinal-fusion surgery, he'd become a heavy user of opiates.

David wanted to end his addictions. His committed internet searches had convinced him that psychedelic drugs—especially LSD—were achieving remarkable results in treating just that. I've been involved with psychedelic research since the mid-eighties, even before the current resurgence of interest from official channels; David came to me because my name appeared in many of his searches. I show up in scientific papers, or on panels, or as a medical monitor. And my office is not far from his home.

I could tell David was determined and resourceful. There's a network of people like him, online and off, who are keenly interested in psychedelics. I knew it wouldn't be hard for him to find somebody to give him LSD in a therapeutic setting. But I advised him against it.

I went to med school in the eighties, just when we were starting to learn about a disease that was mysteriously killing Haitians, gay men, hemophiliacs, and people injecting drugs intravenously. As tough as it can be for a psychiatrist to predict future behavior, I was pretty sure that people were going to keep on having sex and doing drugs. I made the case back then that arming people with condoms and clean needles should be a top priority to prevent the spread of the disease because the biological drive to procreate is immense. But there is also a biological drive to alter our consciousness; it is found throughout the animal kingdom and human history. Like with sex education, preaching abstinence from drugs is a recipe for disaster. The best thing we can do is to create interventions that minimize the harm people suffer and educate them about ways to do dangerous things more safely.

Harm reduction continues to be a huge preoccupation for me—it's one of my central concerns as a doctor. And that's why I tried to steer David away from LSD as his first psychedelic experience and toward psilocybin, the active ingredient in magic mushrooms. There are practical issues to consider: the average LSD trip lasts a long time, a good twelve hours or more, which makes it tough for both the patient and the guide. And challenging experiences happen in a small but statistically significant number of people, often about four hours in, when a metabolite of LSD starts to build up.

We'll discuss this in depth in chapter two, but his experience with psilocybin, which has a much shorter peak period—in a therapeutic setting with the help of an underground guide— did prove effective. After one session, he simply discontinued his opiate use and hasn't relapsed since.

David's experience is not unique. I've been hearing countless stories about people making major changes in habitual behaviors after one or two psychotherapy-assisted sessions with MDMA or psychedelics. And the scientific literature is beginning to back up these anecdotes with strong data, the major reason that the FDA is fast-tracking a number of psychedelic-assisted therapies for approval. Soon, psychedelic therapy will be considered an option, especially when other, more conventional treatments have been tried and have failed.

I believe these medicines should be a key component in our collective treatment plan. We need powerful medicine to deal with the drastic consequences of our ever-increasing isolation. One of the hallmarks of the psychedelic experience is a transcendent sense of unity. We are all connected. We all belong. And it takes a strong dose of that to overcome the crisis of separateness that we're suffering from now. But we have to be careful, because the body's reactions to separation are a necessary adaptation for our survival. It's a positive feature of our animal physiology and not a glitch. We've evolved to be social creatures that can perform at our best only when we're intimately connected to others. This is something the body knows instinctively. And so it creates a state of unease, symptoms of anxiety and depression that normally would impel us to connect with others.

For thousands of generations, separation from the safety of the tribe meant exposure to danger. We're hardwired to react to rejection and ostracism as if they were existential threats: our nervous system enters a state of alarm, elevating the heart rate and shutting down nonessential functions like digestion and repair of damaged tissue. From a biological perspective, maintaining this state of hypervigilance is costly, and diseases accrue the longer one persists in this state. Other processes, like learning and memory, sleep and immune function, depend on a stable and supportive environment to flourish. They all suffer, with predictable consequences, the longer one is deprived of the protective support of human contact.

But there are some immediate fixes that are easy to pull off, and they can help relieve the tension that comes with isolation. For all the complexity of our physiology, at base level our bodies operate on a binary system. When we're in that state of hypervigilance that accompanies chronic loneliness, our bodies are controlled by the sympathetic nervous system, and we hold steady in fight-or-flight mode: the breath and the heartbeat quicken, our reflexes become hair-trigger, our pupils dilate. The adrenal glands kick out the stress hormones cortisol and adrenaline. Blood sugar rises in case we need fuel for a sudden burst of energy. You can see what this leads to in the long run: we become overweight and snappish, too hyper to relax, too stressed out to sleep. And we wear down fast, because there is no bodily repair in this state of unrest.

From middle school through medical school, I must have learned about the sympathetic nervous system a dozen times. Fight or flight was always sold as the key to our survival. But as a psychiatrist, I now know that the key to our survival lies on the flip side. Flip that switch and the body reacts in a completely different way. This second state is controlled by the parasympathetic nervous system, and it may well be the cure for all of this chronic stress. This response goes by many names: rest and digest, tend and befriend, or my favorite: protect and connect. Usually I just call it "para," which means "next to" (because the parasympathetic nerves run alongside the sympathetic ones). The parasympathetic system is meant to be the body's primary condition, our natural state of balance. It's the mode we slip into spontaneously when we relax and feel safe, when we're falling in love, taking care of a baby, lying side by side, when we're among friends, giving comfort or getting it, or when we're in awe, standing at the edge of the Grand Canyon or staring up at the Milky Way.

Fight or flight can be enormously helpful when you are in actual danger—if you are being chased by a tiger or you spot your stalker across the street. Luckily, when loneliness threatens to turn a fleeting reaction into a chronic condition, there are some simple things you can do to slam on the brakes. I call it "flipping over into para," and I keep a list for patients. Nothing on this list is hard to do.

How to Flip Over into Para

1. Breathe. That's easy enough. And there's one trick to make it even easier: breathe through your nose. Okay, two tricks: make sure your exhale is longer than your inhale. It doesn't have to be extreme or out of proportion. An exhale that's slightly longer than your inhale is fine. I have a patient who's been doing this simple technique for ten minutes at a time—several times a day and before bed, using one of the many breath control apps you can use on your phone as a guide—and as a result has lowered his blood pressure so much that his doctor took him off his medication.

2. Breathe through your left nostril. There are a number of peer-reviewed studies tracking the effects of breathing through one nostril or the other or both. These investigations use precisely calibrated instruments to measure metabolic rate, oxygen consumption, galvanic skin response, and blood pressure. They're all designed to test the benefits of yogic breathing practices known as pranayama. The researchers tested left-nostril breathing against right-nostril breathing and both against normal breathing. Some added yoga exercises to the regimens. But all of the studies noted positive changes—lower heart rates and blood pressure, even weight loss—with single-nostril breathing. They also noticed more pronounced benefits in reducing sympathetic nervous system activity—that is, less time in fight-or-flight mode—

coming from left-nostril breathing. And all you have to do to experience this increased parasympathetic activity is gently place one finger beside your right nostril and press down until you're breathing only from your left nostril. The yogis call breathing from the left side the cooling breath, and it does slow the heart rate. With left nostril breathing, the lung on the left side expands more than its partner on the right. Maybe this means that the heart, which is on the left side, too, gets more oxygen and works less. You can check the notes on NaturalMood.com and read the studies, or you can just breathe through your left nostril and relax.

3. Do nothing. Just stop. Sit. Drop whatever you're doing. Put your phone away. When I get to this point in the list, patients get suspicious, thinking that what I'm really trying to do is get them to meditate. And they start giving me pushback. "I just can't stop thinking," they say. I have to remind them that nobody can stop thinking and that meditation is a lifelong practice aimed at noticing, and dilating the spaces between, the thoughts. To do this, try placing your attention gently on the breath. Try to be as fascinated by your breath as you are by your Instagram feed. Meditation doesn't have to be complicated: if you stop what you're doing, sit down, breathe through your nose, and pay attention to your breath instead of what you're going to make for dinner, don't tell anybody, but you're meditating.

4. Do some yoga. Yoga unifies the mind to the body—it means to yoke or bind—and the movements, synchronized with the breath, slow and control heart and respiratory rates. You don't have to be able to put your foot behind your head to benefit. As in one through three above, you just have to pay attention to the breath. Yoga puts you back in your body, which is where you want to be to stay calm.

5. Singing. It doesn't matter what you sing. Sing show tunes or death metal, lullabies or laundry lists. You could chant. You could play a wind instrument. All of them get you to the same place: your exhale is longer than your inhale.

6. Floating. Just get yourself into a lake or a backyard pool and lie there with your arms and legs spread wide. As soon as you put yourself in that vulnerable position, there's no way you can stay in fight or flight. It's a heart-opening posture. If you can get to one, try a sensory-deprivation tank, where it's dark and soundless and the water is body temperature, saturated with Epsom salts so you float effortlessly, like you're in the Dead Sea. Since there are no sensations there to distract you, the body stops paying attention to sensory input, and the mind feels freed of boundaries. I remember one time I floated in a tank: it was so quiet that the only way I knew I was existing was that I could hear myself blink. I'd had no idea that blinking made a noise.

7. Havening. Havening is a self-soothing technique. You cross your arms like you're hugging yourself and you stroke your upper arms downward, from shoulder to elbow, over and over. There are plenty of how-to videos online. It's easy. You can add affirmations—"I am safe, I am cared for, I am looked after, I am loved." Some people will have problems with that last affirmation. The idea of love can encompass feelings of heartache and loss. So you can take or leave the affirmations, but havening, the physical act of self-soothing, is a simple and efficient way to lessen anxiety.

We'll be adding to this list in the chapters to come. The first recommendation—to breathe—becomes especially stronger and more interactive as we progress through the stages of connection. Eventually, the list will include touch and sex, opening ourselves up to laughter and tears, and then on to the ultimate openness: awe. We'll see how this progression from isolation to oneness can help us, as William James put it, "experience union with something larger than ourselves, and in that union find our greatest peace."

This is a practical book, not a course in miracles. Think of it as a cookbook with recipes for connection. We'll stay grounded, working our way to awe and peace using tools we all have—strong hugs, extended eye contact, hand-holding, orgasm, and child-rearing. Even when we're looking at the action of breakthrough drugs like psychedelics, we'll see how they act on our own network of receptors, and how our bodies produce similar compounds naturally that help us access this state of oneness on our own.

The chapters that follow are arranged a lot like the list above, with a simple strategy for progress. We start from the most basic unit, the self, uncovering strategies to connect with ourselves first. We'll work through dramatic success stories, to see how people like David are overcoming trauma and adverse conditioning to reconnect with a sense of themselves—or to experience it for the first time. As one patient put it after overcoming his own profound self-alienation, "It gave me the experience of feeling alive for the first time in my life."

We'll follow that by looking at our basic drive to connect

as a couple. We'll see how the sexual chemistry in couples with "good chemistry" really works, and how we can harness the body's own store of hormones for a deeper sense of oneness.

Then we'll look at family and childbirth—our own ground zero for establishing a sense of connection. Next come our communities, and how our natural drive to form tribes can either divide or unite us.

Keep in mind that there's one key chemical that will reappear often. It acts as an agent of intimacy, empathy, and connection, driving a cascade of chemicals that affect receptors in the body's internal opiate and cannabis systems, enabling social learning, moderating fear, and even helping to disperse pain in someone you love. I'm talking about oxytocin, which is produced in massive amounts during childbirth and nursing and orgasm, and less massive amounts in any act of bonding or connection you can name. Some people call it the love hormone, the cuddle hormone, or the moral molecule. Touching, hugging, and cuddling can stimulate its release, helping to cement the ties that bind. As much as adrenaline and cortisol fuel the sympathetic state of fight or flight, oxytocin is what enables tend and befriend, the parasympathetic state.

Whenever there's social recognition, oxytocin enters the picture. It multiplies the feeling of trust and openness, and it alters your physiology—and, research shows, it does it quickly, within two seconds. The hypothalamus, where oxytocin is produced, and the amygdala, the brain's fear center, are connected by a direct network, meaning the oxytocin can have an immediate effect, reducing anxiety and dissolving the sense of threat. These doses of oxytocin are triggered by any act of trust or bonding, from eye contact to handshakes, to hugs, to cuddling. It's all just a matter of degree. Connection requires a level of openness and trust, and oxytocin enables that behavior to flourish. Following the ways oxytocin works in the body will help us trace the path of our connectedness at every level.

Which will bring us to our last stage of connection— stepping beyond our communities and into our connection with animals, nature, and the earth. We'll see how awe can enable learning and transcendence can help moderate fear in the face of death. We'll look closely at the transformative experience of awe engendered by psychedelics in a therapeutic setting.

I don't want to give away the plot twists or the ending, but each step in this expanding circle of connectedness is all centered on a single point: oneness. That's what triggers the good chemistry, and that's where we'll end.

And, if you turn the page, it's also where we'll begin.

CHAPTER 1

THE FIRST CONNECTION IS WITH THE SELF

There is no coming to consciousness without pain.
People will do anything, no matter how absurd, in
order to avoid facing their own soul. One does not
become enlightened by imagining figures of light,
but by making the darkness conscious.

—CARL JUNG

Maybe the central idea of this chapter, "oneness with the self," sounds obvious and self-explanatory. That's not how it looks from my chair. There are so many ways to feel estranged from—or disappointed, deluded, defeated by—yourself. I can't say I've seen them all, but I can tell you that I often encounter patients with a deep, even fundamental divide in the self. This divide may as well be the spiritual common cold. As Paul Simon sings, "Half of the time we're gone and we don't know where."

The struggle to connect with the self—and if it weren't a struggle, I wouldn't have a job—is an interior one. Connecting with the self, both the body and the mind, requires the exercise of perception. Although you can't really draw a line separating the body and the mind, for discussion purposes we can subdivide perception into proprioception for the body and interoception for the mind. Proprioception, at the simplest level, is just a sense of where your physical body is in space. It requires feedback from the muscles and joints. Interoception is the awareness of inner body sensations. It engages the same multilevel sense of yourself, but the feedback you're reacting to is different. Knowing you're upset is a form of interoception. So is recognizing hunger or horniness. But many of us have learned to quiet our interoception or ignore it altogether. Some habitually suppress any input from a side of themselves that split off as a result of trauma.

Even something as simple as wondering, "Where did I put my glasses? That was dumb of me!" is an example of splitting off, judging, and criticizing the self. This is a fairly benign example of the observing ego, as we split into actor and observer. These separations can turn malignant when we make a split habitual and keep that division a secret, even to ourselves. What we hide from others, we hide from ourselves; the secrets we keep from others metastasize into realities invisible to our own awareness.

In the next few pages, we'll be looking at the cases of a few people who have suffered a radical divorce from their own self. The circumstances of each case are, to use an unscientific word, heart-wrenching. But what's strange and troubling and memorable about their experiences is not how extreme they are, but how familiar they may feel.

Of course there are some quick fixes for connecting with the self, like rubbing your lips with your fingertips. That's a simple move that facilitates embodiment (feeling fully present and at home in our bodies) and tickles the parasympathetic nervous system awake—another shortcut for flipping into para and settling into yourself. But more complex situations require more powerful medicine. That's where psychedelics can come into play. Psychedelics help to release the neuronal hold of certain structures associated with selfhood, identity, and ego. This letting go can have the effect, in many cases, of a kind of mental reset button. (I like to think of letting go as an open hand, not grasping or reaching, but open to catching what lands while also allowing its escape. This is a useful concept not just with the self, but with partners and family members.)

We'll be investigating psychedelics (which include cannabis) in this chapter with a greater focus than we will in most chapters. That's partly because connecting with the self, learning how to create a calm and receptive state and then taking the steps to do so, is a prerequisite for connecting with others. Think of conversation not just as an exchange of ideas, but also as an exchange of silences, of openness to the other. Cultivating openness is a little like setting the table before the guests arrive: all by yourself you're creating the conditions for connection. It's true on a cellular level: the activity of mirror neurons in our brain helps enable our sense of empathy, which drives connection with others. A high percentage of mirror neurons are designed to respond specifically to movements of the lips, which underlines our focus on food, language, and sensuality. And the energetic response of the mirror neurons is its own reward: think of the buzz you feel watching a great dancer. These specialized brain cells play an important role in understanding the mind states of others and in developing language and communication skills. Mirror neurons help us link perception with action. Like when I spit a mouthful of water all over my laptop because the character in the movie I was watching just spit out his bloody tooth. (I may have an overabundance of mirror neurons, but hey, it makes me a solid shrink.) When you listen to someone talking, your motor areas specialized for speech start firing. It's like you quietly mimic them and what they're saying, as you're hearing it. Neural mirroring facilitates social behavior by helping us to understand the minds of others, making intersubjectivity possible. And mirroring another person's facial expressions is crucial for recognizing emotion and, more important, for feeling it. (A reason why you should forgo the Botox.)

Awareness of others—connection—goes inward as much as it goes outward. But we're also focusing on psychedelics here because they light up the interior workings of the individual mind, unlocking profound and often permanent change. In psychiatry, that's often exactly what we're aiming for. But before we can reach that state of robust health, we have to start where we are, and with what it is we're actually craving when our addictions take hold. We are trying to soothe our sense of alienation and the damage it can inflict.

RAT PARK: ISOLATION BREEDS ADDICTIVE BEHAVIORS

In the late seventies, a few years after the start of the war on drugs, Dr. Bruce Alexander, an experimental psychologist at Simon Fraser University in British Columbia, began to raise questions about one of the core principles of that war—the demonization of addiction. The concept owed too much to flawed sixties-era experiments, he thought, where confined lab rats got injections of whatever drug the experiment was testing: heroin, morphine, cocaine, amphetamine. All the rats had to do to get their fix—directly into the jugular vein—was press a lever.

One of the many issues with those studies was that the rats didn't have much else to occupy their time. The sides of their cages were made of sheet metal, so they couldn't see the other rats in the cages stacked around them. They didn't get an exercise wheel, since running around in one would have tangled up the catheter attached to their necks. The only real source of stimulation in their solitary confinement came through the little lever that mainlined drugs straight into the bloodstream.

Left alone in setups like that, rats could be relied on to press the lever over and over, to the point of death. Studies with similar designs repeatedly came to the conclusion that the drugs under review were hopelessly addicting, and that addiction led to death. The results helped persuade policy makers that there was a class of drugs so dangerously addictive that the government shouldn't hesitate to mobilize the weapons and tactics of war to protect the public from such a threat.

But Alexander knew that lab rats used in scientific studies—docile, red-eyed, mostly albino—all descended from ancestors who were, in his phrase, highly social, sexual, and industrious. Maybe they were merely reacting to extreme isolation by numbing themselves whenever they had a chance. What if other, healthier life choices were made available to them besides intravenous drug use? Wouldn't that be a better model for the way humans actually live?

So he and his colleagues built an alternative environment to test the idea: a giant plywood box with platforms to climb on, cedar chips to build with, tin cans to hide in, and plenty of other rats to have sex with. The scientists even painted a mural along the walls with dark silhouettes of a Vancouvery landscape of fir, spruce, and hemlock. They loved it, and the rats loved it. They called their rodent utopia "Rat Park."

The results seemed to confirm their hypothesis. While the caged rats continued to self-administer morphine at a dangerous rate, the free-range, social rats barely touched the stuff. Formerly caged and drug-dependent rats, released into the company of their peers in Rat Park, chose plain water over morphine water. They tried inducing addiction in both the caged and the Rat Park rats by providing them nothing but morphine water, following that regimen with days when drug-free water was provided as an option. Presented with a choice, the caged rats continued choosing morphine, but the Rat Park rats preferred to suffer withdrawals, skip the drugs, and return to a normal social routine.

According to Alexander, the study brought him and his coauthors local fame when it was published in 1981, but it "sank like a stone" in the world of addiction theory. It wasn't until the 2000s, with the spread of the opiate crisis and the growing realization that the war on drugs had proven a spectacular failure as health policy, that the ideas from Rat Park finally began to gain a wider audience. In 2004, Lauren Slater included Rat Park in *Opening Skinner's Box*, her roundup of the great psychological experiments of the twentieth century. In 2008, my friend and colleague Gabor Maté, a Canadian doctor and vocal critic of the war on drugs, published his deeply moving book *In the Realm of Hungry Ghosts: Close Encounters with Addiction*, which pointed to the spiritual void at the heart of addiction. He cited the Rat Park experiments prominently. In 2015, Johann Hari published *Chasing the Scream: The First and Last Days of the War on Drugs*, which gave a thumbnail history of the demonization of addiction and again relied on Rat Park as a cornerstone. Hari's TED talk compresses the book's central argument—that the opposite of addiction was not sobriety but meaningful human connection—into fourteen minutes. At last count, the talk has been viewed 15.1 million times.

Alexander made his own contribution to this reevaluation with the publication in 2008 of a book he'd been working on for thirty years, *The Globalization of Addiction: A Study in the Poverty of the Spirit*. In the aftermath of Rat Park, as grant money for more rat research dried up, he turned to humans, not to subject them to experiments but to review historical precedents and clinical data from psychology and sociology. He found plenty of examples of runaway addiction in populations that had become socially and culturally isolated— Scottish highlanders after the land clearances, First People herded into reservations, Orkney Islanders hired to work in the fur trade in remote Canadian trading posts. It's an impressive work with an unusual detached tone: rock-solid scholarship from a man who doesn't expect to be believed.

Still, he seems happy for the late burst of appreciation for Rat Park. And he has no objections to the popular authors who are recasting his research into what he calls "a popular parable, which seems to shed light on the deepest nature of addiction." He says his most basic finding after all that research is that people use addictions—not just to drugs but to all sorts of things: gambling, pornography, shopping, video games, their phones—to adapt to the destruction of common culture and to overcome the resulting sense of extreme dislocation. Our addictions, he says, are a symptom of our alienation. But in chasing that promise of fleeting comfort, you may find more problems than the pain you're trying to avoid. Please just remember that oxytocin is a pain reliever, literally and figuratively. When in doubt, hug it out.

OSTRACISM: ALIENATION FROM OTHERS (AND YOURSELF)

Alexander's theories fit my own life story. To some degree, alienation led me to drugs. I was lucky, because after a few years exploring drugs of all varieties, the curiosity they inspired led me to psychoneuroimmunology, the study of the effect of the mind on health, or, more technically, of psychological processes on the nervous and immune systems.

I remember finding the journal *Psychoneuroendocrinology* one afternoon in the stacks of the library as a premed student at Penn. This covers the intersection between behavior and hormones. I read it cover to cover, barely moving for hours. The brain, I learned, has its own full-service apothecary. I was in heaven. But I'm getting ahead of myself.

Drugs became a part of my life early on. In eighth grade, I was part of the in-crowd, the popular kids. Life was good. We got together on weekends and drank a little and smoked. I liked the way cigarettes made me look tough and cool. I was a bit of a tomboy. My best friend was Toto, a girl my age who I hung out with all the time.

One weekend I threw a party, and some of the kids found a copy of *Hustler* magazine under my bed. (I liked the letters section: "I never thought this would happen to me.") By today's standards, with pretty much any flavor of pornography just a Google search away, it was fairly tame. But back then, if you were an eighth grader looking for sexual arousal, *Hustler* was about as hard-core as you could get. If you want to picture what it was like growing up in suburbia in the seventies, I found my copy at a construction site a few blocks from my house. After the crews went home, I climbed into an empty truck and there it was on the passenger seat.

The in-crowd kids got to thinking: Julie kept an explicit magazine devoted to naked women. Julie had a really close friend, Toto, who was practically always by her side. Julie was a tomboy who smoked and talked tough and climbed into trucks. Since I'd just broken up with a boy I'd dated for the past two months, my so-called friends decided I was bisexual. From then on, whenever they saw me in the hall or waiting after school for my sister to pick me up, they'd call out, "Hey, Bi!" or "See ya, Bi!" or their favorite, "Bye, Bi!" which would leave them doubled over laughing.

The pleasure they took in yelling at me eventually wore off, but the ostracism that replaced it was even worse. It wasn't subtle. I wasn't in their crowd anymore, and the public shunning drove the point home. All of my friends, unanimously, had decided not to be friends with me anymore. My isolation was on constant display, a casual bit of cruelty that confirmed their own sense of cohesion. It probably made them feel good about one another. But it was the most traumatic thing that ever happened to me.

When it first started, a boy I'd befriended a few weeks before was bewildered. "I thought you were popular," he said.

"I was," I said.

Another boy I'd known since kindergarten, a close friend I used to talk to on the phone till late at night, went along with the others. It seemed to pain him to do it. But the danger of being iced out if he didn't go along with everyone else was terrifying. I was living proof. And so, not only did I lose my friends, I lost my standing, and I was openly, loudly ridiculed.

Toto endured a weaker version of the same thing, but the next year she went on to Catholic high school and a fresh group of friends. I had to attend public school with the same gang, but also ended up joining a fresh group of friends: the "druggies." They were much more accepting (and fun!) and took me in. Adolescence is a time when your sense of self and social identity emerge. It's a strong need, this drive for identity, and I felt it. And for that, I'm very grateful for my drug-using friends. Sharing and connecting are what keep us as individuals, and as a community, healthy and functioning. The drug community caught me when I fell, and I've been catching them ever since. One way is by fighting for drug-policy reform. Even though problematic drug use stems from trauma, poverty, stigma, and isolation, we persist in treating a health and social issue by criminalizing those who suffer. Even in the medical community we can be stigmatizing and punitive with drug users, adding the burden of "treatment trauma" to a person's already difficult experience.

What's important to realize is that all of us are suffering, and we medicate ourselves in various ways. Every childhood has trauma. I feel like cross-stitching this on a pillow for my office. None of us gets exactly what we require growing up. At some crucial moment, our needs weren't met. In adolescence, social pain hits particularly hard. Shunning leads to isolation, which interferes, on a chemical level, with learning and impulse control, just for starters. If you take a rat out of social housing and shock him and put him back with his friends, he'll remember where he was shocked if you put him in the shocking cage again. But if you take him away from the group, shock him, and then put him in isolation, he doesn't learn where he was shocked. Isolation interferes with memory formation, and if you want someone to learn to play by the rules of society, you need to keep them within that group, where peers can model healthier behavior and give feedback and consequences for various misbehaviors. I understand there are times when people need to be taken out of the group, but I am here to tell you that they will not learn and grow and change if they are ostracized, shunned, or isolated. This is why I challenge some of the protocols of "cancel culture." Integration is what's healthiest, nearly always. Try "calling in" a person; educate and enlighten them before you resort to "calling them out."

Isolation also fuels addiction, and it can directly cause suicide. Unfortunately, sometimes this same urge is directed outward, leading to violent behavior. Think of all those lonely people quietly radicalizing in isolation. It's not a coincidence that mass shooters are invariably described as loners. Has there been one yet with lots of friends and a busy social schedule? In more ways than one, isolation is a killer.

ALEXITHYMIA: ALIENATION FROM
THE SELF

The first step to any sense of oneness—or maybe the precondition—involves connecting to the self. Unfortunately, there are so many ways to grow alienated from ourselves—including via the phones that we always have within arm's reach, distraction machines designed to keep us looking anywhere but inside ourselves. But before we take up any of the habits and devices we use to avoid getting to know ourselves, I want to introduce a patient, Josh, whose alienation from himself and his own senses was profound.

If accomplishments were all that mattered, Josh might seem like a candidate for contentment. He was a partner in a leading law practice, adept at conversation, a graduate of an elite law school, and a wizard at contracts. He was married with two kids, both girls, born seven years apart. One was attending an expensive private school; the other went to the kind of New York City preschool that's harder to get into than Harvard. But it didn't take long to sense his lack of ease. He would fidget and avoid my eyes, and he could occasionally get stuck worrying over some minor conversational detail or question. Outwardly, he was highly capable, with perhaps a hint of Asperger's syndrome in his affect. But the complaint he presented—that he couldn't feel his feelings—led in another direction: alexithymia.

Alexithymia is not a common or even an empirically validated condition, but it's useful in clinical settings. Josh complained that he could see other people experiencing what they would identify as joy, sadness, or anger. But, he told me, "My emotional experience of life is much narrower. I don't have any theories about why and I don't have any notion of what the experience is that I'm lacking." He couldn't put common emotional experiences into words and had no stories to tell to illustrate his own emotional life—both classic signs of alexithymia, a term coined in 1973 by the chief psychiatrist at Beth Israel Medical Center in New York that comes from the Greek for "no words for feelings."

But Josh was painstaking and tireless when confronting a problem. At first he thought that meditation might help him explore that inner world he felt was missing. Before he came to me, he'd started meditation, and, typically, he went at it with remarkable determination, signing up for ten-day silent meditation retreats. When he began, he said he couldn't "find his breath," a description so anomalous that the leaders of the retreat, people who'd conducted "hundreds if not thousands" of meditation interviews, had never heard the complaint before and didn't know what advice to give him. Some wondered why, if he wasn't having any emotional experiences, he even wanted to go on a retreat.

Josh kept at it, signing up for more retreats and logging the hours. He recognized that his experience of meditation was different from what others reported but credited his practice with giving him more focus, greater powers of concentration, and a keener sense of proprioception (the ability to know where the body is in space), which he expressed in terms of a dawning ability to "sense inside myself."

He was having lunch with another meditator, and this acquaintance gave him an Adderall, thinking it might help him with meditation. The next morning, Josh took the pill and had an incredible meditation that left him with a tingle in his body that continued throughout the day. This tingle was a dramatic experience for him.

This willingness to try new things—as Josh was doing first with meditation and now with Adderall—is not a typical trait among alexithymics, who usually score low on openness in tests of the Big Five personality traits (openness, conscientiousness, extroversion, agreeableness, and neuroticism). Further, Josh proved to be conscientious about his openness. His eye-opening experience with Adderall pushed him to read up on the ongoing psychedelic research at Johns Hopkins University and investigate psychedelics in a therapeutic setting.

That research set him on a hunt for mind-expanding drugs. But his legal training made him wary of possessing a Schedule I drug, so the process of acquiring psychedelics, which he pursued entirely on his own, took him a while. When he finally did have the chance, in a dance club, to take MDMA, a drug known to increase oxytocin, he described it as a "bigger than big experience. It gave me the experience of feeling alive for the first time in my life, of *feeling* feelings, and realizing that they weren't literary fictions but real things." He said he felt switched on, as if he was seeing color and three dimensions for the first time. In the club, despite what he called one of his "lifelong peculiarities"—namely, never having been able to hear music and move his body to it—he was moving to music and not just hearing it but feeling it as if for the first time. He was finally able to dance.

He recognized one of the characteristics of alexithymia—that of never really feeling that you exist—as true for himself. The MDMA had helped him revise that perception. It had given him an awareness of what life could be like. He called it an accelerant, catalyzing a connection to his body. He wanted to prolong the experience, to extend it into daily life, and so he began a schedule of microdosing LSD, taking subperceptual doses of ten micrograms every third day.

A microdose is roughly one-tenth of a normal therapeutic or recreational dose of any psychedelic. At this low dose, attention and concentration are enhanced, and cognitive flexibility and creativity increase. Josh also found that microdosing helped him with proprioception—his awareness of the body, of the interior feedback from the body. His regular routine of microdosing resulted in more frequent experiences of embodiment, experiences that continued to be revelatory to him. He especially liked to take what he called his "medicines" (his microdoses of LSD) on his meditation retreats. It was on one of these ten-day silent retreats that he had another breakthrough.

He'd been assigned kitchen-cleaning duty with two other retreatants. One of them couldn't make it, and the other guy left early, leaving Josh by himself, with no way to communicate his irritation, since he'd been sworn to silence. He went back to his room and started journaling, when, as he put it, he "noticed some tension on my periphery." Since the retreat had left him "present and quiet," he grew more and more curious about this tension. It felt to him like the tension wanted to move, so he let it move. Without directing it, his hand formed into a fist, and he felt what he called "a tension and a fire in my body that I had never experienced in my life before."

He was angry.

Again, what Josh was reporting was nearly the complete opposite of what people aim for on meditation retreats. Many go because they have problems with anger or other over-whelming emotions that they hope to soothe or moderate. But here was Josh welcoming an experience that he recognized as new.

Josh continues to microdose off and on, and has taken up conscious or ecstatic dancing in place of meditation, a form of expressive, self-exploratory, and often interactive dance that is frequently done in large groups. These two, in combi-nation, seem to be opening Josh's awareness, allowing him to connect to others and to himself in ways he had not suspected were even possible before his microdosing. The awareness has also brought him a sense of regret—another emotion that he can now describe. "I have a much greater sense of my own existence and significance," he says. "I know this is going to be a long journey. But I'm suddenly far more connected to myself. I have two daughters, ages thirteen and six. But in a sense, they have had two completely different fathers. The six-year-old has an excellent father and the thirteen-year-old, unfortunately, when she was born, didn't."

MICRODOSING, INTUITION, AND INTEGRATION

By microdosing, Josh was hoping to extend his experience, enhance his feelings, and so facilitate his sense of his own body and the flow of energy he'd discovered in dancing. It grounded him and brought him to life at the same time. As we'll explore in depth later, taking hefty doses of psychedel-ics (so not microdosing, but macrodosing) can open up new ways of thinking and seeing as well. At that level, mystical experiences are common, and so are epiphanies of universal love and connection. But microdosing psychedelics allows you to take just a tiny slice of that huge pie. Typically, one-tenth of a mystical dose is sufficient. For LSD that may be around ten micrograms or so; for dried mushrooms, it'd be around two hundred milligrams, but some people start lower or go higher.

At low doses, psychedelics facilitate immersion into experience. I was privileged to know the late Sasha Shulgin, a great Harvard-trained chemist and brave psychonaut (one who explores inner space), who is sometimes described as the "godfather of Ecstasy." He wrote about a "museum dose" of various mind-expanding drugs, one that's low enough to spare your coordination and social functioning, but high enough to infuse your surroundings with sparkle and wonder. There is a growing trend within the business, tech, psychonaut, and life-hacking communities to use small doses of psychedelics to enhance creativity and focus. Microdosing psychedelics is all the rage in Silicon Valley because these chemicals bring about a synergy of inspiration and concentration and can help to engender longer stretches of the typically transient flow state, when everything else falls away but the doing.

Psychedelics help to quiet the default mode network—the neural circuitry that devotes itself to contemplating ourselves, our memories, our plans, our social status, and other avenues of self-absorption. Meditators will often describe it as the monkey mind—that constant stream of self-talk that is so difficult to silence. But it goes deeper than that, calcifying into habits of mind, a preference for well-worn neural pathways that can constrain a more fluid response to stimuli. It is this default mode network, often abbreviated DMN, that gives us our sense of separateness from others. Dampening this input from the egocentric circuitry creates an expanding sense of self, of boundlessness. Psychedelics also help connect disparate parts of the brain that don't always communicate. The brain becomes more open-source as it hyperconnects. Perhaps, for that reason, these small doses help to spark imagination.

I'll never forget my first meeting with the lovely Countess Amanda Feilding of the Beckley Foundation in the UK. She let me feel the divot in her head from her trepanation treatment in South America. (This is an ancient treatment performed to target psychiatric symptoms, no longer done in the United States, involving releasing pressure through a borehole in the skull.) Feilding has made it her life's work to fund and organize scientific studies of psilocybin and LSD to discover how they affect neuroplasticity, neurogenesis, and inflammation, which would be valuable in treating a range of disorders, from depression and addiction to neurodegenerative diseases like Alzheimer's and multiple sclerosis. Many psychedelics are anti-inflammatory, which means they can modify immune response. This will no doubt become a burgeoning field of study, but I've been particularly interested in neuroplasticity, the ability of the brain to forge new connections, since my mom went to grad school when I was a teenager. She came home from class one night and excitedly told me that the brain can rewire itself if it's damaged. Now, decades later, we know that this capacity for structural reorganization, which underlies learning, memory, and cognitive flexibility, can happen throughout our lifetimes. Many things can trigger neuroplasticity, including exercise, meditation, significant experiences, environmental enrichment, antidepressants, and various psychedelics.

More recently, Feilding has opted to focus on microdosing. When she spoke at the annual Horizons psychedelic conference in New York City in 2017, she contrasted microdosing with what she described as the "peak experience therapy" of macrodosing. "As a smart drug to improve well-being, mood and cognitive functioning," she said, "the microdose experience has an entirely different set of characteristics from the macrodose: it improves mood and vitality, enhances focus, boosts creativity, and increases motivation and drive, all, importantly, while leaving the user in the driving seat." (When one is macrodosing, the overwhelmingly intense experience itself becomes the driver, not the user!) Like stimulants Adderall and Ritalin, microdosing can be used as a cognitive enhancer, to some extent. But where psychedelics and stimulants differ is in their ability to engender divergent thinking, allowing us to make creative leaps through looser associations.

Josh started his therapeutic journey with the hope of discovering his feelings and wound up trying to connect to his body. In the process, he ended up spending a lot more time in para. As he'd be the first to say, this process is not always as straightforward as it sounds. Embodiment is about our connection to our animal selves, to the meat, as it were, of our existence. To deny or repress our own animal nature—or never to have felt it at all—is to cut ourselves off from our life force. When we are embodied, we are bonded with the self, feeling our feelings and trusting our body's signals. This allows us to hear our own quiet voices, and this connection is the basis of intuition and authenticity.

This is not just psychobabble and jargon. The location

that oversees these processes is the insula, an area deep inside the brain thought to be involved in self-awareness. The insula helps us to process "gut feelings" and to recognize bodily sensations, particularly how these sensations tie into emotions. I ignored the message of these gut feelings once, when I was working at Bellevue. It was also a time when I was lecturing medical students on violence and safety, psychosis, and drugs of abuse. In the safety lecture, I'd remind students that they are animals, that their brains are wired, exquisitely and anciently, to detect threat. If they would only pay attention to that little voice in their heads—the insula!—and heed their fears, their brains and bodies would never let them down. The problem, I warned them, comes when we notice those faint alarms but then stuff them down so we can "man up."

But that's exactly what I did back in the psych ER, and I got punched in the face for it. Right before I went out to reinterview one of my patients, I was joking around in the nurses' station about getting hit, saying that I'd been there long enough and I was due, as if I needed to be baptized in violence to be legitimized as a Bellevue staffer. How could I have known ahead of time that this would happen? Because my body already knew. Some part of my intuition from my first exchange with this patient had put the idea in my head: this guy is dangerous. But instead of heeding the warning, I turned cowboy—a pretty accurate picture of the way I could sometimes behave back in the nineties, and especially at Bellevue. I went against the advice of my own lectures and ignored the warnings of my own body.

Were you taught to ignore fear, to pack it away the way I was? We need to dismantle these behaviors. I assume little boys heard these admonishments more than girls did, though I've met quite a few women who remember, as I do, being told not to be scared or sad, or at least not to share those feelings. And not only did we learn to squelch our natural alarm system and ignore the signals of the fear center, we were also taught to disregard our hunger and our libido. This last nugget of admonishment will be familiar to women in particular. Part of becoming an adult, we were told, is to tame those appetites because they are too powerful for us to control. And while we were being trained in this way to quiet our deepest fears and suppress our innermost desires, we cut ourselves off from our intuition and from our bodies.

In the worst-case scenario, in the face of true and significant trauma, people try to disown the "person" who suffered the traumatic event, and so they split off from the self that was abused. This goes along with a fundamental denial—that the event didn't happen—and those who suffered a trauma think, *Well, it didn't happen to me.* Once someone starts segregating parts of themselves like that, what is left gets smaller. They live life using only some of the self and expending a lot of energy to keep the other parts quiet. More incidents of shame only cause more splintering, and less of a self to survive on.

The only way not to fall apart is to come together; this is known as integration. Getting all the facets of the self to work together is a necessary step for emotional health and authenticity. You can't afford to shelter a saboteur among your fractured selves. This is why the idea of a unified self is so crucial. Self-hatred comes from a split somewhere. When there are divisions within the self—when we're ignoring bodily signs of hunger or horniness, or not listening to our own quiet, intuitive voice that knows right from wrong, when we pretend that we can walk up to a dangerous person without getting punched—this is sabotage.

If you want to know how someone feels, just look into their eyes. This eye contact experience goes in two directions—out to another and in to ourselves. We cannot fully participate in this encounter while censoring and excluding a significant percentage of our own self. We're wired from infancy to focus on the gaze of others for signals of love, safety, danger, threat, and other more subtle emotions. When we read the eyes this way, the information is processed through the insula, the seat of our intuition. Inner perception of the physiological condition of the body is known as interoceptive awareness. Fragmented people have a hard time with this. They seem evasive. They can't lock eyes. They look away. And they are perpetually moving away from experiencing their own emotions.

To overcome that kind of double-edged evasion, we have to get back in touch with our emotions and calmly and truthfully convey them to others, often just after articulating them to ourselves. This is key to connecting with other people. It's just as crucial for reconnecting with the self.

Studies using neural imagery point to the insula as the command center of self-awareness. Increased insular functioning has been correlated with increased empathy. The insula, for example, controls the rate of the heartbeat and brings it into sync with the heart rate of a companion, a key mechanism in helping to enable empathy.

The insula has several parts to it, back, middle, and front (or in medical speak, posterior, medial, and anterior). Sensory pathways from the rest of the body enter via the posterior insula and are then represented and integrated in the mid-insula. By the time the stimuli move to the front part, thanks to the integration of information in the mid-insula, we're generating subjective bodily feelings as well as emotions. The front or anterior insula is involved in many experiences, from drug cravings to epiphanies to maternal love to weighing information to make a decision. People who are particularly anxious show increased activity in this area, and its hyperactivity has been linked to a feeling of diminished control.

One survey by Dr. Bud Craig at Barrow Neurological Institute in Phoenix, Arizona, gave a short list of activities that stimulate the anterior insula: dyspnea, or shortness of breath; the Valsalva maneuver (the thing you do when you bear down to move your bowels); exploratory sensual touch, like massage; itch; genital stimulation; sensations of cool or warmth; exercise; wine-tasting by sommeliers or anyone trained to connect the olfactory and memory networks of the brain; and distension of the bladder, stomach, rectum, or esophagus. He cataloged its role in cognitive control, decision-making, perception of time, visual and auditory processing, risk, emotional awareness, singing, and awareness of the self and the body. The list is so extensive that he came to a general conclusion that covers them all: the anterior insula should be "considered as a potential neural correlate of consciousness." In plain English, the anterior insula is the source of awareness.

Why does it help to know this? It lets us look at our biology, knowing that it can't be separated from our psychology or our social relationships. Empathy and embodiment are deeply enmeshed, just as thoughts and emotions are. How you think affects how you feel emotionally, which affects how your body functions. During my medical training at Temple, "the biopsychosocial model" was ingrained into all of us prospective doctors. You had to see the patient not just as their dysfunctional body parts, but as part of a larger dysfunctional whole: thoughts, emotions, and social status collaborate toward wholeness and health, or conspire to bring on disease and pathology.

In a 1961 letter from Carl Jung to Bill Wilson, founder of Alcoholics Anonymous, Jung speaks of a mutual friend's alcoholism: "His craving for alcohol was the equivalent on a low level of the spiritual thirst for our being for wholeness, expressed in mediaeval language: the union with God." "Holy," "health," and "hale" all come from the same root word, meaning "whole." To heal is to restore to a state of wholeness. That's my first job.

Josh's path to integration—his embodiment and the merging of all of his splintered selves—is leading him through body awareness, which in turn is leading him into a new-found emotional awareness. Microdosing and the divergent thinking it makes possible are facilitating his progress. He's an extreme case, but also an instructive one, since so much of his awakening has grown out of his simultaneous attention to his body and his feelings. For every breakthrough, it was impossible to divide his newborn bodily sensation from the dawning awareness of his emotions.

Cannabis can help people integrate, too. It affects areas of the brain involved with just these processes. A study of blood flow (which indirectly measures brain activity) in people given THC showed increased flow in not only the frontal parts of the brain involved in cognitive and emotional processing, but also in the insula, thus altering interoceptive awareness.

CANNABIS, QUEEN OF THE
MEDICINAL PLANTS

In 1988, the year I started medical school, two researchers at the Saint Louis University School of Medicine, Drs. Allyn Howlett and William Devane, discovered receptor sites in the brain that seemed specifically designed to respond to compounds found in cannabis. A little more digging revealed that these receptors were among the most prevalent in the brain.

In 1992, the year I graduated from medical school and began my residency, Devane paired up with Dr. Lumir Hanus, a researcher at the Hebrew University in Jerusalem. Working together in the lab of Dr. Raphael Mechoulam, who first isolated THC, the principal psychoactive element in cannabis, this international team identified the endogenous, or naturally occurring, THC-like compound that the body produces on its own to act on these receptors. They dubbed this cannabis-like compound "anandamide," after the Sanskrit word "ananda," or bliss. The discovery of anandamide was followed by other compounds with more prosaic names, like 2-arachidonoylglycerol (2-AG). Together, they're known as the endocannabinoids—the cannabis-like compounds produced by the body—to distinguish them from phytocannabinoids, the cannabis-derived compounds produced by cannabis plants.

These discoveries kicked off a research race, as teams tried to unearth the way these compounds might actually work in the body. Soon, cannabinoid receptor sites were discovered throughout the body—and not just the human body, but also in all mammals, truffle mushrooms, even primitive organisms like sponges. These widely scattered receptors, which could be found in every organ and gland throughout the immune system and connective tissue, seemed to constitute a separate, highly functional network that plays a key role in maintaining homeostasis in immune and metabolic functions. This network, now known as the endocannabinoid system (ECS), has been a rich field of study for research scientists, and might be better known and studied if it weren't for the obstacles our government has erected.

I was amazed to uncover this entire saga for the first time, eighteen years removed from medical school, when I was editing a book on cannabis and its role in medicine, politics, science, and culture. It seemed impossible to me that I, a card-carrying drug user and longtime student of all things psychoactive, could have missed this. But despite the medical value of this discovery, to this day, very few medical schools include study of the ECS in their curricula. The findings are not contested, and the science is not controversial. Very few people, except a few diehards in government agencies charged with policing drug laws, argue against the potential benefits of treatments that target the ECS or seek to exploit its many therapeutic functions. But the federal government of the United States continues to classify cannabis as a Schedule I drug, obstructing research both at American universities and, through diplomatic pressure, at research institutions abroad.

This elaborate system of cannabinoid receptors didn't evolve over millennia for the sole purpose of smoking pot. It seems to have worked the other way around. Cannabis has flourished partly because it contains compounds that mimic or enhance preexisting chemical reactions occurring in the body. Once humans recognized this effect, they wanted to ensure that they always had a steady supply. As one of the first domesticated plants, cannabis joined a select group of agricultural necessities that spread from China and the Eurasian steppes to Europe and the Middle East and beyond, valued not only as a food or textile, but also for medicinal and spiritual purposes, back when medicine and transcendent religious experiences were more intertwined.

The ECS seems to work in coordination with the parasympathetic nervous system. For example, learning only happens when the body is in para, and cannabis and CBD promote neurogenesis, or the formation of new brain cells and connections, i.e., learning. Cannabis in its many forms helps to put the body into para, and can help remove the obstacles to connection that we place in our own way, increasing our sense of and delight in embodiment. While psychedelics can help reshape the landscape of the mind, cannabis can help support and encourage a sense of connectedness, highlighting bodily awareness, especially the sense of ourselves as creatures in a green and natural setting. They can act as adjunct therapies in the search for oneness.

Let's first identify the key players in the cannabis branch of treatment. Many people know about THC (tetrahydrocannabinol), the main psychoactive chemical in pot that gets you high. Once less well-known, but recently exploding in popularity, is CBD (cannabidiol), the second-most-common chemical in the flower. CBD is nonintoxicating, but it is psychoactive. While THC can make people forgetful, CBD does not diminish memory. In fact, some of my patients who used to take stimulants to treat their ADHD now use CBD instead. They find it gives them a calm focus. From a psychopharmacologist's perspective, weighing clinical effectiveness against potential side effects, the use of cannabis and its derivatives is proving to be both broadly useful and gentle on both body and mind.

While both THC and CBD are anti-inflammatory and antioxidant painkillers that quell nausea, there are major differences between the two. THC can make you a bit fuzzy or make it hard to stop eating. (So just don't start. Munchies solved.) CBD tends to cut appetite and promote focus. THC, especially in large doses, can make one anxious or self-conscious, but CBD can effectively decrease anxiety. This may be because CBD alters the shape of the cannabinoid receptor, where THC docks, weakening its ability to bind them together.

The two key activators of the body's naturally occurring cannabis receptors—both the ones first identified by Drs. Howlett and Devane in 1988, known as CB1 receptors, and the cannabis receptors dispersed throughout the body, which are known as CB2 and were discovered later—are the endocannabinoids anandamide and 2-AG. If you give stressed-out mice both anandamide and 2-AG, you will see solid antianxiety effects (e.g., these naturally occurring neurotransmitters are key players in flipping the switch from a stressed state to a receptive one). You can get approximately the same result with CBD, which does two things: stimulates the release of anandamide and, maybe more important, inhibits its rapid breakdown by the enzyme fatty acid amide hydrolase, or FAAH. That means that CBD promotes anandamide availability and prolongs the blissful state that it brings on. The end result is a destressed, resilient, and relaxed state.

Research shows that THC also acts on receptors in brain areas involved in memory (hippocampus) and fear (amygdala) processing. CBD also has fear-mitigating effects; animal studies support the theory that cannabinoids (both THC and CBD) can reduce the fear response, and animal models of PTSD respond well to both cannabinoids. Overwhelming numbers of anecdotal reports of people with PTSD show them faring better while using medicinal cannabis, particularly for quelling nightmares. A recent study of PTSD patients linked their cannabis use with milder episodes of depression and fewer suicidal thoughts than nonusers. Clinical studies have been tricky to do in the United States due to bureaucratic obstacles, and even when they are performed, the quality of allowable study drug makes it hard to prove efficacy.

For practical reasons, treatment with CBD may often be preferable to using cannabis. While whole-plant cannabis may not be an option for many people (it makes some people more anxious, euphoric, or "scatter-brained"), there is solid data on using CBD alone to treat anxiety, and I recommend it consistently to my patients. Although it is often used as a sleep aid, it is not reliably sedating in all people. Often it helps to alleviate symptoms of depression without altering normal sleep patterns, which is an issue in many prescription medicines used in psychiatry. In rat models of depression (you don't want to know), CBD has shown rapid and sustained antidepressant effects, which may be a result of increases in BDNF (brain-derived neurotrophic factor) levels, a powerful protein that encourages synaptic growth (synaptogenesis)—new brain cell connections—and improves short-term memory. CBD has also been shown to attenuate the aggressive behavior that can be induced by social isolation. Did you know that animals get more aggressive when they isolate?

There are some people who respond more to CBD alone, while many others do better with whole-plant cannabis, which contains both THC and CBD. Medical cannabis users perceived a 50 percent reduction in depression and a 58 percent reduction in anxiety and stress following whole-plant cannabis use. A study led by Dr. Carrie Cuttler of the Department of Psychology at Washington State University discovered that "two puffs were sufficient to reduce the intensity of depression and anxiety, while 10 puffs or more produced the greatest perceived reductions in stress." One interesting finding: women reported larger reductions in anxiety from cannabis than did men.

Cannabis is commonly used to treat insomnia. Some of my patients smoke it, while others prefer to eat a small amount of an edible a few hours before bed. It can also be used to treat what are called "parasomnias," sleep disorders characterized by abnormal movements, behaviors, or perceptions during sleep, like jaw grinding, sleepwalking, or nightmares. In fact, nighttime cannabis is a mainstay of alternative treatment of PTSD, where nightmares of trauma are common.

I'm particularly intrigued by the antipsychotic effects of CBD. The first reports of this came out in the early eighties, and it turns out CBD can have a role in treating both schizophrenia and psychosis in general. I have worked with a few people with schizophrenia and bipolar disorder who, by titrating up on CBD doses, have been able to taper down on their prescription antipsychotic medicines. In high doses, CBD can act much like other mood stabilizers and antipsychotics.

Some caveats: CBD and Valproate (Depakote) do not mix. Ditto for some blood thinners and chemotherapy agents. And please understand I am not advocating that anyone with a psychiatric illness stop their meds abruptly or un-supervised. But I am suggesting that people educate them-selves and their treating clinicians about the potential therapeutic use of cannabidiol as an "add-on" to traditional therapies.

You can see the pattern—cannabis and CBD seem to of-fer gentler alternatives to drugs with more problematic side effects. Joe Schrank, who founded High Sobriety in Los An-geles and Remedy Recovery in San Francisco, two cannabis-inclusive rehab facilities, says, "Cannabis is the condom of the drug war." Just as condoms help reduce the spread of HIV/AIDS, cannabis use reduces binge drinking and opiate-related morbidity and mortality. Recent studies show that the more people have access to cannabis, the fewer pursue illegal opiates and die from overdoses. First, cannabis increases the pain-relieving effects of opiates without altering the levels of those medicines in the blood—so a combination of the two would allow for lower dosing with fewer side effects. In an open-label study of chronic pain patients, medical cannabis use resulted in improved pain and functional outcomes, re-sulting in significant reduction of opioid use. Another ob-servational study of people with lower back pain on opiates long-term showed that nearly half of them were able to tran-sition to using just cannabis.

More studies from researchers like Drs. Yasmin Hurd and Julia Arnsten are showing that just administering CBD can effectively lower opioid use and help reduce opioid-related morbidity. And because cannabinoids are anti-inflammatory, they're not just masking the pain as opiates do; they're getting at the underlying source. It's the same thing with oxytocin. It can treat physical pain and enhance wound healing, but it also can soothe emotional pain. Simply put, cannabis helps to put the body in para. And just as opiates do, cannabis can act as a psychic pain reliever.

The positive effects of cannabis may be even more sweeping than that, because just like oxytocin and THC, CBD is associated with the growth of new brain cell connections (or neuroplasticity). In one promising development, CBD seems to help modify neuronal circuits that have been disrupted by long-term substance-abuse disorders, helping to repair and rewire the brain's reward structures in ways that make many people less likely to act upon the triggers that previously sparked addictive behavior—what scientific papers call "reducing the salience of drug cues." When I offered testimony to the New York State legislature about our medical cannabis program, my first recommendation, before I even began to read my statement, was that they allow opiate addiction as a qualifying condition. Several states have followed suit. Both THC and CBD, together or alone, can work in this way, easing these compulsions.

You know what else works? Oxytocin, that essential molecule that is secreted in childbirth, nursing, hugging, or even just when you're looking fondly across a room at someone you love. There was a slogan in the 1990s, "Hugs Not Drugs," that was popular during the Reagan era of Just Say No. Now that I understand oxytocin and drug addiction better, I'd say that slogan reflects a neurological reality. If people are sad and scared, they will want to soothe themselves with anything that acts like a drug, which is nearly everything—food, sex, gambling—if you abuse it enough. If oxytocin tamps down the amygdala, the fear center, then people feel safe, which equals less discomfort and therefore less of a need to self-soothe. Then they won't have the same pressing need for these drugs.

In animal studies, oxytocin has been shown to inhibit the development of tolerance to alcohol and opioids and to reduce drug-seeking behaviors, reward, and craving with cocaine, methamphetamine (speed), and cannabis. Oxytocin can attenuate the withdrawal symptoms from addiction to morphine. It may be that over time, oxytocin will be used clinically to help people modify their behaviors, especially those that are fear-based, or designed to quiet the fear.

In no small part, substance-use disorders are learned behaviors, relying on mental circuitry that is strengthened and reinforced with each individual incident of drug use. As the effectiveness of the drug diminishes over time, a well-established consequence of prolonged use, the comfort that a habitual user experiences in the rituals of drug use can begin to take on as much or more importance than the actual experience of the drug itself. This is not to minimize the physical damage that prolonged use can inflict. The body's dependence on the drug is real. But so are these behaviors. In a sense, what we used to call a "drug habit" (the currently preferred term is "substance-use disorder") can actually be seen as two things: the drug and the habit. The neuroplastic effects of cannabis in its many forms can be a very effective tool in treating the latter, not because they substitute a milder or less damaging addiction (they don't) but because cannabis can, by helping create new neural pathways, dampen the triggering effect of drug cues and reduce their salience. So can psychedelics and so can oxytocin itself, the neurochemical enabler of neuroplasticity.

Keeping in mind that certain substances help the brain "rewire" itself, it may make sense to you that cannabis has been used to help people stop smoking crack. CBD alone has helped cocaine and methamphetamine users avoid relapse, and it may also reduce demand for cigarettes. Dr. Chandni Hindocha, of the Clinical Psychopharmacology Unit at University College London, has shown that a single eight-hundred-milligram dose of CBD significantly reduced smokers' response to cigarette cues. Another study showed that cigarette smokers who used a CBD inhaler whenever they felt like lighting up cut their nicotine consumption by 40 percent in one week. CBD has proven so powerful at diminishing the salience of drug cues to drug users that it may be effective as a treatment for people who are addicted to a wide range of substances and behaviors.

In the addiction business, some clinicians are slow to adapt, and there is a "tyranny of dead ideas" that refuse to die. Concepts like "clean" or "dirty" just don't work anymore to describe people involved with drugs. Early adopters of California's medical cannabis programs reported that their patients were also using cannabis to cure their alcoholism. The term "Cali sober" became a thing, and still is. A series of studies showed that patients who use medical cannabis do reduce their alcohol intake. One study compared the density of CB1 receptors in alcoholics versus social drinkers, and found that even after abstinence, there were fewer receptors in the addicted group, so they may be "self-medicating" this imbalance with alcohol, though honestly they'd likely be better off using cannabinoids. In studies of alcohol dependence in mice, CBD reduced alcohol consumption, motivation to drink, and relapse rates. CBD also reduced alcohol-induced brain damage in rodents and can lessen alcohol's damaging impact to the liver. Thanks to studies like these, the place of cannabis in a harm-reduction framework is more widely accepted, with promising results in helping people lessen their dependence on other, more harmful drugs.

The neuroplasticity that cannabis and CBD promotes is a key reason that I've been on a campaign, along with Doctors for Cannabis Regulation, to persuade the National Football League and their physicians that it's a good idea for their players to rely more on cannabinoids and less on opiates. Painkillers only mask symptoms, sometimes enabling further damage to occur. Cannabis-based medicines can often treat the underlying issues that are causing the pain. In addition to pain and inflammation control, there is mounting convincing scientific evidence that cannabis or simply CBD alone may help to protect the brain from injury, treat brain-injured patients (like those football players with chronic traumatic encephalopathy), and help to lessen the risk for age-related cognitive disorders like dementia.

This has implications beyond the NFL. Dementia is characterized by an increase in excitatory brain chemicals, free radicals, and inflammation. Stimulating the ECS can combat all of these. We know that activating CB1 receptors facilitates the growth of new brain cells. Cannabis can also help to rid the brain of the plaques and tangles that typify Alzheimer's disease. In recent studies, both THC and CBD acted as neuroprotective agents, helping to clear the brain of amyloid accumulation and the accompanying inflammation, the pathological responses typical of Alzheimer's disease. The American government holds a patent on using cannabinoids as neuroprotective agents [patent #6630507] even though they continue to list cannabis in Schedule I, meaning there is supposedly no accepted medical use. Is this an example of hypocrisy on the federal level? You decide.

Despite the mountains of results, there is still a struggle within the medical community to recognize that cannabinoids can treat diseases. As you can tell, I am well beyond that point. I'm advocating for wider acceptance of cannabis as a defense against mental decline and dementia as well as a tool to help a body and mind on the path to oneness with the self. Cannabis enables wellness, as part of a parasympathetic lifestyle that includes exercise, sleep, meditation, and an anti-inflammatory diet. In turn, keeping your stress down by flipping into para also keeps inflammation down, which can mean less pain and lower rates of many diseases that have their root in inflammation. It should also be noted here that many of the classical psychedelics are potent anti-inflammatory molecules.

What makes you stressed? Being separated from your body and your breath, and being separated from your own personal integrity and authenticity. Cannabis can help to de-stress in so many ways, while heightening the sensations of being in your body. What else can make you stressed? Paradoxically, both being separated from those we love and spending time with those same people. Isn't life funny? If you smoked cannabis, you'd think so.

MDMA-ASSISTED PSYCHOTHERAPY
AND INTEGRATION OF THE SELF

Sometimes the self can grow deeply resistant to efforts at reintegration. Trauma, as we've seen, can split us in pieces, separating parts, segregating a side of ourselves, alienating wounded and vulnerable facets of a person from the functional part—or semifunctional parts—that we use to act in the world. MDMA therapy has been getting positive results addressing these traumas, especially among people who have suffered from treatment-resistant PTSD. The results have been so encouraging that the FDA has designated MDMA-assisted psychotherapy a breakthrough therapy, meaning it recognizes that preliminary clinical results have demonstrated substantial improvement over existing therapies. It's a very promising development in the world of psychedelic studies.

This new designation accelerates the process of drug development. MDMA-assisted therapy is going into phase-three multicenter trials—the final phase of studies, one of the last steps before official approval. I'm proud to be a medical monitor for these studies, as I am of my longtime connection to MAPS, the Multidisciplinary Association for Psychedelic Studies, a nonprofit research organization and drug development company that is sponsoring this work.

"Breakthrough" is the right word for these therapies. In the phase-two stage, the subjects in the studies had an average of nearly twenty years in therapy and had taken multiple different medications and combinations of medications, but still suffered from severe PTSD. In the trials, the protocols involved preparatory sessions, then a treatment session with MDMA, followed by integration sessions to help the participants make sense of the startling changes experienced with MDMA. This cycle repeated two or three times, depending on the study.

MDMA acts by releasing serotonin into the synapse, the area between two neurons or nerve cells. Dopamine is also increased, as is oxytocin. So the person is in a place where they are attentive and motivated to talk (dopamine) and also to connect and trust (oxytocin), and they feel calm and centered (serotonin), willing and able to do the tough work of digging up, sifting through, and making sense of trauma. This last piece is due to a dampening of the fear response mediated by the amygdala, which can be hyper-responsive in people with PTSD. Both oxytocin alone, and MDMA alone, can quiet this emotional center of the brain, called "the repository of truth" in a long-admired book by Dr. Arthur Janov, *The Biology of Love*. The effects of these permutations in neurotransmitters and connectivity are particularly useful at making psychotherapy go deeper, faster, and more comfortably. Usually uncovering trauma takes years. It is painful and slow work. Here, the work is done over months, in several sessions.

The trials demonstrated that the greatest progress tends to happen in the first session. Trained therapists administering the drug and actively assisting throughout the next six to eight hours were amazed to watch the process: patients often seemed to recover "basically overnight." The people who experience this change—who have felt the reintegration and with it the seeming disappearance of their symptoms of PTSD—are often surprised to learn that such a potent treatment is not yet FDA approved. One group of veterans in the phase-two study started a lobbying group to convince Veterans Affairs that the treatment should be the new standard for veterans.

Dr. Chris Stauffer, an assistant professor of psychiatry at the Weill Institute for Neurosciences at the University of California, San Francisco, is working on the current round of trials, and he spoke about the experience. He was surprised by some of the adjustments he had to make to participate fully in the twists and turns of an MDMA therapy session. "I had to unlearn some of the things that I've learned in my Western medical training," he said. For example, the prohibition against touch, which is often the thing psychiatric patients need most. There is still the framework of consent throughout, and much discussion in the preparatory sessions about requests coming from the participants. "So there's a lot of concern and permission and all of that," he says. "But sometimes people want to, like, hold your face for five minutes."

The MDMA sessions can also validate novel therapeutic systems in dramatic ways. Frequently, Stauffer said, patients will spontaneously start talking about different parts of themselves, even giving these separate parts names and describing their appearances individually, giving further support to the idea of a fragmentation of the self. There's an effort in the MDMA sessions to make the experience inner-directed—the patient will often lie on a couch wearing eye shades and headphones—so it can be surprising when the introspection turns into something entirely different. "We had a patient recently who, during her MDMA session, started talking about having this vision of a bunch of people sitting around a boardroom table. She realized all of the people were her and they were trying to figure out how to work together," Stauffer said. Through the course of her treatment, they identified these individuals and discovered which ones were in conflict. "It's kind of like doing family therapy."

In fact, he says it can be helpful to follow protocols from a type of therapy called Internal Family Systems (IFS), developed by Dr. Richard Schwartz out of his work with people seeking treatment for eating disorders. The standard treatment for eating disorders at the time Schwartz started was behavioral therapy—essentially, a system of punishment and reward aimed at reinforcing targeted behaviors. But in listening to his patients, he soon found it valuable to identify different parts of the self, which he divided into three categories: the exiles, who suffered the trauma; the managers, who protect the exiles and deal with the world; and the firefighters, whose method of protecting the exile involves distracting attention from the feelings of hurt or shame, often with impulsive or addictive behavior.

The IFS model recognizes that each of these figures has a role to play, and the goal is to get all of them to work together. The big contribution that Schwartz made, in Stauffer's view, comes in asking consent from the different protectors directly, asking them to step back, so that the "capital S self" can access the vulnerable parts of the psyche that split off. "I didn't know about this before these trials," Stauffer says. "So it was hard for me as a student of psychiatry to understand. If someone had taught me that, I would have been, like, 'What the hell?' But having experienced it, talking to these different parts of people directly has really helped me understand the mind more."

He gave an example from the current trial. One participant, Maria S., a woman in her thirties from a large family in Missouri, had been four years old when her father left the family. One afternoon at her grandparents' house, her mom and her mom's new boyfriend came to pick her up, along with all the rest of her siblings. Once they were all loaded into the family minivan, her uncle (her mother's brother-in-law) came out to the car and shot her mom's new boyfriend in the face at point-blank range. It was, even in the best of times, a chaotic family, but in the aftermath of that horror, no one thought to take care of four-year-old Maria. She was left to fend for herself.

Stauffer had seen training videos. Often, people describe their parts and protectors, and sometimes a therapist can engage them directly. For the most part, the subpersonalities come across as roughly the same age as the participant. But when the original trauma, and the subsequent splitting of the self, occurred at a young age, in this case below the age of five, it's not unusual for the participant in the MDMA session to embody that child and speak as a four-year-old. "So the first part that came forward from this boardroom scene was this angry four-year-old child. I can't remember what she first said, but my co-therapist and I watched this thirty-year-old woman as her whole body transformed into that of a four-year-old child. It can be pretty intense. It almost seems like an exorcism. You're talking to this demon who needs to be exorcised."

At first Maria's four-year-old self was hesitant, thinking she'd get in trouble. But when they told her she could scream into a can or hit pillows, the kind of classic therapy routines that, under normal circumstances, people are too self-conscious to commit to in a psychiatrist's office, Maria went at it with abandon, and Stauffer and his cotherapist held up couch cushions, providing counterresistance while she wore herself out. When that seemed to be coming to an end, they asked her what she needed next. And she said, "A hug." So they both sat by her side with their arms around her while she cried for nearly twenty minutes.

In the next MDMA session, Stauffer encountered more voices, more selves. First came a manager type who was adept at dissociating, deflecting attention in a socially acceptable way whenever conversation circulated near sensitive topics. When they asked the dissociator to step back, Maria described a recurring dream—almost a life condition—where she felt weighed down, walking through the city with a huge weight descending on her from above and powerful gravity pulling at her from below, so heavy that she found it hard to take a step. Once the dissociator had stepped back, a whole collection of characters and emotions seemed to pour out of her, Stauffer said, almost like purging. It was as if she had an army, each of them willing to say, *You can't have access to your vulnerable self, you can't handle it, you shouldn't trust anyone.* But one by one, the two therapists asked them all to step back. And once they did, Maria sat between them in a state of weak, raw vulnerability. She wanted to hold Stauffer's hand and practice looking into his eyes.

The first MDMA session had been filled with the yelling and punching of the four-year-old. But Stauffer said that was nowhere near as intense as simply sitting and being present in the second session. "It felt like I was making up for all of the neglect she'd been through in her whole childhood," he said. "Looking into this woman's eyes and holding her hand—there's so much that we don't understand yet, things we can't measure that are going on in the room. Her looking at me was calming to her, like she was learning how to bring the parasympathetic nervous system online, taking in calmness and acquiring an ability not to be so hypervigilant. But for me, it was the opposite experience. It felt like I was being activated. And this was an exchange of energy that we don't understand yet—or at least I don't."

Maria went home after that session and began looking at herself in the mirror for ten and fifteen minutes at a time. This was not something that the therapists had suggested. She came up with it herself. It seemed to calm her, to rekindle the experience of the MDMA session, to stare at herself and flip into para. She realized that even looking in the mirror at herself, she was averting her eyes, which made her see that she'd been doing the same thing with the rest of the world. It's not hard to see why. The original episode, being a witness to murder at four, wasn't her only trauma. She'd suffered years of physical and emotional abuse through her childhood and teen years until she moved out. That experience had left her with the habit, or maybe the protective strategy, of avoiding eye contact at all costs. It posed too great a risk.

One of the risks in the aftermath of these enormous changes, Stauffer pointed out, comes when the participant returns home—to the web of relationships in her daily life. Sometimes this network can act to reinforce or re-create the trauma. They may go home and their symptoms have disappeared. In Maria's case, she said that the feeling of weight, of constantly being pulled down by gravity, a feeling that never quite left her, had entirely disappeared. But the worry, from a therapeutic standpoint, is that the partner, or the larger circle of friends, would pull her back into the dynamics that had previously defined her life.

To help get past such hurdles, the therapists offer to bring in the partner to the integration sessions in the aftermath of the MDMA-assisted therapy, to talk about the big changes and how they can help the system shift with these changes instead of working against them. "Sometimes people end up breaking up," Stauffer said. "But we encourage people not to make major life decisions in the afterglow of the treatment." Maria had a boyfriend who also had a history of trauma, and she did consider ending the relationship. And when the therapists offered to bring him in for a session, she insisted that she didn't want that. Instead, she took what she'd learned in the sessions and tried it at home. She said that when she and her boyfriend got into a fight, as he was getting upset, she was using the calming techniques she'd learned on herself.

Then Maria turned to her boyfriend and said, "Listen, why don't we take a deep breath together and I'm going to hold your hand and let's see what sort of sensation comes up"— exactly what she'd done in her MDMA session. And this became part of their crisis tool kit, something they would do together, holding hands and making eye contact. Soon, according to Maria, he was making nearly as much progress as she was, even without access to the therapists and the MDMA sessions. It seemed as if, having discovered these in- struments of connection in herself, she could teach him the exercises and model the kind of behavior that allowed him to find a new balance in his life too.

This transitive effect—that the MDMA-assisted therapy

of one partner in a couple could positively affect the other partner, even without access to the drug or participation in the therapy—recalls another study, from 2012, when Drs. Omri Weisman and Ruth Feldman, at the Gonda Multidisciplinary Brain Research Center at Bar-Ilan University, outside Tel Aviv, gave a group of fathers oxytocin in a nasal spray, then had them interact with their babies. Oxytocin, the hormone that the body secretes in massive amounts during childbirth, nursing, and sex, promotes "affiliative bonding," as the studies say. Not surprisingly, Weisman and Feldman found that doses of oxytocin measurably increased the fathers' quality and amount of interaction with their babies. But what did surprise them was that the levels of oxytocin in the babies' blood increased by roughly the same amount—even though they had never been given a dosage.

MDMA acutely increases oxytocin levels, which amplify the prosocial aspects of the drug: you become more open and trusting in general. In MDMA therapy sessions, that means that you bond with the therapist, reliably improving the outcome of the therapy. Because of that increased therapeutic alliance, because you trust both yourself and the therapist, you're able to open up about brutal childhood traumas that you never dared to speak about before. (For some people, it is the first time that their stories are fully heard or believed. I have several patients who were molested by their doctors or coaches, and then betrayed by their parents, who could not face that truth.) And because of the therapist's compassion, you're also likely to be more compassionate toward yourself, to forgive yourself and others associated with trauma. One of the ways that oxytocin works is by quieting the fear center—the amygdala, small bilateral almond-shaped segments of the brain that are particularly active in patients with PTSD. So because the fear center is, in a sense, turned off, you're not in fight-or-flight mode, and you're able to look at the trauma without rejecting or repressing it.

The trials are helping to reveal the factors that make MDMA therapy so profoundly transformative for people with PTSD. We can better understand the chemistry of fear and compassion, the way we process traumatic memories, and how chemically triggered neuroplasticity can help "rewire" the brain. One of the reasons Maria's treatment was so successful is this neuroplastic rewiring. She became less fearful about discussing her trauma, in part because the traumatic memories carried less fear with them. In the phase-two trials, over two-thirds of the participants no longer met the requirement for PTSD. Many of the subjects were able to decrease the amount of psychiatric medications they were taking, thus lessening or eliminating long-term side effects of antidepressant or anxiety medication, like weight gain, depressed libido, and decreased motivation. Subjects reported experiencing life in a new way, responding to old triggers with new behaviors.

In fact, one of the most exciting characteristics of all of these new medicines—CBD, MDMA, and psychedelics like LSD, DMT, and psilocybin mushrooms—is their ability to stimulate neuroplasticity, allowing the brain to make new neurons and connections. There is a term being used lately, "psychoplastogens," to describe this group of drugs. Nothing new has been added to the arsenal, but the grouping points to a new emphasis in psychedelic circles on the reopening of a critical learning period that is made possible by this family of medicines.

But maybe we don't have to be so technical. After Maria's treatment, she used simple tools to reconnect with herself and to connect with her boyfriend: staring in the mirror, making eye contact, holding hands, deep breathing, showing patience. As different as their experiences and their treatments were, both Josh and Maria learned to cultivate interoception, the ability to monitor what they were feeling. In dramatically different ways, both of their treatments seemed to jump-start their emotional intelligence, helping them to sense and understand the feelings of others and to catalog and handle their own. We know what helps this process: meditation, cuddling, havening, breathing, yoga, nature walks—anything that can put you in a parasympathetic state. Remember these watchwords: "observation" and "self-regulation."

FOLLOW-UP

I got a letter recently from a patient I hadn't seen in years. During the time I was treating her, she was experiencing significant spells of depression and struggling with ADHD. On top of all this, she was drinking a lot. She was young and impulsive, and I worried about her. In the spirit of concern, I also spoke with her mother. Well aware of the limits of her ability to intervene, she thanked me for all I was doing to keep her daughter well.

It clearly wasn't enough for Tina, though. After many years of treatment, she disappeared from my practice, and I didn't hear anything from her till this morning, as I was finishing work on this chapter. Tina wrote:

Hi Julie,

I'm not sure why I'm just now choosing to write to you; the healing process is filled with twists and turns.

I want to let you know I've been off all pharmaceuticals for well over 3 years. The physical withdrawal was months long and brutal, but on the other side I discovered I never knew life could feel so easy. I have more energy, I can think clearly, I can decipher and express my emotions. I am actually quite a stable human being, it has been a joy to uncover.

I have done some work with plant medicines on Maui and in Peru. Through this blessing I have been able to identify root causes of the depression and anxiety I have struggled with. It turns out I am not "sick" at the core, but rather had emotions inside that were asking to be experienced. And in this way released.

I have been angry with you at times. I felt betrayed once I realized I was actually well. Like you wanted to keep me thinking I was sick. I still don't know if this is true, but I am hoping that your intentions were good, and maybe you didn't know another way. Either way, I am welcoming in compassion and forgiveness.

I am married to a wonderful man who is also on a spiritual path. I am teaching yoga to tourists and finding it fulfilling and healing. Most days I can experience a real sense of peace.

I don't even know if you will read this. But I wanted to share.

Aloha Julie,
Tina

It's hard to imagine a better letter or outcome. Her feelings of anger to a former prescribing doctor are consistent with successfully withdrawing from medication, something that from the sound of it she managed on her own, after considerable struggle. And dealing with her anger now, head-on, in a rational adult manner, in a spirit of compassion and forgiveness is a good sign. It certainly fits with being a happily married yoga teacher in Hawaii on a spiritual path! It seems likely that she found more ways to be in para, and no doubt there was some amount of neuroplasticity at play in her response to her explorations with mind-manifesting medicines.

But in a more profound sense, I am gratified that she has found a way to get at the root causes of her depression and now feels released. As a doctor who is keenly interested in what Tina calls "plant medicines"—which, judging from her geo-tag of Peru and Maui, I would take to very likely mean ayahuasca (a psychedelic tea) and possibly psilocybin—I am happy to hear that the experience was first of all safe, and beyond that, beneficial to her.

Not everyone is in a position to do deep spiritual work, but as I age and public acceptance of these modes of healing increases, I mention this work to more of my patients. I'm certainly an advocate. In some ways, the best avenue, from a legal standpoint, for me to learn about a patient's experience is the way I did with Tina, after the fact, when the precise circumstances are of secondary importance compared to the discovery of her therapeutic progress.

But as a doctor, I know that I have an obligation to my patients. Many of them arrive in my office declaring their intention to investigate these experiences. That was the case with Josh. Once I've learned of a patient's intentions, I feel deeply invested in the outcome. Above all, I want it to be safe—I never want to get that call from an emergency room when there are so many ways to guide a patient toward a positive result.

One key element to a positive outcome is focused intention. From a therapist's perspective that means eliminating thrill seekers who are simply looking for some kind of medical sanction for recreational use. For the serious, the therapist has to help provide a sense of what to expect: every clinical design includes preparatory sessions that not only lay out the format of the treatment session, what might happen in the six to eight hours while the psychedelic medicine is active, but also create a sense of trust that will allow the patient to venture into what will almost certainly include new and unpredictable territory. At this point, there is plenty of clinical data to demonstrate that the presence of a trained therapist acting as a guide, someone who is experienced negotiating the full range of behaviors and reactions and practiced at steering participants through troublesome stretches, has positive benefits, far beyond their ability to ensure that first no harm will be done.

My obligation doesn't end there, though. I am doing everything I can to advance the study of these experiences despite the legal difficulties. As Josh could tell you, anyone with a web browser can discover a highly active network of psychonauts, along with life-hacker-style DIY instructions for obtaining or, for the ambitious, concocting nearly anything on a psychedelic shopping list. Some doctors like me wish that there were sensible legal ways to advise and assist people through this dark market. Until there are, I'm here, trying to direct the traffic on an internet-era version of the Underground Railroad.

In fact, there is emerging evidence that women are experimenting with psychedelic self-treatment the way Tina did, and in increasingly large numbers. Given the history of bias against and underrepresentation of women and their unique health issues in scientific research, I feel the need to speak up for our issues from a medical perspective, at the very least.

But the point of all this is not to promote the psychedelic experience as an end in itself. Here and throughout the book, case studies of clinical experiences with psychedelic substances have a broader use: they serve as dramatic illustrations, illuminating the workings of the interior world. One of the remarkable characteristics of these experiences comes in the aftermath. A big reason that psychedelics are gaining a broader acceptance now is that evidence shows they are transformative but not addictive. People try to segregate the recreational model from the medical one, when both can be therapeutic. Whichever model you're working within, what's most important is to minimize harm and maximize benefit.

For our purposes, Maria's story is instructive not just for her dramatic breakthroughs during her MDMA session with Chris Stauffer. It's also important to pay attention to what she did *after* her treatment, as she set about maintaining the gains she made through integration. Those simple steps, her regimen for long-term maintenance of her once-fractured self, are available to anyone: make eye contact, hold hands, have patience and compassion. I keep a list handy, and I often send it to patients (especially in August, to tide people over during family vacations). None of it costs money, except maybe buying a notebook.

Here's my list, because we all have to get down to basics:

Be present.
Unplug.
Feel.
Journal.
Make art.
Dance.
Breathe through your nose.
Make joy a priority.
Connect.

You know what else is good? Silence. It also encourages neuroplasticity and neurogenesis.

Staying fully present, stilling the default mode network, and bringing the parts of yourself that have been scattered back to a sense of oneness sounds easier than it is in practice. Silence, taking the time to do nothing, to notice your thoughts but not get caught up in them, takes concentration. And there's one more thing: That negative voice in your head isn't the truth. The truth is in your body. Embodiment is a prerequisite for peace and joy.

If you'd like to rest here, self-partnered, integrated, and content, by all means, please do. But if you're game, these tools for oneness within the self are exactly what we need to help us take the next step: connecting as a couple, moving out of alienation and disconnection and into the intimate awareness where two become one.

CHAPTER 2

CONNECTION WITH A PARTNER

The meeting of two personalities is like the contact of two chemical substances: if there is any reaction, both are transformed.

—CARL JUNG

As we now know, connecting with the self is not always simple. As Josh discovered, the body can be unresponsive, whereas Maria felt extremes of emotion that left her feeling under siege. Meanwhile, the world we live in offers so many escapes and easy outs—distractions, compulsions, addictions—that leaving is often much easier than staying. Sometimes connecting with the self can feel like an impossible dream.

Luckily, there are practical steps—some as natural as breathing, others on the developing edge of psychopharmacology—that can help keep us balanced and receptive. But one thing about connecting with the self: it's always there. If you want to work on oneness, you don't have to make an appointment and you don't need to ask anyone's permission. You can just get on with it. That's one reason psychoactive substances can be such prominent therapeutic tools in connecting with the self. These medicines also have a profound effect on the neurochemistry of the brain. But the place where all these breakthroughs happen is interior and individual, and your permission is the only one required.

Now we'll take the next step, to connect on the most basic human level: one to one, person to person. We'll see that oxytocin is the glue that can help people form lasting attachments, and we'll learn about a study using MDMA, a powerful oxytocin releaser, in couples where one member has PTSD. So yes, mind-manifesting medicines play a role not only in connection with the self, but also in helping two people to come together.

We'll also dive into the neurochemistry of lust, romance, and mating, all those waves of hormonal signals that take us from the heavy surf of initial attraction to the calmer waters of long-term attachment. From a genetic standpoint, this is job number one for the body, the main point of evolution. But much of the neurochemistry designed to give us pleasure, bringing us together (and then, once a child is born, keeping us there), is the same chemistry that kicks in during addiction. It turns out, people can get addicted not just to masturbation or sex, but also to lust or falling in love. These things are designed to feel better than anything else, and once the mating dance begins, the body starts pulling out its biggest special effects.

Often sex, or the promise of sex, is what drives our connectedness. It's how we're built. But just because the body is exquisitely designed for sexual connection doesn't mean the world will offer you high-quality opportunities to connect. Also, keep in mind that not everyone is comfortable with closeness. Different attachment styles that grow out of the varieties of parental bonds—ambivalent, avoidant, and secure—can influence our style of connection in adulthood. For some avoidant people, being united with another human being is a terrifying prospect, something to escape at all costs. For others, it's clear they're ambivalent, approaching and then scurrying from intimacy. These behaviors may stem from childhood trauma or be strongly affected by the type of oxytocin receptor genes we carry. There's a simple test to determine which gene you carry, and that information may provide an explanation for some habits, good and bad, as well as a possible blueprint for healing. So pay attention to how anxious or relaxed you are at the prospect of attachment. It's vital information in moving toward oneness. And remember: conflict, whether within one person or between two, is growth trying to happen. So often, you need to move out of your comfort zone.

Observation and self-regulation, key components in creating emotional integrity and authenticity in the self, can work between two people as well. Think of it as a "vibe check." When you're connecting with a partner, it's important to watch for the sudden appearance of the fight-or-flight instinct. Forget conscious uncoupling—let's try conscious coupling. Check in with yourself to see how calm and open, versus agitated and defensive, you are in any given conversation with your partner. If you are in fight or flight, you won't be able to do the most important thing, which is to stay open and connect. Stay in the room, in the present moment. Don't run away from hard conversations or difficult feelings.

In fact, just as engaging with the self, flipping into para is an important first step in nearly any intimate interaction. One exception: let's acknowledge that testosterone-fueled behavior can play a significant role in sexual dynamics—it's the hormone pressing the gas pedal in the earliest moments of sexual attraction. But the more intricate choreography of attachment that follows the first frenzy of attraction only happens when we're in para, so it's important to cultivate that relaxed and receptive state. It helps to think of "tend and befriend," one of the nicknames for para, as two steps in a coordinated effort: we tend to ourselves in para, relaxing, breathing easy, allowing the body to repair itself. This is the optimum state for befriending, making time for the required maintenance that helps a relationship thrive. It almost doesn't matter which happens first; caring for someone will put you in para. Try it: give somebody a foot rub and you'll relax too.

Some of the complex dynamics of relationships are reflected in our tendency to project the unwanted or repressed parts of ourselves onto others, determining who we're attracted to. We re-create our earliest environments as we replay the hurts and insecurities that arose in our childhoods. If our parents were attentive, warm, and reliable, we'll be drawn to that type of stable relationship in adult life. But if our caregivers were uninvolved, aloof, wrapped up in their own issues, or inconsistent, that may be the type of person we choose to attach to. Either way, we're bound to unconsciously project our fears and angers onto our partners. After the magic of early connection comes the power struggles, as we jockey for emotional position, one-upping each other in getting our needs met, often at the expense of meeting the other person's needs. Again, I'd recommend the idea of an open hand; let things come and go without becoming too invested in the outcome. It's easier to stay in para when you think this way. (And it'll be easier to raise a toddler.)

I'm not saying it's easy to stay calm. Sometimes the very things that attracted us in the beginning become the things that drive us crazy after we've been together for years. This isn't a coincidence. These reflect some of our deepest core issues, and they won't go away without our full attention and compassion. That same projection, often based on deeply buried childhood patterns, can play into rivalries that spring up in intimacy. Imagine reacting to some trait in a partner that reminds you of your own weakness, then holding them responsible for that entirely internal struggle. Hard to untangle, right? In the worst cases, this dynamic can give simple everyday transactions a crippling undercurrent of psychodrama as each of you grows exquisitely sensitive to the slightest indication of familiar patterns of conflict. Also worth noting: some of us (myself included) are genetically predisposed to be both prosocial and also more sensitive to social slights and exclusions, owing to differences in our oxytocin receptors.

Doing yoga taught me a few things. I can stay calm in a difficult pose if I breathe slowly through my nose, and this translates into most other difficulties in life. But also, I've learned that the hardest postures are the ones I need the most. They reveal where I'm weaker or less malleable. It's no different in a partnership, but the focus is on psychological flexibility, as opposed to the rigidity of being stuck in your ways. As you might guess, psychological flexibility correlates with resilience and adaptability, physical and mental well-being, while inflexibility correlates with many psychiatric symptoms and disorders. If you train someone in cognitive flexibility, their therapy outcomes improve, as they go from avoidance and disconnection to acceptance and connection. For example, recent studies coming out of Johns Hopkins, where they've been doing psilocybin research for years now, show that this change in psychological flexibility is what mediates the subsequent decreases in depression and anxiety symptoms. An increase in openness, a key personality fixture that was once thought immutable, is at least one of the reasons why the Johns Hopkins psilocybin participants are getting and staying better. Active imaginations, an appreciation of beauty, novelty seeking, and a capacity for deep emotional reflection are some features of this personality trait—and what psilocybin users have after their experience.

In conscious coupling, partners take turns being the other's therapist, to some extent. They each stretch their behaviors to meet the other's needs. This compassion, understanding, and altruistic giving create a corrective experience and are the foundation for what happens next: they each heal the childhood wounding in their partner. If each person stretches toward the middle, they widen their shared repertoire of behaviors. This encourages growth and healthier behavior in both partners. Each partner has the blueprint for the other's growth. That has certainly been my experience with my partner, Jeremy. It's not always easy or pretty, but if we can work our way through an issue and repair whatever rupture has occurred, we come out the other side stronger for it. Think of it as maintaining a therapeutic alliance, just as a therapist would with a client.

Further, just as individuals need to harmonize their own feminine and masculine qualities, so do couples. Balancing the yin and yang that each of you brings to the table will benefit both of you and lead to more unity in your partnership. Jeremy is more yin and I am more yang, but between the two of us, we create a balanced wholeness.

At the root, connecting with a partner one-on-one means using all the tools in the communication starter kit: being open, listening, making eye contact (the "anchoring gaze"), smelling, touching. We have biological drives for more than just mating, giving birth, and raising children. We also have a drive for peak experiences. When you're connecting to another person, many of those experiences are close at hand. Meditative states, being in a daze or state of "flow" together—an intense level of absorption in any shared activity that lets the world fall away—are moments of losing the self, or ego dissolution. This may sound counterintuitive, but ego dissolution is not something you have to do alone. In fact, it may be easier when you're not.

We know that psychedelics can initiate moments of massive ego disintegration, but these smaller yet satisfying everyday versions of belonging can also add up: getting or giving a massage, having your head scratched, hugging your partner, dancing together in a crowd. These pleasurable states of prosocial behavior reflect positive changes in neurochemistry, with spikes in oxytocin, dopamine, endorphins, and endocannabinoids. They also inaugurate new ways for the brain's networks to fire together, giving us a break from the well-worn pathways of our individual neurotic monkey minds. Being in para, especially in a flow state, helps us enter the right mindset for coming up with new ideas, thanks to improved access to unexpected neural networks and connections.

One surefire way to access this checklist of rewarding chemicals is through orgasm, which can catapult us into an altered state in the short term and, with practice, can strengthen and reaffirm deeper social attachments. Some orgasms can lead to brief out-of-body experiences (thanks to the intense but short-lived naturally occurring psychedelic compound phenylethylamine). This is a happy occurrence, and of course it feels good, but it's also good for you, your partner, and even your whole family. Orgasms reduce mortality, and they're good for your heart and the rest of your cardiovascular system.

I don't want to reduce the science of connection to sex alone. But we also shouldn't overcomplicate things. It turns out that your own body has all the best drugs already; we just have to learn where they're hidden: in plain sight, in the stash box of connection.

LOVE IS THE DRUG

Sometimes I use words like "stash box" to give you a clue that I've had some firsthand experience with drugs. We all write what we know. In this case, it's also the right vocabulary. Sex, orgasm, falling in love—they're overwhelming, mind-altering experiences. All the feel-good chemicals in the body's chem lab start flowing in your own proprietary blend: testosterone, estrogen, dopamine, norepinephrine, endorphins, endocannabinoids, phenylethylamine, oxytocin. People falling in love, for instance, are under the influence of a generous pharmacopeia and exhibit a familiar syndrome of behaviors: they're fixated on the object of their desire to the exclusion of others, can't concentrate, forget to eat, are sleepless, and engage in risky behaviors. They are obsessed (and quite possibly delusional about all that their love interest can provide) and usually feel amazing.

Brain scans of people falling deeply in love look suspiciously like brain scans of cocaine addicts. They both light up specific pathways, kicking dopamine production and distribution into high gear. Remember, dopamine is less about pleasure and more about fixing onto and driving rewarding behavior. It's the chemical of tenacity. Blood flow increases to the caudate nucleus, an area fed by these dopamine neurons. The caudate nucleus is a key motivator in goal-oriented behavior. So the addict fixates on the next fix and the lover fixates on the object of desire. Their high levels of dopamine, especially in the intense early phases, ensure that attention is paid and rewards are expected. Yes, the process will eventually lead to pleasure, but that's not dopamine's job. First of all, oxytocin is the chemical that enacts the pleasure of social engagement. But the pleasure itself comes from the brain's internal opiates, primarily, and then also the cannabis-like molecules, the endorphin system and the endocannabinoid system.

Details aside, this is one of the pitfalls of the pharmacology that accompanies dizzying romantic connection: megadoses of brain chemicals can be followed by periods of acute withdrawal when the object of your desire breaks it off. All juiced up with dopamine and nowhere to go. What happened to all my good chemistry? The comedown in this cycle is bad. I see grieving, heavy drinking, sugar binges, and overspending in jilted patients. Or they can't seem to leave their bed or stop crying. The whole roller-coaster ride starts right up again if they get back together with an ex. But don't let hot make-up sex fool you into thinking that everything is right with the world. Junkies feel good, too, when they relapse.

One thing that all those internal chemicals may not help you with is the exercise of good judgment. High dopamine usually means low serotonin, the result being obsessive fixation and poor impulse control. Your brain makes a point of noticing every aspect of the object of your obsession and keeps you focused and ready to act again. Introspection and good judgment don't have anything to do with these early stages of attraction, also called limerence.

As a psychopharmacologist, I could never concoct a medication regimen to compete with the drug-like intoxicants that your brain comes up with in the early glow of a relationship. I've had patients quit my practice when they fall in love because they think they don't need to be on meds anymore. And they're probably right. One way to sustain operations at this pitch is to keep breaking up and starting over, with your ex or someone else, catapulting yourself in and out of the dopamine rush of infatuation.

The chemistry of initial attraction is robust enough to lead some people into behavioral addiction, junkies of serial attraction. They fall in love, stay high for three to six months, and when the magic fades they move on to the next partner who can provide a new version of the same thrill. For narcissists especially, those first few months are the best. (Talking about yourself begins a smaller version of the pleasure chemistry of falling in love. And some people get off on that more than others.) Or, some may get "addicted" to the power of swiping left, of upgrading, of dismissing and rejecting people. With expanded options, people often become even pickier. Or analysis paralysis sets in; too many choices cause them to choose no one.

Not only is upgrading often an option in real life, but the plethora of fantasy mate choices on porn sites or "dating" apps forces more specificity in the fetishes. As with so many people with addictions, over time they need a bigger rush, a bigger risk, to bring them that same reward. With every new relationship, there's a new level of danger. To some people, this danger is part of the thrill. That underlying element of risk, and the adrenaline surge it provides, is part of the draw for many people who pursue affairs, boldly or in secret.

But the next round with a new infatuation rarely provides that relief. Do you remember all those rat experiments of the sixties and seventies? One principle the researchers discovered, thanks to the rats, is known as "partial intermittent reinforcement." If you give a rat a pellet every time it presses a lever, it'll walk away if you miss a few in a row. You haven't created enough interest for it to keep trying, and, hmm, I guess this machine isn't giving out anymore. But if you reward it randomly, it'll keep coming back to press that lever forever, because, hey, you never know—this time might be the charm. This is the principle that keeps people sitting at slot machines hoping for a payoff, and keeps the rest of us checking our social media apps. It's also one of the mechanisms that keeps some people using drugs even though the consequences aren't always great, and will keep others in relationships when the bad outweighs the good. Partial reinforcement is the most powerful type of reinforcement there is. Because it's almost enough, it keeps us coming back for more.

One of the driving forces behind this appetitive behavior is dopamine, the neurotransmitter of attention and drive. It's the gas pedal for both the mating process and addiction. The chemistry of sex, love, and attraction has been refined over hundreds of thousands of millennia with the sole purpose of making procreation irresistible. The closer you get to the possibility that you may have sex, the stronger the drive. Near misses actually spur our behavior more than pure wins, which is why playing hard to get makes sense, neurologically, and why unrequited love is often harder to get over than a consummated affair. Unattainable partners, "the one that got away," will haunt your brain just the way a drug user might spend forever trying to recapture the overwhelming rush of that first high.

Recent research has been illuminating the ways that our behavior on the internet and social media can be ruled by this same appetite for the unattainable. Adam Alter, who does research into psychology and marketing at the Stern School of Business at NYU, has studied the rise of behavioral addictions and social media platforms. His definition of addiction—something you enjoy in the short term that undermines your well-being in the long term—has tragic consequences for the addict, since, according to Alter, one property of addictions is that you can't tell that they're addictions until *after* the damage has been done. "A behavior is addictive," Alter says, "only if the rewards it brings now are eventually outweighed by damaging consequences." So the damage keeps accumulating as love junkies dive into one failed romance after another—because you can never get enough of something that almost works, remember? And there's something called hedonic habituation, which is the brain's way of adjusting to pleasure over time, where you need a bigger hit to get off.

It's not within the scope of this book to review all the mistakes that people make at this stage in sexual connection, as the flood of hormones and neurotransmitters begins to subside and the rational mind begins to submit the relationship to a review. That's the point where attraction can turn to attachment—or it's the point where reality hits and you remember that you actually can't stand many of the things you've recently been thinking you could never live without. For love junkies, this is the time to start all over with someone new. For the rest of us, it's time to roll up our sleeves and dig in. If we're going to stay in a relationship, we've got lots of work to do.

CONNECTION AFTER THE STORM OF ADDICTIONS

David K., the patient of mine I mentioned in the introduction, was a serial addict, and a serious one. Peeling away his addictive behavior led to a surprise outcome—and an instructive one for anyone interested in establishing a real connection. When he came to me, he was trying to find a way out of eight years of opiate addiction that had started with a prescription for Vicodin after a spinal-fusion surgery. "I don't think it helped with the pain at all," he told me. "Advil can take away pain. The Vicodin just made me not care about the pain. It made me feel great. So, it was like, 'Hit me again. Doesn't matter. I can take it.'"

David was prosperous and seemingly functional, running his own talent agency in New York. He was also resourceful. Within months of that first prescription, he had multiple doctors writing him prescriptions on a regular basis. David settled into a serious substance-abuse disorder. But it wasn't just drugs: his history made it clear that he was also addicted to some behaviors as much as he was to whatever substance he'd settled on at the moment. He seemed to have a knack for constructing one private hell after another.

He'd started drinking in college and soon became an alcoholic—so drunk some nights that he'd drive through New York City traffic with all the windows down in the middle of winter, one eye closed because he was seeing double. He added cocaine on top of that and experimented with Seconal (a sedative), and then moved on to various stimulants. But because he successfully quit each of his addictions one by one, by himself, with his own willpower, he kept convincing himself he was in control. Then, once he had stopped, just like the love junkies, he'd find something else to fill the void. By the time he picked up his opiate addiction, for instance, he'd been sober from alcohol for fifteen years.

There was deeply buried pain behind that carousel of substance use, what he referred to as "the usual crap about growing up." His father was a Broadway actor, a heavy drinker with an anger problem, who came home late every night and took his frustrations out on his oldest son. So even though David was now in his mid-sixties, and his father had died decades ago, when he said, "Hit me again. I can take it," I knew exactly to whom he was referring.

At first I thought he might respond well to MDMA, which had recently been designated as a breakthrough therapy by the FDA for treating post-traumatic stress disorder. I'm a medical monitor for three MDMA-assisted psychotherapy studies: one is designed for training psychotherapists, the second is aimed at treating people suffering from PTSD, and the third is for couples, where the PTSD of one member of the dyad is an issue for the dynamic of the relationship. But it was another study I'd only read about, Chris Stauffer's study at UCSF (he was Maria's therapist), which had been getting tremendous results giving MDMA to people with substance-use disorders and PTSD, that made me think of David. His lingering issues with the abuse he suffered as a child and his recurrent episodes of substance abuse made me think he might be a promising candidate.

But David said his two sessions of MDMA therapy with an underground therapist on the East Coast didn't leave him with "any lasting sensation of understanding or progress," although he reported having a "pleasant experience." (It's worth mentioning here that there's a possibility that he has a genetic variant that affects the oxytocin receptor that can mute the MDMA experience.) That's when he suggested LSD. He'd already done a lot of homework on the subject before we met, reading all the groundbreaking psilocybin studies that showed how reliably it induced a mystical state. He became a fan of LSD pioneers from the first wave of academic research in the fifties and sixties who showed the promise of the drug for treating alcoholism. He was convinced it might help him find a way out of his addictive behaviors.

David had already shown that he was resourceful and determined when it came to drugs. I knew he could find both LSD and a willing therapist to act as his guide, but as I said earlier, I suggested mushrooms, which contain psilocybin.

(The psilocybin that is administered in most studies in these pages comes in a pill form. But within psychedelic studies, many people use the terms "psilocybin"—the pill and the psychoactive chemical—and "magic mushrooms"—the actual fungus that contains the psychoactive chemical—interchangeably.) The advice grew out of practical reasons—a trip on mushrooms lasts about six hours, while LSD can continue for up to twelve or more—and because mushrooms tend to be easier to navigate, with fewer "bad trips." (Although it should be stated plainly: challenging experiences on psychedelics can often yield a lot of unconscious material to sift through later, part of the integration process.)

David's guide for the earlier MDMA treatment that he'd been dissatisfied with had given him the same advice. So one Saturday he arrived at her place around eleven a.m. and took his dose of mushrooms. Because he hadn't eaten anything that day, the effects came on quickly. He said it was like "being strapped to a 747, rocketing into the stratosphere." After he got past that sensation, he said he began to sense what I'd been talking to him about—connectedness and oneness. He called it a beautiful, calming experience. The fear he'd spoken to me about—his primary issue of fear of empathizing and connecting, the one fear that even OxyContin couldn't get rid of—had disappeared.

He left the experience fundamentally transformed, although it took a while for him to register how profoundly he'd changed. He went straight home and got into bed and stayed there for a week. By the time he reemerged, he was free of his opiate addiction. Nine months later, he's still drug-free.

Maybe even more important, before his experience with psilocybin mushrooms, he'd been on the brink of splitting up with his wife—a cabaret singer he'd been married to for twenty-two years. For the two years before he came to me, he'd been abusive, he said, although he was quick to add that he'd never hit her. His experiences with his own father had left him with a lifelong distaste for physical violence. But in many ways, he worried that his verbal abuse and hair-trigger temper might be even worse than the violence he shunned. She was a sweet woman, he said, with no defense against the fury he was directing at her.

But now, in the aftermath of his experience with psilocybin, his life at home has been transformed. His wife has called the change in him since his treatment "miraculous." Before he'd never understood how people could listen to music and cry, even though he loved music and had been to hundreds of his wife's concerts. But now the concerts had become transporting, a way to tap into the sense of awe and transcendence that he'd felt during his treatment. "It's almost like the emotional dam got chipped away and broke down," he said. Previously not one to express a lot of emotions, he was "a basket case" when his dog died.

His wife, who'd had no experience with drugs of any sort, had been understandably suspicious of his eagerness to experiment with one more substance. But when the two of them ran into David's guide (at a Grateful Dead concert!) after the treatment, his wife told her, "Whatever you did, thank you very much—because it worked." David's summary was in line with hers. "This stuff shouldn't be illegal," he said. "It should be compulsory. The world would be a much different place."

David's saga is a success story because the behavior targeted by the therapy really did disappear. But the metamorphosis didn't end there. Dr. Robin Carhart-Harris, at the Centre for Psychedelic Research at Imperial College London, has a theory that psychedelics work to relax the precision of "high-level priors"—neuroscientific terminology for "the influence of strongly held personal beliefs"—leaving the subject open to "bottom-up information flow, particularly via intrinsic sources such as the limbic system." He refers to this model as REBUS, for "relaxed beliefs under psychedelics." In other words, psychedelics help you shake free of deeply ingrained patterns and foundational beliefs and prejudices, leaving you open to new input, insights, and emotions. In David, this meant that not only did he break free of his addiction, but he also emerged from the experience acutely sensitive to a range of emotions that his previous high-level priors had blinded him to. His marriage, which had survived more than two decades of serial addictions and his recent abusive behavior, suddenly thrived on his newfound openness and eagerness to connect.

EVERYONE ELSE DISAPPEARS

Dopamine is not the only drug-like neurotransmitter surging through the body in the early phases of attraction. Norepinephrine, a chemical cousin of adrenaline, also floods the system, causing your palms to sweat as your heartbeat quickens and keeps you in a state of nervous excitement. Norepinephrine revs up your senses, helping you catalog every one of your loved one's quirks, along with how each one makes you feel. The brain is formulating and filing emotional memories, particularly for salient behaviors that could be interpreted as good for coupling or parenting. This puts certain brain areas into high gear: the anterior cingulate cortex, where attention, emotion, and memory interact, and the insular cortex, which processes emotion. Of course, learning happens better in a state of heightened attention and focus, so this mix of dopamine and norepinephrine provides a good chemical foundation. They combine to produce a cocaine-like effect: euphoric, energetic, mentally alert, sensitive to sight, sound, and touch. Sleeping and eating take a back seat to information-gathering and obsessing.

Norepinephrine also enables the release of estrogen, leading to receptive mating behavior. What exactly constitutes mating behavior in humans is not as codified as it is in lab rats, where it can be precisely measured by the number of ear wiggles and back arches, cues that would signal sexual arousal if you were a rat. Obviously, there are plenty of cues for sexual receptivity in humans—a glance that lingers, a toss of the hair, wetting the lips, smoothing the clothes in a way that mimics a caress or emphasizes a secondary sexual characteristic. Of course, none of these equals consent, but they're moving in that direction.

But the body doesn't stop at stimulating chemicals; it adds in some mighty relaxers as well. Endorphins, our naturally circulating opiates, soon join the neurochemical rush, creating a pharmacological equivalent of a speedball—a mixture of heroin and cocaine. To add to this high, the early thunderclap of attraction—that feeling of love at first sight—is often accompanied by a surge of the trippy phenylethylamine (PEA), which floods the brain in those instants of initial magnetism, adding to the first-kiss feelings of dreaminess and giddiness. Naturally occurring phenylethylamines have a half-life in the body of about thirty seconds, which may have something to do with the timing of and eagerness for second and third kisses.

Obviously, the sex hormones—testosterone and estrogen—play a crucial role in attraction, enhancing sexual desire (testosterone) and receptivity (estrogen). Researchers of "sexual incentive motivation," the scientific term for horniness, point to the role of estrogen and progesterone in both proceptive behavior, especially in women, designed to initiate or escalate sexual activity, and receptivity to the act itself. Estrogen and progesterone also enhance the love and trust circuits, because oxytocin works better in this hormonal milieu, which means you may be more open to loving and nurturing behavior from a potential mate versus others in your sphere.

Lust—the part of this process that's mostly fueled by testosterone—is short-lived, and it's quite possible to lust after more than one person at the same time. But the complicated neurochemical cocktail of attraction and infatuation won't let you fall in love with two people at once. Oxtyocin reinforces that singular focus; repeated sex only multiplies the exclusionary effect. The flood of oxytocin after orgasm is one of the key chemicals in the luxuriant feeling of satisfaction, a feeling reinforced by further skin-to-skin contact (which reliably triggers more oxytocin release) in the intimate aftermath of sex.

But testosterone, in both sexes, is the hormone of lust. Men and women with higher levels of circulating testosterone have more frequent sex and more intense orgasms. Men who are injecting testosterone on a regular basis, thinking it may enhance their performance in sports or finance, have more sexual thoughts and more frequent morning erections. A woman in a receptive state thanks to high estrogen levels can experience a surge in testosterone from inhaling pheromones. Interestingly, men who are falling in love may see their testosterone levels dip, maybe to keep them from scaring away a new mate with their horniness (or aggressiveness). So a woman's testosterone levels rise while the man's dip, bringing libidos on both sides into chemical equilibrium.

The specifics of how this chemical choreography might change when the attraction happens between gay men or lesbians or nonbinary people is hard to pin down, mostly because there's so little research. But there's been enough clinical work to verify what's obvious, that same-sex couples experience the same rush of hormones and neurotransmitters and go on to form the same lasting attachments. Brains (and all the other available sex organs) light up with the same intensity. It's as true in the lab as it is anywhere else: love is love.

THE GOOD OXY

Then there's the baby talk. In the early phases of attraction, whether gay or straight, lovey-dovey words like "baby" and "sweetie" remind us of our very first, crucial relationship as a babe in arms. Just as in early childhood, we need to be securely attached to someone who'll care for us. We adopt the words of a baby and mother to re-create that primary attachment and primal bliss. The chemistry that accompanies each state—a mother falling in love with her baby, the baby falling in love with mother, and lovers falling for each other—takes advantage of the same pharmacological machinery. Oxytocin enables a cascade of feel-good chemicals like endorphins, endocannabinoids (the body's natural cannabis-like molecules), dopamine, PEA (the trippy one), and anything else it can muster up to create a cocktail that feels amazing. Falling in love, having sex, reaching orgasm, bonding with baby—they're all pleasures your brain can give you, and we should bow our heads in thanks.

The most concentrated dose of the brain's mind-altering chemicals may come from death, but orgasm (*la petite mort*) comes close.

Here's a short list of practical things you can do to promote it.

1. **Timing is everything (part one).** The midpoint of the menstrual cycle, around ovulation, is when you're more likely to be horny. Feel free to take advantage of this timing, but keep in mind this is also when you are most fertile. (Nature is not messing around here.) There is sometimes a second surge in libido right before your period is due, but with PMS, that can get complicated. It's possible you're fighting more, or harboring more resentments, during this phase.

2. **Pacing and courtesy.** Women take significantly longer than men to warm up to orgasm, which means men have to hold off a bit. This can be challenging on both sides. Talk about it ahead of time if you can. Simultaneous orgasm is great for movie lovers, but in real life it can be elusive. A simple *I'll go after you* from either partner can do wonders for taking the pressure off everyone.

3. **Learn the territory, then map it out for your partner.** Find out what feels good to you and then gently communicate

that to your partner. This sounds obvious, but it rarely happens in practice. The key to good sex is being in your body, with the openness and curiosity to see how good you can feel. Learning to masturbate yourself to orgasm is the first step in sharing it with others. For communicating, show when you can, and tell when you can't, but gently. Egos bruise easily, but more so when we're naked.

4. **Dream sequence.** Do not judge your fantasies. Let them go. Fire-breathing dragons, alien probes, mud people— branch out! The thing that gets in the way for most is our minds, our thoughts, and our judgments. Focus on your body and the way it feels, feed yourself narratives if you need to, but allow yourself the freedom of pleasure. You've earned it, I'm sure of it. And in my experience, the more of an alpha you are, the more your fantasies run submissive. It's normal. Stop feeling bad about it and take advantage of any edge you can get in the run-up to release.

5. **Timing is everything (part two).** Be honest about your level of interest in sex and how much time and energy you're willing to put in. Sometimes it's going to be *Not tonight, sweetheart*; other times maybe the right answer is *I can be convinced*, or *Only if we're done before the meatloaf is.* Whatever you're feeling, be honest with yourself and your partner. Take a thorough inventory of your own appetite before you share where you're at. If you're not into it, be honest. And if you're going to do it, go all in. Often, once you get started, you'll get interested in something along the way.

That ultra-relaxed feeling you get after orgasm? That's mostly oxytocin. Yes, it's the hormone of bonding and trust, but it also makes us feel great, giving pleasure through the endocannabinoid system and via endorphins. (So that's the feeling that opiates are mimicking, the missing feeling that so many people are trying to find a pill-shaped substitute for.) Oxytocin surges when lovers lock eyes across a crowded room. We read emotions in others' eyes, and oxytocin enables this behavior. Looking away, turning away, or doing anything that threatens bonding (like fighting with a romantic partner) can trigger the stress hormone cortisol, which gets in the way of oxytocin and the resulting cascade of feel-good chemistry. This is why conscious coupling is healthiest. Mindfulness can moderate the negative impact of these cortisol bursts, or it can quicken the body's recovery from them. With mindfulness, even if your cortisol surges, you can remain calmer.

You can also feel the good chemistry settle in during a long hug, a sensation that's underscored as dopamine triggers the reward centers, reinforcing the positive feelings of physical contact and encouraging more attachment. Remember, women have more oxytocin receptors than men, and oxytocin is more effective in the presence of estrogen.

Oxytocin is also the reason that it's probably easier for a woman to fall in love in the first half of her cycle, when estrogen surges and then peaks at ovulation. Oxytocin not only creates feelings of pleasurable connection, but it also lowers the heart rate and blood pressure, quiets the fear center (the amygdala), and makes it easier to open up and trust strangers. This idea that "love is letting go of fear" has a strong basis in biology. And the fact that at higher doses oxytocin can make you forgetful and cloud your ability to think critically probably doesn't hurt, either. We all look better in soft focus.

THE SHIFT FROM ATTRACTION
TO ATTACHMENT

Many of the components of the pharmacological combination generated in attraction stick around for the attachment phase, with a few noticeable exceptions. Once you've been together for a few months, perhaps half a year or longer if you're lucky, the special chemistry of limerence fades, and a stronger but gentler feeling takes its place: security. Sociobiologists call this cycle of coordinated rewards "pair-bond formation," a term only marginally sexier than other dry terminology like "adult affiliation" or "partner attachment."

While the early phases of attraction may be red-hot and passionate, attachment is calmer, cooler, more relaxed and solidified. Attached love is sometimes called "companionate love." There is familiarity and a sense of peace, primarily due to oxytocin, the key player in the transition from testosterone-fueled novelty seeking to the preference for familiarity, which parallels the move from attraction to attachment. Oxytocin is the common denominator in each phase, enabling two people to get closer, to overcome their suspicion and their defenses, to trust and connect. Oxytocin exerts a stabilizing influence, decreasing the likelihood of drug addiction or its behavioral counterpart, serial romance, and helps turn dabblers into devotees.

Committed love creates a feeling of satiety: you have all you need; you want for nothing. This is likely courtesy of serotonin. Serotonin and dopamine often seem as if they're on a seesaw—when one is up, the other is down. Dopamine got to be the star for a good, long time, but now it's serotonin's turn in the spotlight. This means rational circuitry, courtesy of the frontal lobes, is back online, so there should be less of what I sometimes call the "delusional state of infatuation." Also, no more impulsivity and OCD-like behavior (given that the gold-standard pharmacological treatment of OCD calls for medicines to enhance serotonin's availability). In fact, a study that examined people in early infatuation showed brain scans similar to patients with OCD. When these lovers are scanned later on in the attachment phase, those similarities are gone. So in this next stage, there's less fixation and aching need because both dopamine and testosterone levels are normalized, creating less fire or drive for novelty.

But let's not forget about adrenaline junkies. Because there are people who thrive on chaos in a relationship, and whether you call them vampires or disruptors, we need to be aware that the rules don't apply to everyone. There are also psychopaths (born that way) and sociopaths (made over time), who can't seem to connect or practice empathy. And then there are the people who've been so traumatized in the past that they are afraid of falling in love. So there are many exceptions in how people's brains process the possibility of attachment. Sometimes the prospect of a committed love relationship is terrifying.

OPPOSITES ATTRACT
(AND THEN REPEL)

Pheromones are hormones that act outside the body on members of the same species. They float through the air, passing along insider information that ranges in usefulness from mildly helpful to timely and critical. Other animals rely on pheromones to sense social rank, detect the presence of food, or alert nearby creatures to immediate danger, thanks to the vomeronasal organ, a tiny sensory apparatus located in the septums of snakes, amphibians, and a number of other mammals besides us. It's detectable in human fetuses in the womb, but, most researchers believe, it disappears sometime before birth, and its presence, in us at least, is vestigial.

But that doesn't mean we're out of the game. Of all the senses, smell is the least mediated, with the fewest cellular connections between the outside world and the brain. Two areas are directly stimulated by smell: the amygdala for emotion and the hippocampus for memory. We still detect pheromones through the nose, which relay vital information about immune status and mating compatibility that we absorb, often without being consciously aware of the exchange. That doesn't mean that this chemical data doesn't register. It does, and with a degree of precision that we're only recently coming to understand. Human pheromones seem to act on some deep nonverbal circuit of sexual awareness, detecting suitable candidates for mating and providing input on genetic desirability or current sexual receptivity.

The pheromones seem to work differently depending on your sex and sexual orientation. Men, for example, appear to be able to sense ovulation via pheromones. In one study, lap dancers at a club in Albuquerque saw their tips spike on days they were ovulating and drop significantly during their periods. In another, men in relationships engaged in more "guarding behavior," like calling, texting, or dropping by, during ovulatory peaks, especially if the woman in the relationship was perceived to rank higher than they did in sexual attractiveness. Another study, explicitly designed to register only the effects of olfactory cues, e.g., pheromones, showed that male bar patrons who smelled a T-shirt worn by an ovulating woman drank more than men who smelled a T-shirt worn by women at other points in the cycle. These studies suggest that men, whether or not they have any awareness of their reactions or any conscious intent, respond to covert cues of sexual receptivity or peak fertility.

Women have a subtler take, or maybe a more critical interest in the outcome of any mating. When presented with a choice of sweaty T-shirts that men had slept in for several consecutive nights, women preferred ones from men whose immune systems were significantly different from their own. You might not have known that this was a big item on the list of things you're looking for, but the smell that triggered the positive response in women seems to be a marker for something called the major histocompatibility complex (MHC), a set of genes that serves as a kind of catalog of preprogrammed immune responses. And this gene complex is present and active in the sweat glands to such a degree that a man's odor can serve as an accurate genetic signature, like an airborne LinkedIn page itemizing his immune-response profile. As a result, women can smell enough to eliminate potential mates whose immune responses nearly duplicate their own. This strong reaction to scent is highly adaptive (good for evolution), since it suggests that any child the woman might have with her immuno-opposite would have an enhanced resistance to a greater range of diseases. It's no joke. Ignore these cues and you might have conception problems or, if you do conceive, risk transmitting a shared weakness in the form of a genetic disease.

Women respond differently to these pheromones at dif-

ferent times in their cycles, too, becoming more likely to select their MHC opposites the closer they get to ovulation.
But during menstruation or approaching it, women pick men
whose MHC profiles are closer to their own, as do women
on the pill. The pill, which to some degree acts by fooling
the body into believing it's already pregnant, seems to in-
terfere with pheromone detection too. Women on the pill
are more likely to pick men with an MHC profile similar
to their own, as if they were seeking the company not of a
genetically desirable mate but of a supportive relative who
could help raise a child.

That's why it's important to meet people in real space,
face-to-face, and not just online. It's crucial to find out if you
like the way someone smells. It's something I ask my patients
regularly. If a partner smells good to you—and I don't mean
their cologne choice, I mean their real signature biological
scent—if that arouses you and comforts you, it always will.
It's a sign of a healthy connection and biological compatibility. Your body is showing you the way.

Too much similarity between partners means not enough
genetic variation. In the plant world, when you mate two different strains, you often end up with what's called a "vigorous hybrid." Ideally children should inherit different traits
from each parent, especially immunities to different illnesses
that make them stronger. One of the many reasons I'm not a
huge fan of the pill is because oral contraceptives take away
that naturally enhanced sense of smell that happens with
ovulation. They also alter your pheromone-detecting capacities, so your medication may end up influencing you to pick a
partner who smells more like "brother" and less like "other."

There's another danger, too, that taking the pill could

shift your sexual priorities, making you inexplicably lose interest in an attractive partner once you're on the pill, turning somebody irresistible into somebody not so much. It can work the other way, too, where when you come off the pill, your partner smells different to you, or you start to notice an enhanced sense of smell around ovulation.

As noted before, research into the effects of pheromones has focused on heterosexual response, but several studies have shown that both straight women and gay men respond in a statistically comparable way to androstadienone, a pheromone present in male sweat and semen, and that straight men do not, a study that has been taken to support the idea of a biological basis of sexual orientation. Gay and bisexual women also respond to estratetranol, a pheromone first detected in the urine of pregnant women, but their responses are less robust than those of straight men. (Scientific research lags behind social changes, which is why data for the sexual response of the nonbinary is thin to nonexistent.) In all cases, these responses occurred "in the absence of awareness," when the odors were masked by the scent of cloves.

A dynamic similar to the one observed over the course of a woman's cycle operates on the psychological level—opposites attract, and then over time, the growing familiarity seems to reverse, or at least fray, those forces of attraction. And what's frustrating is that in the same way that pheromones seem to register on a preconscious level, short-circuiting the mind as they engage the sexual impulse, these tricky psychological forces seem to act on a level that's also untraceable or at least highly resistant to analysis.

We're drawn to our psychological opposites for the same

reason that we're looking for our genetic opposites: we seem to know on some level when a relationship will produce a vigorous hybrid of complementary natures, a synergy energized by our differences. People falling in love often feel as if they've met their match, ready to say, "You complete me," like Tom Cruise in *Jerry Maguire*. But underneath that magnetism, floating around like pheromones, there's a complex dance of projection.

People are good at spotting projection in others, and often point it out like a parlor game of "gotcha." The classic example is the trio of GOP congressmen—Newt Gingrich of Georgia, Bob Livingston of Louisiana, and Dennis Hastert of Illinois—who led the way in impeaching President Bill Clinton for his sexual relations with Monica Lewinsky. Ironically, or maybe predictably, each of those three politicians was exposed at one time or another for their own infidelities and/or sexual misconduct. If your career depended on your sexual life remaining a secret, would you take the lead in making someone else's infidelities national news? It doesn't make sense. In fact, it's foolish and reckless and hypocritical. But that's how projection works. We hide our shadow selves from others and from ourselves, pinning the worst parts of us on our partners or our rivals, calling out our own undesirable traits by pointing them out in others instead. ("If you spot it, you got it.") In relationships, in families, and in race relations, we accuse others of all the things we can't accept in ourselves. This "us vs. them" mentality is the basis of sexism, racism, xenophobia—and also supreme marital woes.

Even though projection can seem hard to miss in others,

it's not easy to spot in yourself, partly because we get good at hiding our ideas, feelings, and attitudes, especially our unpleasant and unresolved ones, like shame, blame, and responsibility. And, maybe because we're still attached to these emotions and entanglements, we hide them close by, projecting them onto others we come into contact with most often. Since projection is so complicated to pull off and so costly to maintain, it's not really something you'd bother to try on a casual acquaintance—one good reason why our closest relationships, in love, at home, at work, can become so stressful. The people we're closest to hold up a mirror to us, causing us to walk away from our fights, partly because we see so much of ourselves in the people we're fighting with and partly because the resulting feelings are unbearable. So we go back and forth between spending time with our family and friends, all the people we say we love, and then retreating into solitude. Once we're alone, we get our connections online, the kind that let us stay isolated, showing only small, perfectly curated slices of who we really are.

Projection plays a big role in the thrilling early stages of attraction. Often the traits we're looking for in a partner are the ones we don't have, because they've been rejected in us, shut down by our parents, our friends, or the society we live in. We've learned to hide or repress these traits. In a way, this only adds to the appeal when we finally meet someone who appears untroubled by all the strict prohibitions we grew up with or place on ourselves, the voices that kept us from indulging in forbidden behaviors that come so easily to them. All of a sudden, you're seeing those forbidden behaviors in action in someone else, and not just anyone—someone who's so sexually attractive that you can barely sleep or eat.

Just to be close to them and their almost threatening self-confidence (or their tender diffidence, if you're the one with all the threatening self-confidence) can look and feel liberating, exhilarating even.

This appetite to access parts of ourselves that we've been denied isn't surprising or uncommon. In a teenager, it's part of normal patterns of rebellion and self-assertion, and parents hoping for healthy outcomes should encourage (or tolerate or ignore) this behavior. But later in life, this dynamic—being drawn into an obsessive new relationship with someone who seems so unlike everything you'd imagined before—can be deeply fulfilling, offering a chance for the maximum personal growth that comes from being close to someone whose traits are vastly different from yours.

When opposites come together, there's a synergism, a whole that's greater than the sum of its parts. Especially in that first stage of initial attraction, where even just looking at your shiny new love can leave you with a warm oxytocin rush, you may not quite feel like yourself anymore. And in a way you're not. You're blending with the partner you're obsessing over, and oxytocin is reordering your brain, growing new connections, reshaping you as you fixate on them.

Why couldn't we forever stay in that early blush of love, that magical time when the chemistry between our two brains was united, bathed in the same neurochemical cocktail of attraction? Back then, when we were physiologically synchronized and chemically engaged, our partners were perfect. Falling in love is a deeply medicated state, even if it is natural, a cross between obsessive-compulsive disorder, hypomania, and just plain delusion. And more than that, we're wired to pursue our opposites—which feels amazing at first and is great for creating more humans. But it can also be a setup for disaster.

With the right partner it's worth hanging in there, moving together from attraction to attachment to long-term commitment. There's tremendous value and endless variety in real intimacy. And there are solid medical and psychiatric benefits to be had from getting married and staying that way, like lower levels of the stress hormone cortisol, lower risks of heart attack and stroke, and an improved ability to fight chronic illness. And believe it or not, there is less anxiety and depression in committed, attached relationships. So marriage may be an effective solution to our chronic disconnection.

But in long-term relationships like marriage, the opposites-attract dynamic can easily turn into an "us vs. them" mentality, and can be painful. Sometimes our beloved is an "us," but other times we'll recast a partner as "them." In an effort to avoid examining the complexity of our own issues, we project qualities we disown in ourselves onto our partners. Projection is something to keep in mind when you're bickering. Many of the accusations you're leveling at "them" could be just as true if they were applied to you.

Over time, and sometimes with increasing frequency, we can start to be irritated by the traits we were first attracted to, the same ones that have been rejected and trained out of us by our parents or friends, our tribe, our Midwestern or West Coast or Eastern European upbringing, whatever forces made us what we are, for better or for worse. And so we replay the lessons we learned in childhood, and the repressed parts of the self, now so recognizable in a partner, get rejected all over again.

In my case, I got subtle messages and formative reinforcement from my father whenever I acted fearless and independent. I also caught on to the flip side of that preference—and I don't know whether I came up with this on my own or not—that I should not behave in ways that seemed scared or needy. Eventually, I grew up and went out on my own, calm and confident, and fell in love with someone who gave himself permission to feel need, who drew people in with an air of sadness, a doleful gaze, and patience with pain, both his own and that of others.

What can happen now if I react to something he does before taking time to breathe and think things through, is I can get impatient and riled up by those same traits I was initially attracted to. I see behaviors that I rejected, the same things that made me unlovable to my father, and I short-circuit. I go back to the childhood lessons I learned and reject my own undesirable behavior all over again, but this time it's Jeremy's behavior that I reject. Unfortunately, all too often, these childhood scenes take hold of both of you and become part of your marriage. If you're lucky and you can communicate about it, you can develop shorthand for when it's happening. "Oh no, we're doing that thing again where you treat me like your smothering mother," or, "You're putting me in the role of warden again, honey."

The optimal outcome, the way out of the dead end: you accept and embrace all the disowned traits in your partner, and that helps you accept them in yourself. Opening up to loving and accepting these things, in your partner and yourself, helps make you whole. If you don't work on this, the feeling that's so strong in the early attraction phase—that there's someone who really does complete you—can turn dangerous and fill your partnership or marriage with projected self-hatred.

The way out is not simple, not because the steps are difficult, but because it's so hard to recognize and then admit these problems. Projection drives a lot of conflict in any dyad, and it takes a lot of work to ferret out and overcome. The opposite of projection in a relationship is reflection. Therapists are professional reflectors, or they should be. We repeat what the patient has said so they feel heard and understood. We also help a patient reflect on their own issues, their own internal struggles, by making them visible. In this case, reflection is one of the first steps on the road toward integration, making sense of it all, making a coherent whole out of disparate parts and separate personalities.

It's hard to do this anywhere, but especially in an intimate relationship, partly because the projections can become habitual, almost invisible by virtue of their familiarity. But recognizing and addressing them is crucial. Hammering out disagreements helps you accept yourself—and your partner—and reclaim your lost and rejected parts. And the benefits of doing this are doubled: not only does working on these conflicts strengthen our oneness as a couple, it also strengthens our oneness as individuals, which as we established earlier is the foundation for any successful relationship. Remember, in any marriage, each partner holds the blueprint for the other's emotional and spiritual growth. If you stretch toward the center, you will be able to reclaim your repressed parts, which helps to make you whole.

Yes, you and your partner are opposites. That's the point. You'll create strong hybrid offspring if you mate. Stop fixating on how you can make your partner more like you. Between the two of you, you can make something bigger than either of you ever could alone: an effective team.

As much as couples may seem different, they do grow together, discovering areas of connection and similarity despite their initial differences. You learn to accept yourself and the image of yourself you see in your partner. And this closeness can bring on another problem: couples often come to act like rivals. Rivalries almost always arise between people or groups or even brands that are more alike than different: think of Sunni and Shiite, Arab and Jew, Coke and Pepsi. Rivals fight over the turf they share. The word "rival" comes from the word for river, and rivals were people who shared the rivers, at first as associates with equal rights to a common good, and in later meanings, as competitors for the same scarce resources.

Rivals are people who have the most in common. They may strongly believe in their uniqueness, but outsiders missing subtleties would look at the two sides and not see much difference. Half the time, it's basically brothers fighting brothers. Rivals project their unwanted qualities onto the other. All of the repressed, the hidden, the "evil" parts of ourselves get lobbed onto the other bank of the river. They're persistent problems. But just as we had a simple list to flip into para when we were trying to connect with the self, we can do things to help connect as couples, starting with simple statements.

In arguments, it's helpful to mirror what your partner is saying to you. Just repeating what someone said—without adding any extra spin—will, first of all, give both of you time to breathe and calm yourselves. And by using their words exactly as you re-create them, you show you're paying attention. You hear them; you get them. That simple act helps to validate the viewpoint, and most important, it can stem the flow of cortisol and give oxytocin a chance to get back in the game. Being heard, understood, and validated will keep you in para.

And don't forget about mirror neurons. We're built for mimicking motor behaviors, yes, but also for empathy, which means you can put yourself in someone else's shoes and guess what they might be going through. Oxytocin helps with this process. What's great about a dialogue format is that, thanks to the power of language, repeating your partner's statements helps you empathize with their position: just saying the words of an argument gives you insight into the thinking of the person who said it. It's part of the magic behind prayer and acting and hostage negotiation. Speak the words calmly, as gently as possible. Let them settle between you. I promise, just being heard, feeling heard, will bring the emotion down significantly for your partner. (And in clinical studies, empathy helps decrease the perception of pain. It physically makes things hurt less.)

Now, in a way, you have a shared perspective. There are phrases you can use after mirroring as a shorthand to validation, too, things like, "You're making sense," or "I can understand why you're feeling that way." Feeling seen, heard, empathized with, and validated will smooth the way through an argument. If nothing else, when you don't know what else to say, this habit of mirroring will buy you time, give you a mini time-out, and temper a reaction you might regret.

It's important to practice these habits when you're calm and seeing eye to eye. You probably won't feel like running through a set of exercises designed to flip you into para in the heat of an argument. That's why it's important to have rituals you practice at other times, simple exercises like taking thirty seconds to stare into each other's eyes. It may feel foolish at first, but it works. Try synchronizing your breath—it's nearly impossible not to feel empathetic when you're in the middle of timing the rise and fall of your breathing to each other. You'll sense the give and take—who's taking a longer breath, and whose shallower breath is expanding? Do these simple things and you'll have a muscle memory of intimacy to draw on when things grow heated.

It can feel intrusive if somebody's trying to force an intimacy exercise on you, especially if it's just when you want to say something you're mad about. So practice getting in sync at neutral moments, for something to draw on when you need it. Jeremy and I pay attention to arrivals and departures. We try to check in with each other before we leave the house, and especially whenever we come back home. We've observed over the years that those are naturally bumpy times for us. It's great to have a welcoming ritual for every return. Knowing it's coming is a big mood enhancer, helping to flip me into para even before I open the door. There are all kinds of ways to change our chemistry so that we're more open to connection.

FINDING TRUST

Back to Josh, my internally disconnected patient who found a pathway from segregation to integration through micro-dosing and music. The last time I saw him, he gave me some amazing follow-up information. His marriage has gone from being "on the brink of divorce" to being "in the best place it's ever been." They have taken ayahuasca together twice, and a third time he refrained, and instead held space for his wife while she drank the psychedelic brew. He says she feels so remarkably changed that she has taken a new name, and they "are in a much different place." Josh was beaming as he relayed this information to me, adding that his friends and coworkers are so excited for him, marveling at the way he's grown and blossomed. His transformation has affected his other relationships as well.

So it seems clear to me that even though psychedelics can catalyze personal growth and assist in working through early trauma, they can have a positive impact not just on the partaker, but on their friends and family. In some cases, psychedelics taken as a couple can help both members of the dyad at once. Think of David, whose marriage improved after his psilocybin session, and of Maria teaching her partner the coping skills she'd discovered in her MDMA treatment. I came across an article in *VICE* about couples taking mushrooms together with the tagline, "It was like we could see into each other's souls." They reported having deep conversations they didn't even know they needed, and a satisfying sense of reconnecting. But I've known since the mid-1980s that MDMA is particularly suited to couples work. I have spoken to therapists who were using it before it became illegal, and the two things nearly all of them told me were that it was good for processing trauma, and it was great for couples therapy. Luckily, a recent study set out to prove just that.

Dr. Candice Monson is a Ryerson University professor, in Toronto, and the director of the IMPACT Lab there, dedicated to "investigating methods to prevent, assess, and care for trauma." She cowrote the treatment manual for cognitive behavioral conjoint therapy (CBCT) for PTSD, which expands cognitive behavioral therapy to the treatment of a couple, simultaneously—that's the conjoint part—where one member of the dyad suffers from long-term PTSD. Cognitive behavioral therapy is a branch of psychotherapy. It's structured, almost like a college course. And like a college course, it's meant to be implemented in a finite number of treatment sessions. The goal is to get at the thinking behind a condition, to help alter, possibly permanently, the way a patient, or, in the case of conjoint therapy, a couple, thinks and feels. "I say, a little bit tongue in cheek, if you have to get a mental health condition, PTSD is the one to get, because relative to other disorders, it's much more treatable and once it's treated people tend not to relapse," says Monson. "With CBCT, you're going after the cause and not just managing the symptoms."

After significant success treating PTSD using CBCT alone, Monson joined a MAPS study that used MDMA-assisted CBCT therapy for PTSD, hoping, she said, to "catalyze treatments that we know work, not just add a therapy to a drug." In matching the primary mechanisms of the drug to those of psychotherapy, she was targeting the drug's ability to provoke and enhance "openness, expansiveness, the idea of wanting to connect."

The study was voluntary. But she pointed out that the willingness to undergo this particular treatment together seemed to be an active ingredient in the success of the therapy. The novelty, the bonding that occurred around taking a medication that alters your consciousness, the readiness of the couple to go through an adventurous experience together—it all added to the effectivene_____me cases, Monson noted, it was not t_____ary PTSD but the nonafflicted partn_____reaction to the medication. It wasn't_____o'd had the original traumatic exper_____oked by the drug. Often the person w_____retaker for the other person in the _____active phase, a positive outcome in_____oals of the therapy is to overcome the_____ciated with trauma.

With or without medication, a key goal of CBCT is externalizing the disorder—making it something that exists between the two of them and not something for one person to suffer alone. Even when the traumatized person is experiencing something unquestionably interior like recurrent nightmares, Monson points out, the primary complaint is not that they hate nightmares. They worry about the interpersonal damage—because of the nightmares, they can't sleep, and because they can't sleep, they find it hard to be with their partners or connect with their kids. They withdraw from life, avoid crowds, friends, and commitments. This avoidance becomes a prominent feature of their life. People in this situation don't complain about nightmares; they complain about loneliness and social constriction. Like so many others with different presenting conditions—substance-use disorders, treatment-resistant depression, social anxiety—at the root they're suffering from a lack of connection.

"Traumas, by their very nature, are interpersonal," Monson says. This idea is so simple it can be easy to miss: nearly all traumas are caused by someone else. Or they're simultaneously experienced in a community—in the case of veterans, they happen in or to a unit or among a crowd in a battle. "So trust is disrupted, the sense of interpersonal safety is disrupted, and the ability to get close to someone else, which is so inherently interpersonal. In a way, that's how conjoint therapy got born—to treat that interpersonal element. And that was the reason to match it with MDMA, because there are so many interpersonal effects of the drug that enhance openness."

As we explored earlier, the results have shown that the MDMA helps stimulate memories of the trauma, but it also creates conditions where that trauma can be reexperienced in a new setting of interpersonal satisfaction and intimacy that seems to override, or at least lessen considerably, the lasting effects of the trauma. This altered memory reconsolidation may be a main mechanism of action of MDMA, and may stem from increased oxytocin levels experienced during the trip.

Monson had gone through a clinician training program to understand the effects of the drug and how it might mix with psychotherapy. Her most prominent recollection of her experience was what she called a sense of "Teflon euphoria—like no matter what's coming or what was going on, it couldn't hurt me. It's not threatening and therefore I could work with it. That's a really powerful ingredient in therapy, but especially with PTSD, where people are so phobic of their internal experiences and memories."

Remember that MDMA stimulates the release of oxytocin, and so fosters empathy and compassion. That oxytocin circulates in the body but also, thanks to the direct connection between the hypothalamus, the oxytocin producer, and the amygdala, it disarms the sense of fear and enhances trust.

Since oxytocin is also associated with neurogenesis and neuroplasticity, the profoundly prosocial behaviors have a chance to become wired into the brain and remain in place after the MDMA session.

She cited one couple in the study, a combat veteran and his wife. He had been involved in a gruesome, bloody scene with civilians. And under the influence of MDMA he became deeply immersed in those memories, almost to the point where it became a dissociative episode. In the midst of all this, his partner got up and sat next to him and started saying, "You know, I'm here with you," as if she, too, were there in his memory. He kept on talking as if he were going through it and she kept on reassuring him, as if she were there, too, comforting him, while the experience continued around them both. Afterward, they both commented on how powerful that moment had been. Unlike her husband, she'd been fully oriented to the fact that she was in a room in a lab. He'd continued to go through the experience, but later said that he'd suddenly felt as if she were right there beside him.

Monson said that CBCT therapy often achieved a similar result, but the MDMA made it a less intellectual and more visceral experience. If you can evoke emotion, Monson said, you can facilitate learning, which is one of the reasons that traumatic events—or any highly charged emotional situation where the adrenaline is flowing—become seared in the memory. But positive emotions, and the good chemistry that accompanies them, promote learning, too. And under the influence of MDMA, the veteran could reshape the experience in a new and unexpected framework, as an intimate interaction with a loved one. Recalling it later, the traumatic event had lost much of its terror, and he would become tender, even tearful, recalling it. "I felt like you were there beside me," he said. "So then I could go through the experience without it tearing me apart." MDMA can help strip away one of the central elements of a traumatic experience, the feeling of inner personal violence and sense of abandonment, the persistent fear that there is no one to protect you.

Monson considers herself a scientist first—in other words, she was drawn to this experiment for practical reasons: MDMA-assisted psychotherapy promised to improve outcomes for people with social anxiety disorders and traumatic stress–related conditions. But scientists can still have heartfelt reactions. "People can certainly be immersed in these dissociative experiences without drugs," she says. "But they're heightened under medication, and in that case, he had his most intimate loved one around to go through it with him. That's kind of the essence of life, isn't it? To feel that someone's got your back and is with you in the hardest of times— even if memories are the hardest of times for you."

So we can see that observation and regulation, focusing and relaxing, are not only foundational when bringing peace to the self, they are crucial in building a bridge of peaceful connection between two people. However, keep in mind that if you're going to stop, focus, relax, and open up, you need to stay there for a bit. Staying is a prerequisite for any real growth.

If you can be with yourself and not run away from your own consciousness when the going gets tough, if you can be with your partner and not flee when there is conflict, these behaviors will help keep you connected, integrated, and strong. It's the same thing in parenting—staying in the moment with your child, choosing attachment over avoidance.

It scales up well also. Stay with your family to work out your childhood traumas, stay integrated in the community to tend to your town's conflicts, stay connected to the planet to help reverse the damage we're doing.

Stay with me as we head into the next sphere, yet another crucible of connection: the family.

CHAPTER 3

CONNECTION WITH THE FAMILY

What usually has the strongest psychic effect on the child is the life that the parents have not lived.

—CARL JUNG

Sometimes being a doctor means not trusting other doctors, or at least avoiding them whenever possible. Doctors love to intervene. We're not trained to stand by and watch something take place in its natural progression. I knew enough about childbirth to insist that when I had my first child (and my second), I wanted a midwife, no epidural, no C-section, and no medical interventions. Then again, I *am* a doctor, one with a history of experimentation with drugs and a professional interest in the body's own neurochemical cocktails. So apart from all my emotions about childbirth and motherhood, the psychonaut in me was curious to experience whatever natural anesthesia my body would provide.

And, hoo-boy, I wasn't disappointed. I remember feeling, in my professional judgment, really high. The contractions had a bell-shaped curve: I'd ride the pain up and the plateau would nearly break me, but just when I thought I couldn't take it anymore, the pain would ebb away. In between these regular contractions, I felt altered—not stoned exactly, but blissed out, probably thanks to the beta-endorphins, one of the body's most potent natural opiates. On top of that, I felt clear-minded and alert. My pupils were dilated, which is one of the side effects of many psychedelics and stimulants, but not opiates. I kept telling Jeremy how great I felt, how impressed I was with my body's stash box. When the brain needs to, it really knows how to throw a party.

Even though I wanted a doctor-free delivery, pregnancy didn't mean that I had to abandon my own professional principles. I read thirty-five books on pregnancy, delivery, nursing, and early childhood development before giving birth, trying to get myself up to speed on all that was required to get my child through those crucial first moments and all the years afterward. I took a class on nursing, and another one on hypno-birthing. I spent hours listening to audiotapes to facilitate a fast, easy birth. They must've worked, because my daughter, Molly, came out in a hurry, even though she had one arm raised up in defiant victory.

In a sense, childbirth is ground zero for oneness. The body is throwing everything it has into the birth, and when all goes right—the room is warm and cozy, free of psychodrama or medical issues, with plenty of people around to support you—the sense of connection between mother and newborn can take over. It can be overwhelming. It may seem odd that one of the most concentrated experiences of oneness comes at precisely the instant when you split into two people. But from another perspective that's not what's happening at all. For all the months you're pregnant, there's no boundary between you and your child. They are embodied within. Then, when the baby is born and placed immediately, skin to skin, in your arms, you may feel that nothing can come between the two of you outside the womb, either.

Oxytocin floods the body during birth for some practical reasons, like helping dilate the cervix and strengthen contractions. But it's also working in profoundly emotional ways, promoting the bond between mother and child, the ultimate "affiliative behavior." The hormone is pivotal, involved at every step from conception (especially if conception includes an orgasm, which enhances uterine contractions that help push the sperm toward the egg) to delivery, where oxytocin helps to push out first the baby and then the placenta. These are major, deeply physical events, and oxytocin plays a decisive role on a muscular level. But that doesn't mean we can discount its psychoactive dimensions, as the hormone helps transform childbirth into a euphoric, mysterious experience, the first instance of a life-changing bond.

NEW BABY, NEW MIND

As a psychiatrist who's given birth, I'm totally into the neurochemical pyrotechnics. But in particular I'm interested in the way oxytocin (especially in the high-estrogen environment of pregnancy and childbirth and lactation) promotes neuroplasticity, the massive ongoing rewiring that helps lay the foundation for all the new behaviors of motherhood.

Emotionally significant experiences, various stresses, and exercise can also create experience-dependent changes in the hippocampus (memory center), in turn creating new connections, which translate into new behaviors. Oxytocin enables all of it. (But estrogen is also a key player in the neuroplasticity of pregnancy.)

The reason so many women tell me they feel like their "brain changed" after they became mothers is because they're correct. It does. Although precise counts are hard to pinpoint—oxytocin is released in waves and has a half-life of minutes, both of which make data difficult to gather—the pattern is clear. From the first trimester onward, oxytocin counts begin to rise, promoting nutrition necessary for both mother and child, making sleep easier, and probably contributing to the "glow" people are always pointing out to expectant mothers. The count peaks at delivery—cresting at the actual moment the baby's head crowns—then tapers over the next six weeks, the so-called fourth trimester. This means over nine months, brain reorganization happens both slowly and then all at once: at its most active, pregnancy-related neuronal reorganization can multiply at a remarkable rate of 250,000 brain cells a minute. And it's not just the density of neurons that increases. Their structural network also changes, adding new contacts and realigning circuitry throughout the brain.

One area of the brain that's deeply affected by these increases in estrogen and oxytocin is the memory center, the hippocampus, which reshapes behaviors previously focused on personal needs and survival into new behaviors focused on feeding, protecting, and caring for the child. One critical aspect of motherhood is looking out for the safety of both yourself and your child, so verbal and emotional memory centers are also highly active, scanning for potentially threatening behaviors, like abandonment or violence.

Some women do complain about feeling foggier during pregnancy. My cousin Liz called it "baby brain suck." But you're not actually losing IQ points; you're gaining brain cells and connections. In fact, the effects of birth-related neurogenesis can last for years after pregnancy, a protective effect that accounts for the lower incidence of age-related dementia in mothers, especially mothers of three or more children. While you may find it more difficult to multitask or concentrate on the kind of chores that were second nature to you prepregnancy, this may be related to oxytocin's amnesiac properties helping erase older behaviors and replace them with new patterns. I think this is one reason so many of my patients have been able to quit smoking or drinking when they're pregnant. Adopting a new mindset comes so easily in the neuroplastic stage of pregnancy that it can almost feel as if you just forgot how—or why—you smoked or drank in the first place.

Once the labor is over and you've delivered your baby, the oxytocin can help you transition from the intensity of childbirth to the emotional moments that follow. However, the bond is not immediate or automatic with every mother and child. I remember feeling not quite aligned yet with the gooey little person in my arms right after giving birth; I didn't really sense anything like the bonding all the books talked about until I started nursing. Still, the connection starts taking shape, on a purely physical level, as soon as you take your newborn in your arms. As skin touches skin—contact you can control and should arrange for ahead of time as a top priority—your two bodies begin to coregulate: the baby's vitals respond to the mother's embrace, and the mother's vitals stabilize at the same time. Coregulation jump-starts a virtuous feedback loop between mother and child. Your breathing and blood pressure, elevated by all the pushing in delivery, settle into sync with the baby's. Your heart rate lowers, along with your body temperatures. Blood sugar levels that spiked under the stresses of birth lower in tandem. The same neurochemical cocktail that fueled mutual attraction between partners (minus lust) starts to settle over both mother and child. The baby relaxes on the mother and the mother begins the tender, instinctive rituals of bonding—gentle touch, warm embrace, quiet sounds of comfort and happiness—that will solidify their alliance and prepare the child to enter the world with confidence.

Oxytocin plays a key role here, providing immediate rewards for maternal behavior, so immediate that you may feel surprised by the new maternal instincts overriding other impulses. While the mechanisms are not entirely clear, coregulation also applies to your oxytocin levels. Your higher ones trigger a corresponding oxytocin rush in the newborn, creating a self-reinforcing feedback loop just as your breathing and blood sugar syncing up. At first this exchange is very physical—touch, smell, and body contact set off the mutual surges of oxytocin. But soon sights and sounds—the baby crying or just breathing, mom rushing over or cooing—have the same effect, a reflex that becomes apparent to mothers once the letdown occurs (thanks again to oxytocin), and you start leaking milk whenever you hear your baby cry.

My earliest days with Molly, my oldest, were spent in what

is called mutual coregulation. She regulated my physiological states, and I regulated hers. Her crying triggered my milk to come in; my milk triggered her calmness. She needed to be held and feel safe; I needed to hold her and provide for her safety. The fourth trimester was a limbo between us being one and us being two. It was a tapering off of our unity. Importantly, as she was coregulated, she learned to self-regulate.

Research shows that oxytocin levels are a reliable predictor of a positive mother-child bond. Dr. Ruth Feldman, the researcher from Israel who measured oxytocin nasal spray's effect on fathers' parenting behavior, directed a study that followed mothers from the first trimester through the first month after birth, tracking their oxytocin levels at every stage. The role genetics plays in determining these hormone levels is unclear, but there are some studies that suggest parenting styles do correlate with different oxytocin receptor gene types, called polymorphisms. Feldman's group found that higher levels in the first trimester correlated with strong attachment and more typical maternal behaviors, like affectionate gazing, attentive support, stimulating touch, baby talk, special songs, etc., once the baby was born.

My experience during pregnancy confirmed that. I could feel how my physiological state affected me and potentially my fetus as well. I know that when things are tough in your life during pregnancy, the baby is bathed in the stress hormone cortisol. That can shape development. So, setting aside the fact that I had a planned, wanted pregnancy, I simply felt happy and relaxed because the pregnancy hormones agreed with me. They soothed me, and I learned that estrogen has a great antistress effect, taking the edge off most of my irritability or aggression. I was a kinder, gentler doctor when I was pregnant (with a girl; my experience with the testosterone of a male fetus was a different one).

We've already seen how easy it is to coax the release of oxytocin. So a nurturing environment early on, filled with oxytocin-enriching behavior like attention, hugs, sex, and orgasms, can help set the tone for a positive birth experience. In other words, even though your partner can't take a starring role in mother-infant bonding, their early support can help shape a positive outcome. And the neurogenesis that accompanies elevated levels of oxytocin throughout the pregnancy contributes a lot, preparing the mother for a whole new set of mental and behavioral challenges.

Scientists have tracked how this good mojo helps set the stage for the health and confidence of your child later on in life. There are a number of measures to monitor "vagal tone," a catchall term for the activity of the vagus nerve. When I was in medical school, they taught us that the vagus was called "the wandering nerve," because it courses its way from the brain stem to the heart, lungs, and digestive tract. Vagal tone helps regulate all sorts of functions governed by the parasympathetic nervous system, like heart rate variability and the dilation of blood vessels. Childhood trauma leads to low vagal tones, meaning the child is spending more time in fight or flight. If these bursts of cortisol and adrenaline become the new normal, then that establishes a new baseline, which is a setup for many problems down the road. The CDC recently issued guidelines clearly stating that preventing childhood trauma reduces a child's chances for developing addiction, chronic diseases, as well as mental health problems later in life. Imaging studies of people with depression, anxiety, or PTSD often show similar patterns of weakened inhibitory control (when the frontal lobes can't calm down the emotional centers) and also a modified processing of salience of stimuli, which means how important or threatening any given event is. When you've had multiple traumas, your ability to respond to them becomes impaired. Conversely, when you have multiple social supports, your ability to dampen a stress response greatly increases. This protects you against, and helps you withstand, physical and mental health problems.

To some extent, vagal tone is just a measure of your ability to flip into para, a nearly automatic response whenever you're breastfeeding. Thanks to the combined effects of oxytocin and coregulation, mother and child both tend to flip into para while breastfeeding (maybe not in a train station or pulled over on the side of the interstate, but most of the time), and the ease and frequency of that interaction seems to establish the pattern for a child's ability to self-regulate and empathize—that is, to tend and befriend throughout childhood and later in life. This, along with a relatively trauma-free childhood, helps to ensure a lifetime of resilience in the face of future challenges. (I appreciate that this may be unattainable; consider it aspirational, then.)

This is one of the main arguments in favor of breastfeeding, apart from the fact that it feels amazing and is often the quickest way to soothe a baby. (I also loved how I could eat like a lumberjack and still lose weight. Never before or since.) By connecting with your baby, letting your heart rates and breathing slow down and get in sync, you're teaching your child how to self-soothe. Breastfeeding helps them grow up to be less anxious, less prone to psychosomatic illness, and more adept at emotional self-regulation. Connecting with your infant at this stage also teaches the child how to connect with the self, and studies show that mothers with high vagal tone (which translates into slower, but more adaptive, heart rate and steadier breathing) pass that along to their kids.

The other big reason to breastfeed: it reliably triggers the good chemistry of connection, and seems to reduce both the incidence and the severity of postpartum depression. None of the studies on this are wildly reliable, probably because nobody's in the mood to volunteer to be poked and prodded and monitored any more than they have to right after giving birth. But the results suggest a spectrum, with breastfeeding on one end, expressing milk or partial bottle-feeding somewhere in the middle, and total formula feeding at the other extreme. Those who wanted to nurse but couldn't are more likely to experience postpartum depression than those who chose to bottle-feed.

Whether you nurse or bottle-feed, there are behaviors that help us to bond with baby. Picking up the baby, we soften our voices, smile, nod, touch, and hug, and the child quickly adapts to our mood. The baby soon starts to return the favor. When I moved upstate, out of New York City, I never felt fully woven into the people or rhythms of the town I lived in until my kids came along. The children made us a family and gave us a reason to engage in all the activities in our town, to go to baby-and-me music classes and parent-teacher nights and Halloween parades. Maybe I just got better at affiliative behavior once I had more oxytocin on board, but it did give me that sense of belonging, crucial to feeling knit into our new small town.

However, parenting is not all warm and fuzzy, as anyone who's hung around a playground can tell you. In research settings, aggression is commonly seen in female mammals who are lactating and protecting their young. Oxytocin is not set up for indiscriminate bonding: it also helps us distinguish who's in our tribe and who's not. And when it's tamping down the amygdala's activity, protective mothers can become fearless. Does this help explain some of the playground "us vs. them" behaviors that can spring up?

CONNECTED FROM BIRTH

We're three stages into our journey of connection and starting to see how really interconnected connection can be. We can sing and float and breathe through one nostril and connect with ourselves. We can rip off our clothes and jump into bed and connect with a partner. But once you have a baby and start connecting as a family, you've started living in a three-dimensional world and the connections quickly multiply. I have a friend in town, Jeni Howe, who's tall and radiantly healthy. She looks like she's stepped out of an organic farm-to-table baby food catalog or something. On top of everything else, she coaches her kid's field hockey team. We know each other as moms first, but Jeni is also a doula. She started as a postpartum doula, working with new mothers, but lately she's been focusing on supporting families through the birth process. She helps the mother and her partner come up with a plan they're comfortable with, making sure the mother gets what she needs, whether she's delivering in a hospital maternity wing or having a home birth. On a personal level, Jeni's making sure the mother-to-be is as comfortable as possible during delivery. But giving birth can present challenges, and when they do pop up, Jeni's there to act as advocate (especially if the birth is taking place in a hospital setting), to ensure that the mother and child aren't subject to more medical interventions than they planned for.

Jeni works with the kind of moms we see a lot of out here—women at or nearing forty, who've had a successful career for fifteen years. They've moved out to the country from Brooklyn to have a first home and a yard and a dog. They've got the great marriage and the perfect stroller. All the pieces of life are in place. These are women used to feeling stable and knowledgeable and experienced—and once they have a baby, contrary to all expectations, suddenly all that experience isn't necessarily an advantage. You can't control the birthing process, nor a newborn. You're not getting as much sleep. It's not really popular to say in this culture, but women at forty are different creatures from twenty-five-year-old mothers. "First of all," Jeni says, "you're not as young as someone twenty-five doing the exact same thing. And at twenty-five, you're not really sure what it means to be an adult anyway. So when your entire world is thrown on its head, it doesn't matter as much. It just doesn't have as much impact."

Jeni points to the most recent example of the risks that can come with poise and the ideal life: an interview with Meghan Markle, the American actress who was thrown into the tabloid glare when she married Prince Harry. In front of the camera, the new mother was asked an obvious and human question: "With all that's going on, are you okay?" Markle took a long pause and answered as any sleep-deprived woman might, with a crack in her voice that made it clear that she maybe was not okay at all. "Yes, it's a lot. And also, thank you for asking, because not many people have asked about it." Markle got a lot of blowback, because she had the royal millions and the doting husband and all the support staff a Duchess of Sussex can command. Like, what could possibly be the problem, Your Royal Highness?

The problem is one we've seen before: isolation. "Look," Jeni says. "Meghan Markle is the perfect example of someone who's supposed to have it all. But she's missing the one thing she needs to embrace being a mother, which is having supportive people around and safety and privacy. Obviously, the bond and the hormonal release of oxytocin every time you breastfeed, that's a huge upper. You're getting the love hormone, this incredible blast of endorphins." But Jeni sees firsthand the factors that can upset the bonding experience—you're impoverished or in an abusive relationship or you're isolated by your wealth. "These are factors that just might override oxytocin."

She says she's seen heroic outliers, women you might expect to be in the worst possible situation for creating a lasting connection with their newborn, who seem to be able to overcome their isolation and enter an unexpectedly serene state after giving birth. "I've seen women who are in an abusive relationship or women who are grieving for their own mother and they're just more at peace. They don't like having anyone around. They've got this exquisite monogamous bond between mom and baby and it's beautiful. Some of the happiest mothers are actually grieving over something else."

Dyads like this are rare, and nobody would recommend following their pathway to maternal connection. But the extreme cases point to one of the fundamentals of connection:

no one, certainly not a mother and child, exists in a vacuum. And from a doula's perspective, many of the obstacles to the ideal birth and bonding experience are political. "Being a woman of color is probably the biggest risk factor in childbirth. The numbers are staggering. It's not just poor women in the South. It's Serena Williams and Beyoncé." There are all sorts of factors contributing to this unequal treatment. For one, doctors are less likely to believe African American women reporting pain, which is the problem that Williams encountered. When she reported difficulty breathing—she'd had a history of blood clots but had stopped taking her anticoagulants before her emergency C-section—doctors lost valuable time treating her hematoma because they thought her medicine had left her confused. (Williams was finally able to overcome their skepticism.) On top of this, African American women suffer from hypertension at higher rates, a condition that can contribute to low birth weight and infant mortality. And studies have shown that perceived racism contributes to this hypertension, which puts African Americans at greater risk for any number of conditions, like diabetes and cardiovascular disease. And statistically, she points out, poor African American women are the least likely to breastfeed, removing the ongoing physical and psychological benefits of oxytocin.

Another trouble spot in the population: mothers who've been subject to multiple medical interventions over the course of their pregnancy and birth. If a woman has been through five rounds of IVF, was induced, had an epidural then a C-section, and after the birth had trouble breastfeeding—if the whole birth experience has been medicalized to that degree, Jeni asks, "How does that woman go home with not one bit of evidence that she knows how to do this?"

Jeni tries to push against the model that sees pregnancy as a potential pathology requiring a battery of preventive technologies—blood work, ultrasounds, genetic testing—to ensure a safe delivery. Instead, she preaches the opposite view, that pregnancy just might be okay on its own medically, and the real focus should be on psychosocial preparation. That requires some adjustment of ideals—turning from fetishizing paparazzi shots of celebrity mothers and their "postbaby bods" and promoting social solutions instead, like the family-centric policies that have been in place for nearly forty years at the outdoor clothing company Patagonia. Their programs for on-site child care, lactation programs, and paid medical leave have been rewarded with a 100 percent return rate by employee moms coming back from their (generous) maternity leave.

In Jeni's ideal world, new mothers would be supported by a community of fellow mothers, grandmothers, aunties, friends, and sisters who'd swoop in and make soup and take care of everything, leaving the mother-to-be to the important work of being with her newborn. That may be a utopian vision, but in the meantime, a few towns over, she's opened up a community center she calls Baby Botanica, a real-world collaborative of "birth, growth, and health practitioners," as well as a meeting space for classes, treatments, workshops, and events. It's too early to tell if there's a market to support the place, but as nearly any first-time mother could tell you, even with the regular hits of oxytocin that make breastfeeding feel so relaxing and rewarding, early motherhood can be a lonely and disorienting time. Feeling like you're not alone but part of something nurturing and bigger than yourself could be just the medicine you need to feel connected.

If there's any moment in life where our biology seems to

have conspired to make us stay put—tweaking our hormones, raising some and lowering others, and reshaping our brains so that we have every incentive to just sit—it's right after birth, as you're welcoming a newborn into your family. It's time to protect and connect. This hormonal reorganization occurs in men, too: once a new baby comes home, a father's testosterone levels plummet. Testosterone in abundance may help a man (any male mammal, for that matter) find a new mate, but once the baby arrives, those testosterone-fueled behaviors— aggression, risk-taking, general horniness—aren't all that useful. In fact, it's prime time for all the stuff that comes easily when the body has a little less of it, like nurturing and compassion and fidelity. Not surprisingly, oxytocin and testosterone are often at odds in the bloodstream. When one is up, the other is often down.

People used to think that there were two kinds of men— high-testosterone bad boys and low-testosterone dad types— but a study of 624 men in the Philippines in their early twenties showed sharp drops in testosterone across the board in partnered dads as soon as the baby came home. This was especially true in the baby's first month.

This isn't something guys should obsess about. It's not a sign of fading glory. For one, helping raise a kid is part of male biology just as much as sex drive is. For two, a dad's lower levels of testosterone are associated with positive health outcomes, like lower incidence of prostate cancer and lower mortality rates. There are all sorts of reasons for this—single men drink more, eat worse, suffer more from the damaging health effects of isolation. But maybe the simple reason is the best: being a caregiver triggers the good chemistry that will keep you happy and healthy.

VASOPRESSIN, FIDELITY, AND FREEZING

In men, vasopressin—considered the hormone of monogamy and exclusivity—plays a bigger role than oxytocin does. But these two chemicals are part of the same pathway, and they appear in the same parts of the brain. While oxytocin works better in the estrogen-rich environment of women, vasopressin works well in the testosterone-rich environment of men. But each gender has both of these molecules of attachment and bonding. Vasopressin is present not only in committed male-female pairs, but also in male bonding, aka the "bromance." In prairie voles, the presence or absence of a vasopressor receptor dictates whether a male vole will be monogamous or a player.

Receptors for oxytocin and vasopressin are found throughout areas of the nervous system that regulate emotional and social behaviors, and the reward process that molds them. They work together to form the oxytocin-vasopressin pathway. The pathway is an integrated and adaptive system that regulates attachment and pair bonding, sexual behavior and parenting. These two hormones balance the drives between social engagement and defensive posturing, working a bit like gas and brakes in the battle between love and fear. The effect of their dynamic interaction is to influence our perception of safety or danger. Vasopressin encourages protection of self and progeny, and it typically does this through mobilization (fleeing). Under safer conditions, oxytocin will dominate, supporting sociality, which sometimes requires you, and often allows you, to stay put.

In an acutely stressful situation, you may see both hormones activated, supporting mobilization and escape, but also enhanced bridge-building with people considered to be safe. In this situation, you would protect (progeny) and then connect (tribal members). It is safe to say that men may be more inclined to protect or flee, and women will be more inclined to use social strategies to create safety.

However, in traumatic situations, mobilization with fear would predominate, which means disconnecting. Pull up the stakes and run. If the circumstances got even more intense, or if escape was impossible, the freeze/shut-down response kicks in—the ultimate disconnection. It's left over from our earliest development (called the "reptilian brain"), when playing dead conferred real survival advantages. When people say "fight, flight, or freeze," as if it's all one system, they're lumping in "freeze" where they shouldn't. It's its own thing. It's not just a part of the sympathetic nervous system, because freezing involves para as well. It's a co-creation.

There are different kinds of freezing behaviors. There's immobility without fear (like when a kitten goes limp in order to be picked up by the nape of its neck, or when you're receiving sexual pleasure from someone and have to stay still), and then there's immobility with fear, which happens in extreme trauma. Not only is shutting down a more primitive response in the brain, but it also happens more easily in women (e.g., fainting when given horrific news), which may have to do with oxytocin-estrogen interactions.

Vasopressin, perhaps because it is the defensive-oriented hormone, prioritizing protecting the progeny, is the biggest factor in paternal behavior, helping a dad to watch over his child and bond with its mother. Men have prolactin as well, which elevates as they hear their baby's cry, just as a woman's prolactin levels do. And dads absolutely have oxytocin on board. During the early phases of parenthood, cohabiting parents share elevated oxytocin levels, which are often interrelated. Although some men may be more likely to cheat when their mates are pregnant or are new mothers, it could be that if you allow your partner more time with his baby, particularly skin-to-skin cuddle time, his bond will be stronger not just with his child but with you as well, thanks to both of these hormones. And in the same way that oxytocin and testosterone are at odds, so are vasopressin and testosterone. When more vasopressin is around, monogamy will outweigh competition and aggression, and protecting the progeny will outweigh a search for a new partner. If testosterone levels are higher than vasopressin, then confrontation, infidelity, and the drive for novelty will win out.

Ruth Feldman, the same neuroscientist who measured oxytocin levels in mothers, also tracked the levels in fathers and found that their baseline levels were comparable to those of mothers, even in the first weeks after birth when breastfeeding begins. Obviously, this isn't because the dads are lactating. In the same way that cuddling can increase oxytocin levels in couples, just dads doing dad stuff—playing with the baby, making dad noises, giving raspberries, goofy dancing, whatever they invent to keep the baby happy—is enough to raise their oxytocin levels and that of their baby, too. This means that dads also benefit from the neurogenesis that comes with elevated oxytocin levels, and learn to parent by parenting.

For nursing mothers, the oxytocin rush of breastfeeding is a pivotal part of the prosocial reward system, the body's positive feedback loop that keeps them invested in nurturing their children and keeps our species going. The entire activity seems designed to make moms happy, attentive, and tender (or at least help them overcome a sleep deficit) when they're busy doing what they and the baby are programmed to do. But babies are also irresistible on their own. Nearly every parent can tell stories about feeling helplessly drawn to their child, watching a newborn sleep, smelling a baby's head, listening to their adorable baby snores. It turns out all this cuteness is part of the plan, too: a baby's cuteness unlocks caregiving. And it's not just Bubbe. Even nonrelatives find themselves helpless to resist what scientists call "the attentional prioritization of infant cues."

There is a caregiving system that includes activation of the insula (remember, the intuitive center?) and secretion of oxytocin. It's an adaptive system that is molded by environment, perceiving need in another, being motivated to care for another, and delivering a helping response to someone in need.

The brain circuitry's response to cuteness—the big head and eyes, small chin, full cheeks—is nearly immediate and, it seems, compulsory. All that cuteness gets your attention— apparently parts of the brain, in both parents and nonparents, respond to infant cuteness within 140 milliseconds. It's hard to say which came first—the big eyes or the hair-trigger response. And it doesn't matter, as long as they command attention.

Babies' eyes, like their brains, are disproportionately large at birth. And human eyes are already larger than any comparable primate's. They're more conspicuous, with the colored disc of the iris set off against the white background of the sclera. Human eyes are also dramatically longer horizontally than any other primate's, in ways that make the movement of those colored discs more visible. The eyes of humans emerge at birth already a third of their adult size, and they grow quickly. According to the cooperative eye hypothesis, the darkness of an ape's eyes are designed to disguise the direction of an eye's movements. Ours, by contrast, are designed to enhance the signaling of the gaze, indicating collaborative intentions. From an evolutionary standpoint, this is a big fork in the road. And here again, cooperation and connecting are shown to be foundational, built into our bodies and our DNA.

And it's not just the eyes drawing us in. The noises that babies make are pitched to cut through auditory clutter. And the responses that these cues elicit is nearly universal, going beyond tribal "us vs. them" distinctions. Basically, if you're human, you're programmed to respond protectively. That's one reason the 2015 photograph of the drowned Kurdish baby washed up on the shore of the Mediterranean drew outrage from leaders—and everyone else—around the world.

These powerful instantaneous responses are followed by more slowly developing reactions, and the long lead reactions help parents learn the skills that nurture a child's cognitive and emotional development. Cuteness helps here, too. In just the way that the oxytocin rush of breastfeeding (for mother and child) seems designed to promote connection, cuteness seems to work on both parties—motivating parents and caregivers to interact and provide the child with the attention and stimulation they need. Babies are adorable and fascinating, and that quality helps you invest the time it takes to learn how to be a parent, to overcome any initial nervousness about your competence and learn to tune in to your baby.

See a common thread here? These hormonal systems are all reinforcing one another. Oxytocin makes caring for your baby pleasurable. The neurogenesis that comes with higher oxytocin levels helps you become more adept at caring for your baby, which makes your baby happier, which makes for more oxytocin all around. The factors seem to multiply the positive effects of connection—as long as you stay connected.

Yes, oxytocin works on fathers; however, these benefits don't extend to fathers who don't get involved. And mothers who skip this stage—whether from postpartum depression or because they rush back to work or because their lives have become unsettled by traumatic external factors—also miss out on the benefits of this positive feedback loop. The effects can be long-lasting. A 2014 study in Australia showed that women with weak or troubled bonding experiences with their own mother had lower oxytocin levels as a parent, a setup that's likely to be reproduced if the mother loses interest in her own child in turn.

ACUTE ENLIGHTENED MOOD
(AKA MIRTHFUL LAUGHTER)

Did I mention how cute babies are? They learn to smile before nearly anything else; it's their first facial expression of their own pleasure and is immediately responded to with more of the same. That social smile triggers not only a mirroring grin, but also the oxytocin in anyone who bears witness. Parents of newborns are likely to track a baby's expressions closely, watching for smiles, waiting for the instant when those smiles become intentional and come with eye contact and contented sounds. The first intentional smile usually comes somewhere in the first two months, and until you spot one, even unintentional smiles—the ones that killjoy parents of older children will tell you is "just gas"—can feel like a reward for all the hours you're putting in.

And then there's laughter, the even more infectious behavior that keeps parents coming back for more. Somewhere around three or four months, your baby will laugh out loud for the first time. It may not come in reaction to something funny, but just because she's delighted that you walked in to see her. Laughter puts both of you into para. It dilates the blood vessels and promotes cardiovascular health. Once your baby gets the hang of laughing, you're likely to discover something, when you least expect it, that will send her into uproarious laughter. It's the kind of reward that makes you want to stick around—so it's an adaptive behavior that promotes bonding. A study where they gave women intranasal oxytocin showed that it enhanced the salience of infant laughter. Meaning it made laughter more important. Oxytocin seems to make you pay attention to and prioritize your baby, among other things, which means that you're more likely to be there the next time the baby finds something hilarious. Remember partial intermittent reinforcement and how powerful it could be? How the mouse won't stop pressing the lever if sometimes it pays out? This time, that powerful drive is working in everybody's favor, keeping you coming back, trying new games, finding new ways to stimulate your child, knowing that one of these times, you're going to be there for the sound of your baby's delighted peals of laughter.

This is when the fascination grows, and you start playing all the games that can make a baby smile and laugh—peekaboo and gonna-getcha, poking, tickling, widening your eyes, ducking your head close to the baby as if to scare them. This is all rich territory: the interaction helps cement the bond and stimulate neural growth. Optimally, there should be a synchronized dance between caregiver and cared-for, with babbling and cooing as the baby attempts vocalization and receives verbal feedback for its efforts. Mirror neurons in the baby's brain will fire when the mother moves her mouth or face, assisting the baby in trying the behavior for herself. In fact, this is part of what makes peekaboo a neurological exercise: the mother withdraws her face and creates uncertainty, returns into view with a startling noise that engages the fight-or-flight instinct, then soothes the baby with smiles and reassuring sounds. The entire sequence helps teach the child how to navigate through a variety of mental states (from calm to vigilance to startled and back to calm) in a way that promotes resilience. Also, it teaches a very valuable lesson of rupture and repair. She's gone, she's back—abandonment and reunion. Being able to tolerate this cycle, and even responding with joy, is a crucial social skill. None of this teaching is going to happen while you're checking your notifications.

What's the big deal if I ignore my kid? Well, here's one possibility. Since we know that opiates soothe social separation, you'd be wise to keep your kids supplied with their own natural stores of endorphins, triggered by oxytocin, so they don't have to go looking for an external supply. Remember hugs not drugs? And let's not forget mirror neurons. "Checking out" on your phone is stealing time from just sitting with your kid. The baby in the carriage is supposed to be receiving not just visual attention to ensure safety, but engaging interaction to ensure neural development. Mostly, watching you absorbed in your phone will only prime them for the same behavior.

When people ask me about the "problematic behavior" in their kids, I often end up explaining this: it is a bid for relationship; they're not "doing it for attention." They are starved for connection. They want YOU. Jeremy and I were on the subway watching a mother on her phone, a child in the stroller visibly upset that she wasn't engaging with him, and a father trying to distract and tickle away the child's distress. If someone was trying to tickle me while I was being ignored, it wouldn't go well. It didn't go well for this father and child, either. The child was being taught to ignore their own deep pain. All the screaming and crying wasn't pretty. It was so clear to both of us that the mom just needed to prioritize the kid over the screen.

I could write a whole book about the harm of choosing your phone over your child, and I don't know if it would change a damn thing. But here are a few highlights: Glowing screens like televisions, laptops, and phones put you in a receptive, nearly hypnotic trance. The content doesn't matter. It's the glowing itself that is part of the attraction to our brains. (If I walk into a restaurant with a television on, I find my eyes being drawn to it, regardless of what's on the screen.) We are biologically drawn toward flickering flames for the same reason. Then you factor in the hardwiring we have for hunting and gathering, and you begin to see that the internet not only allows us to do both, but there are pharmacological rewards to be had. Numerous studies are suggesting that things like gaming and being on social media can trigger the good chemistry—the dopamine that gives us tunnel vision, the euphoria of an endorphin rush—that is supposed to naturally keep us hooked into each other.

And because we are also wired to gather in groups—to create dominance hierarchies and cooperatives—the internet enables and rewards this behavior. In some cases, it mimics the good chemistry that we would get from actual human interaction. But not quite, and so we, and then our children, feast on our feeds, hoping quantity will make up for quality. It doesn't. It's all the same gaping connection hole. Put your phone down and connect with yourself, your partner, and your progeny—or you'll miss out on the best parts of life.

PARENTING A TODDLER AND AN ADOLESCENT ARE NOT THAT DIFFERENT

When Molly was hitting not her "terrible twos," but her "f^&*ing fours," I realized that toddlerhood is a lot like a mini-adolescence. There are pushes for autonomy, testing limits, and plenty of power struggles. As a parent, you need to go through this messy phase of disentanglement. (Consider it part of the "unpaid emotional labor" we've all been talking about.) "You're not the boss of me" becomes truer by the year. Kids have their own wants and needs. I tell my patients who are having parenting difficulties two things: It's your job to give your kids what they need, not what they want. And . . . don't bite the hook. Kids will throw out various beautifully tied flies in an effort to get you to engage. Feel free to chant *Om Shanti* to yourself as an invocation of peace: may I not be provoked. Keep steady in giving them the unshakable, secure attachment and boundaries they require, without getting sucked into the conflict. Remember the open hand, not grasping at desired outcomes or getting dug in by attending to misbehavior.

Take a moment to consciously shift gears, from fight-or-flight mode to tend and befriend. In communicating with our partners or our children, when shifting to connect-and-protect mode, we soften our voices and our eyes, we smile, we nod, touch, and hug. Just as with couples, children want to feel seen, heard, and understood. You can use mirroring and validating language to help with this. ("I hear you say you don't want to leave the park. I would feel that way, too, if I were having so much fun with my friends.") We spend a lot of time convincing kids they don't feel the way they say they do. ("Oh, you don't really mean that.") We'd be better off accepting their reality and then taking it from there.

Please try to remember that a lot of "misbehavior" is really just a bid for attention and, more important, connection. So start there. Go ahead and give lots of loving, positive attention whenever they're acting in any way that approximates the desired behavior—or just every damn day. Set clear limits and boundaries calmly. Then ignore (as much as is safe) undesirable behavior. Don't give it any reinforcement, positive or negative. Remember that partial intermittent reinforcement will guarantee a more persistent form of unwanted behavior, so be very careful in how you respond to tantrums. If your kids learn that no actually means no, they won't spend hours wheedling you into a yes. (So save the nos for when you're done making a decision, and not as a starting point for negotiations.)

Keep in mind that adolescence is a distinctive time in brain and behavior development. Impulse control is not yet mastered, as the myelination of the long tracts isn't quite done. In terms of the electrochemical machinery of the brain, it's akin to saying the wiring hasn't been fully insulated. Adolescence is a time of increased risk-taking and intense learning from mistakes. There is a version of this in the animal kingdom called predator inspection, where not yet fully mature adults are more likely to approach than avoid a predator in order to gather crucial information.

Also remember that risk-taking behavior increases when adolescents are with their peers. This is the reason I agree with many states' requirement that with a junior license, multiple teens are not allowed in one car. In one study, just knowing there were other teens watching prompted the driver to act more carelessly.

Adolescence is a particularly challenging time in parenting because our kids need room to explore and make mistakes. Better to be a helicopter pad, giving them a safe space to land, than a helicopter parent, taking away the opportunity to learn by doing.

If you don't know where to begin, try this new parenting idea: teach your child to meditate, read, and play music. Not only will it increase your child's brain development and language and cognitive skills, and have them be better at impulse control and managing their behavior, but these habits will also keep them away from harmful screens. The data are in: those glowing devices are screwing up kids' neural development, which affects literacy skills when they're young and then often causes tremendous social pain and isolation when they're older. When I think about what I went through as an adolescent, and imagine how that would translate into today's online world, I shudder to think of where I would've ended up. More kids than ever are committing suicide or harming themselves, and the data strongly suggest that social media is contributing to these behaviors. In a recent study, every additional hour spent engaged in social media, on a computer, or in front of a television was associated with increased severity of depressive symptoms. We all know this intuitively, and the studies are bearing out our intuitions; the only thing left to do is act.

I'm going to introduce one more concept in parenting before we move on to something completely different, and it's a doozy: psychedelic parenting, aka "plant parenthood." Here's the thinking: if ingesting mind-manifesting medicines (when you have the day, or even better, the weekend off from your parenting responsibilities, can we agree?) can make you more open, connected, attuned, compassionate, or creative, that may actually be a good thing for a growing family. As part of integrating mystical experiences back into our everyday lives, we can more genuinely connect with that sense of curiosity, magic, and wonder that is naturally woven into childhood perceptions. And we can more generously nurture our children, making space for their self-expression and having compassion and acceptance for who they are and will become. Anecdotal stories of parents benefitting from their own psychedelic explorations and education abound. Controversial, yes, but parents can't connect fully with their child if they're not fully connected with themselves.

AN OCTOPUS'S GARDEN

Think back on what you learned when you were a teenager, right around puberty. Is it still in your brain? Those things get "wired in" on a very deep level, and they stay around forever. When I was an adolescent, I learned to play guitar and trumpet (while also learning to use drugs). I believe I will have those skills forever.

Adolescence is a time of intense social learning. The adolescent brain is in an exceptionally plastic phase here, when social signals (like if you're in the in-crowd or out in the cold) can have a stronger effect than usual. This hopefully helps you understand why peer pressure is primarily an adolescent phenomenon, and why parents may have less influence during this phase than during other milestones. A recent landmark study showed that MDMA reopens that window of critical social learning that is exclusively adolescent, effectively turning an adult brain back into an impressionable plastic pubertal one, at least for a few hours.

If all goes well, official FDA approval for MDMA would come sometime between 2022 and 2025. But that approval will likely be limited to the kind of treatments that have been closely studied in clinical trials, like the ones led by Candice Monson and Chris Stauffer, for PTSD. But the encouraging results within the narrow approval guidelines of those studies have prompted many in the field to consider broader applications for MDMA-assisted therapies. And plenty of psychiatrists would love to make use of the therapeutic opening that MDMA facilitates—that impressionable period of neurogenesis that the medicine ushers in, when, thanks to the flood of oxytocin to the amygdala, traumatic memories (and remember, every childhood has trauma) can be reframed in ways that help lessen or eliminate their terror. This cognitive reprocessing, which defangs the traumatic memory, allows the information to remain but the emotional component to be significantly altered.

Luckily, not every MDMA study is aimed at contributing to the incremental advance toward FDA approval. Some of the most exciting research now is looking deeply into what MDMA can show us about the nature of the mind and the crucial reopening of critical learning periods. The legal constraints are not as limiting for animal studies (although research funding often still depends on government review), and this has allowed for innovative and exploratory research that would be off-limits in human clinical trials. In her recent groundbreaking study, Dr. Gül Dölen, a neuroscientist and assistant professor in the Brain Science Institute at Johns Hopkins and the chief investigator at dölenLAB in Baltimore, caused a stir in the neuroscience community when her paper in *Nature* showed conclusively that MDMA could help reopen critical learning periods, effectively turning the adult brain back into an adolescent brain for a few hours.

We've been looking at these periods of heightened neuroplasticity, in parents and infants and now in adolescents. Dölen focused on a very specific type of neuroplasticity—social-reward learning. The brain certainly has other types of learning, some involving cognitive and visual perception and others involving movement and spatial awareness, but social-reward learning appealed to Dölen because she'd been studying it already and there were well-established clinical methods for measuring it. "We started out with social-reward learning critical periods, because we were studying the development of social behaviors," Dölen says. "We had this sense from human literature and just intuition that social behaviors change over your lifetime. You know, teenagers can't get enough of [being social]. But after a conference, I need a couple days of alone time. And kids are much more susceptible to peer pressure but adults are happy to wear ugly shoes if they're comfortable."

Although both her parents are doctors, Dölen originally came to clinical neuroscience from a philosophical slant. As a grad student on an MD/PhD track, she designed her own major in comparative perspectives on the mind, and the question that appealed to her was mindfulness, in particular how we can't really understand mindfulness in ourselves until we understand it in others—that there is no "I" unless there is "you." This led her to the study of autism, since its underlying disruption seemed to be that people suffering from it didn't fully grasp the idea of "other" or "you," and therefore had a limited understanding of "I." Autism research excited her, since philosophy usually trafficked in wonderful thought experiments without any tangible experimental data. And when she joined the lab where she was going to pursue her PhD, her adviser suggested studying Fragile X, a genetic mutation that inhibits the production of a protein necessary for brain development, and associated with autism spectrum disorder.

Actually, Dölen was drawn to Fragile X not because of anything inherently interesting in the mutation. The problem with treating autism is that it's a condition without a single specific cause. Each case is individual, and there are usually a number of precipitating factors and mutations that are thought to contribute to the condition in any single case. Fragile X is really not so much a cause of autism as it is the most frequently verifiable contributing factor. In choosing to focus her research on Fragile X, Dölen was aiming at the biggest target in a diffuse and shadowy syndrome.

To address the deficits that Fragile X causes, Dölen eventually narrowed her focus to a specific receptor involved in brain signaling. She found that suppressing that receptor in mice helped address and improve brain function not only for Fragile X, but also for a number of varieties of autism spectrum disorder. When follow-up studies in other labs reproduced her breakthrough results, several major pharmaceutical companies began to run human clinical trials. It seemed like a promising development. Nearly every other drug treatment for autism had been discovered by accident. This, Dölen said, "was going to be a home run for mechanism-based therapeutic design. But then the clinical trial failed and the whole field was in a funk over it. I especially was in a funk."

When she recovered, she started hunting for crucial differences between her experiment and the human trials, hoping to find the reason that her success with mice hadn't translated to humans. She noticed that the pharmaceutical companies had performed their tests on young adults while the mice she'd done her trials on had been juveniles. There's far less neuroplasticity in young adults. To prove that this was the key difference, she had to create a new experiment and figure out a few things all at once: how to test for both social behavioral impairment and social behavioral learning in mice, do both in a way that relates easily to autism, then verify that the capacity for social-behavior learning that she was tracking in mice might change over the course of a life. When you add all that together, she'd know a lot about critical learning periods in mice.

In Dölen's *Nature* article, she said conclusively that, yes, the critical learning period came early in life, and, even more significantly, it was possible to reopen that critical learning period later on in adults by giving the mice MDMA.

These findings had broad implications, certainly for her ongoing attempts to address autism, the "mean disease," as she puts it. Reopening a critical learning period in adults might afford people with autism spectrum disorder a chance to rewire their brains and help them overcome the social impairments associated with the disease—not to mention the fact that this reopening for social-reward learning might improve outcomes for other types of learning, like motor learning, a great benefit for people trying to recover from a stroke. "Right now," Dölen says, "we're looking for any evidence that what these drugs are doing is just reopening critical periods writ large, and that there's some sort of master key for critical-period reopening. But I can't tell you anything else about that yet because we started that experiment in April and [it's] ongoing."

This brief account doesn't do justice to the twenty years of laboratory wizardry involved in Dölen's research, which relied on breeding specific lines of genetically modified mice (modified to have the Fragile X gene, in particular) and genetically engineering oxytocin neurons to respond to light, advanced stuff that equals or exceeds anything that could be accomplished with a genetic technology like CRISPR. Along the way she's come up with insights into the workings of the brain, and especially into the effects and functions of oxytocin and serotonin.

One key distinction she's discovered is that there are two

types of oxytocin that do different things. One is called magnocellular (or big-celled) oxytocin, and in an electron micrographic scan you'll find many clustered together, ready to release all at once, flooding the entire body. The other type is called parvocellular (or small-celled) oxytocin, and in a scan you'll see only two or three of them at a time. The parvocellular oxytocin remain behind the blood-brain barrier. They don't operate on the body but do all their work within the brain.

It's her observation that these two types of oxytocin align with two types of behavior. The magnocellular oxytocin is important for what she calls Mad Love, while the parvocellular oxytocin seemed designed for Platonic Love. The Mad Love oxytocin goes to work when you're falling in love with a baby or a partner. It's the oxytocin that causes the all-over rush in your body, that makes a mom start lactating when she sees her baby. Platonic oxytocin goes to work when you're forming attachments with a group member. As Dölen says, "When you see your best friend coming down the hall, you probably don't want to start lactating."

It makes sense that the two types of love would be governed by distinct versions of the love hormone. When you're falling in love with a baby or a partner, she says, "The sky is blue, the birds are chirping, and you don't even notice that he doesn't put the toilet seat down." But deciding who you're going to let into your friend group is a trickier proposition. "You don't want to let in somebody who's not going to do their fair share of the work or is going to be a mooch or you know isn't going to have your back when you need it." So parvocellular oxytocin releases at judicious intervals, at a pace that won't cloud your judgment. You don't want to rush in. Instead, you gather evidence to confirm your positive impressions. There's no such thing as platonic love at first sight.

Dölen's research on reopening critical learning periods is exciting, but there's another study of hers that may be even more provocative. Back in the days when she first began studying autism, one big appeal to her was the philosophical one, that autism provided a way to study Theory of Mind, the ability to attribute subjective mental states to others, a capacity that develops over time (asking a two-year-old how someone else might feel is fruitless) and is often missing in people with autism. Theory of Mind has other names—like mind reading or social cognition or cognitive empathy—and is indispensable in the social understanding of others.

Cognitive empathy is distinct from emotional empathy, which is the ability to sense what someone is feeling. Cognitive empathy is the intellectual counterpart of that: the ability to decipher what someone is thinking. You need cognitive empathy to trick people, to bluff or read someone's poker face, to lie, to manipulate, or to do more terrible things. (It can be employed for positive outcomes, too: for diplomacy, for instance, or to negotiate an equitable deal among parties with competing interests.) To illustrate the difference, Dölen likes to compare a psychopath and someone with autism. "If you ask people with autism, 'Why did you hurt my feelings?' they say, 'Because I didn't know I was hurting your feelings. If I knew I would never have done it.' They have no cognitive empathy. Then if you ask a psychopath, 'Why are you hurting my feelings?' they say, 'Because I find it enjoyable. I get pleasure from it.' So a psychopath has no emotional empathy. But by all accounts they have either normal or actually slightly better cognitive empathy.

But for this experiment, Dölen's instincts to follow Theory of Mind led her to the octopus. The octopus exhibits behaviors that suggest that they have cognitive empathy: they hunt by trickery, using a ruse like the ones that high school boys love so much, where they tap you on one shoulder then, when you look that way, circle around your other side. That's the capacity that's missing in autism. (It's also missing in mice—one big reason why Dölen had to go to such great lengths in the lab to measure social impairment.)

Octopi have this capacity, which is normally a sign of higher social cognition. But what especially fascinated Dölen about the octopus is that its brain isn't organized like a human's at all despite this key similarity. Octopi have no nucleus accumbens, the part of the brain that spurs on motivation, translating it into action. They have no dorsal raphe nucleus, which appears to be a key player in neuroplasticity. They have no cerebral cortex, the distinctive highly folded outer layer of the human brain believed to be responsible for higher cognitive functions like language, memory, perception, and consciousness. Their brains are closer to a snail's brain than a human's.

There was another reason the octopus intrigued her: a brain doesn't fossilize well, so there's nothing left that would allow you to study its evolution. By most measures, neuroscience, she says, is behind other branches of biology on evolution—except that there is a tremendous amount of evolutionary information in the genome. If you have a reference genome, you can mathematically calculate the distances between different changes in it, allowing you to reconstruct backward an evolutionary tree. So once someone sequenced the genome of California two-spot octopus, Dölen says, "That was like, Oh my god, we're off to the races."

Octopi are creatures that have solved many of the same complex cognitive assignments that we have—they use tools, solve problems, play, recognize individuals, and store memories—even though we last shared a common ancestor five hundred forty million years ago. Not surprisingly, when Dölen and her fellow researchers tried to match octopus and human DNA, it was only a 60 percent match, about as much as we share with a banana. But when she looked at the part of the gene that encodes for the transporter protein on the receptor that serotonin (and MDMA and SSRIs like Prozac) binds to, it was basically a 100 percent match. They realized that if they gave the octopus MDMA, the MDMA would almost certainly find the serotonin transporters in the octopus and bind to them.

Serotonin is the neurotransmitter associated with satisfaction and satiety, with having what you want and wanting what you have. The confirmation of the serotonin transporter protein on your genes can affect whether you will end up with depression or an anxiety disorder. Decades of research point to a correlation between the short-allele type and these disorders. It was thought that people with the short alleles respond more negatively to emotional friction within a relationship, which could make it difficult for psycho-emotional health. But one lab run by Dr. Robert Levenson at UC, Berkeley, has proposed that rather than predisposing someone to more negative emotional responses, these short alleles may be serving as a "psycho-emotional magnifying glass" that allows all emotions to be more deeply and intensely felt.

Serotonin is one of the oldest hormones in the genome, among the first to appear on the evolutionary tree. And in one sign of its enduring importance, it's exactly the same protein in both the human and the octopus. Over millions of years, different creatures have made use of serotonin to encode different behaviors, but Dölen and her team decided to test for social behaviors, to see whether MDMA would have the same profoundly social effect in octopi that it does in people.

One stumbling block: Octopi don't have a lot of social behavior to enhance. They're extremely private creatures who interact only for the two minutes or so it takes to complete a sexual act. All the rest of their lives, they're aggressive isolationists. This eliminated social behavioral assays where octopi would be housed together. Instead, scientists adapted a framework long used for experiments on monogamy in prairie voles. In the prairie vole version, the rodent is offered a choice of three chambers: one with a familiar partner; another, in the middle, that's empty; and a third with another prairie vole of the opposite sex—the social object. The setup had to be adapted because octopi are so naturally aggressive. In the octopus version, the first chamber contained a toy, the middle one was empty, and the third had another octopus— the social object—safely stashed below an open-weave basket that would serve as a barrier and keep the creatures from killing each other but would still allow them to interact.

When an octopus was put in the three-chambered setup without being given any MDMA, the octopus immediately went to the chamber with the toy and played. "We don't think that's because the toy object was particularly interesting to them," Dölen says. "We think it was just that it was maximally far away from the other octopus." But then when they gave the test octopus MDMA (they used a series of octopi in a number of assays), the normally asocial creature suddenly spent a significantly larger proportion of its time on the social side by choice, with the other octopus, lounging on the basket, touching each other, and exposing their undersides, something they never do. Thanks to the psychedelic enhancement, the test octopus was essentially giving the other octopus an eight-armed hug! When not actively engaging with the other octopus, the test octopi engaged in blissed-out, un-octopus-like behavior, like floating with all eight arms extended in a star shape or tumbling playfully through the water.

The results of the tests suggested several things. The first was simply that MDMA was powerful enough to alter the behavior of an octopus at all, reversing the asocial behavior that seemed to be encoded in its genes for millions of years. The second was that MDMA did the same thing to an octopus that it does to a person—made them open and tender and eager to connect, an outcome that showed how deeply encoded prosocial behavior is in the serotonin system. But as much as anything, what excited Dölen about the study was it showed that, despite the evolutionary distance, it was possible to employ an octopus—a creature with powerful cognitive skills—for neuroscientific research that could further our understanding of the workings of the mind in general.

"The octopus project—to be honest, when I'm having a bad day, because of politics and sexism and baloney in science, when I'm just feeling deflated, the octopus stuff just makes me feel rejuvenated," she says. "Because it feels like pure science. There's no career advantage to it. It's just fun.

It's curiosity for curiosity's sake." But the fact that it's enjoyable doesn't stop her from seeing the broader implications of the study. "If I had to summarize the point of the octopus project in the smallest possible frame," she says, "it's that we are meant to be social. It's in our DNA. And it seems to have been in our DNA for a long time. And don't get me wrong, psychedelics are really powerful, but I think the easiest way to make people be social is to just return to our social roots and turn off the television, turn off the influence of big corporate media trying to sell us thirty different kinds of shoes. Because deep down in our genes what we really want is to be social."

CHAPTER 4

CONNECTION WITH THE COMMUNITY

A man who is unconscious of himself acts in a blind, instinctive way, and is in addition fooled by all the illusions that arise when he sees everything that he is not conscious of in himself coming to meet him from outside as projections upon his neighbor.

—CARL JUNG

Not long ago, after an early yoga class, I went to breakfast at my local diner, seventy miles north of New York City in the Harlem Valley, a patch of rolling hills and farms between the Hudson River and the Connecticut state line. In the parking lot, I saw a car with a #NotMyPresident bumper sticker. There were two dogs in the back seat, and one of the waitresses was sitting in front. It made me like her more, knowing we shared an opinion on the biggest political controversy of the day. Here in the country, closer to the heartland than to the city where Jeremy and I met, I often feel like I'm in the minority (although this area is becoming more of a mix of red and blue, which makes it purple, my favorite color as a kid).

After breakfast, I went to Hannaford to pick up a few groceries with Jeremy, and I chatted amiably with the older gentleman in line behind me—not about anything in particular, just the weather or what was on the menu for dinner. I can't remember what he said or how I replied, just that he seemed like a kind man with pale blue eyes and a sincere smile. As we were leaving, Jeremy asked if I'd noticed his faded NRA cap. I was glad that I hadn't because it might have made me miss out on a nice moment of connection.

We live side by side with the people who watch Fox News and wear the hats. They're at the diner, behind me in line. They're my townsfolk. They're fellow Americans. They're us. Really, there is no "them." When I was younger, I thought that "divide and conquer" meant that if we split up the grocery list, we'd be done shopping sooner. Now I know it's about maintaining power, which means we have to resist our natural impulse to categorize. If you were to divide us by some other measure—our favorite Beatle, or whether we put ketchup on our egg sandwiches—it wouldn't be "us vs. them" anymore, conservatives vs. progressives. As Dr. Brené Brown, University of Houston professor of social work, says: "It's harder to hate up close."

Let's now look at our connection with our community and how we can strengthen it. Connecting at this level is different from the connections we've looked at and tried before, with ourselves, the people we love, and our children. We can't count on the people we meet on the street in the same way, or maybe there's no room in our alienated society for the kind of collective living that's in our DNA. But despite this distance, we are still drawn to places where we can connect, where we can be part of the same effort, on the same team, and contribute together to a vision from which we all draw strength.

In this chapter, we'll continue to look at the opening that comes with psychedelics, but this time we'll also approach it from the other side—what happens when psychedelic medicine helps create a new sense of eagerness to connect and the community doesn't notice. We'll talk with Dr. Rosalind Watts about the Watts Connectedness Scale—a measure of integration that people feel after their psychedelic-assisted therapy session. Watts has been one of the main researchers in an ongoing study of psilocybin-assisted therapy for treatment-resistant depression at Imperial College London. The study showed a tremendous success rate: 85 percent of the people reported a strong positive change after the treatment. But follow-up interviews revealed that the change wasn't happening on a level of symptoms (do you sleep better, have more motivation, suffer from fewer ruminations, etc.). Instead, the participants reported a shift on a deeper level, telling Watts that their day-to-day experience had changed from one of intense disconnection to a strong experience of connectedness—to themselves, to others, and to the world around them. But Watts cautions that these positive changes can erode over the months that follow treatment, especially when patients return, alone and unsupported, to an unwelcoming community that has become identified within the landscape of depression.

We'll look again at oxytocin, as well as the recent research that suggests that while, yes, the so-called hug drug can contribute to cooperation and trust within a group, it also can promote the kind of tribal behavior—ethnocentrism, ostracism, and even violence against an out-group—that has become such an identifiable feature first of online communities, and increasingly of everyday life in the so-called real world.

Then we'll examine how social anxiety can be a barrier in forming strong connections. We'll hear how Dr. Alicia Danforth has addressed this problem in a study of adults with autism, looking at how MDMA helped ease their chaotic sensory and cognitive experience and allowed the expression of natural capacities for interaction that had previously been blocked. Although Danforth's study aimed for results that could be replicated by different teams—she doesn't want the study's positive outcomes to be attributable to test administrators with a magic touch—her own practice shows the effective steps she's taken to make the neurodivergent feel comfortable.

As a contrast, we'll hear from Dr. Brian Anderson, who worked with long-term HIV/AIDS survivors, treating them with psilocybin-assisted therapy, which provided them with measurable relief from demoralization—the loss of meaning and purpose, the helplessness, and the loss of hope. One of the features of his study, before and after individual psilocybin sessions, was group sessions. Subjects prepared together and then went through their integration sessions together—a setup that resulted in 100 percent participation from start to finish—a rarity in a large study anywhere.

You may notice that there are a lot of people weighing in on community. That's because it's a tough subject, one that often calls for a balancing act between different perspectives. Then again, that process is at the heart of connection; ours is a world that you can't come to understand alone.

TRIBAL COUNCIL

In earlier times—before I started this book, but perhaps not before the advent of psychedelic medicine—the tribe would gather around a fire in order to pass along vital information, like where food is plentiful for foraging or what dangerous animals were lurking where. Gatherings like these were not simply practical for trading information. They were also for group ritual, for chanting, and for dance. We can safely say, then and now, that coming together was an occasion for celebration. Group mind, an ecstatic experience of oneness, was our main reason for dancing around that fire. You see this kind of bonding in nightclubs or stadiums or high school gyms throughout the world. That sense of belonging, of connecting, is powerful and alluring, programmed into our genes. It engenders a particular state of consciousness, helping us to feel safe and cared for—a sign that oxytocin is at work. This feeling of connection provides meaning to many in existential crisis, and the chemistry it engenders is heady and rewarding.

But oxytocin is not all rainbows and flowers; it's time we discuss its dark side. Oxytocin does not promote indiscriminate bonding; it actually helps to discern who is in or out of the tribe, and who is friend or foe. As Gül Dölen has suggested, oxytocin, especially the parvocellular variety, can be an instrument of skepticism. In experiments, intranasal oxytocin can promote both generosity toward in-group members as well as spiteful behavior toward those deemed outside the group. This "us vs. them" mentality is inherent in social primates. We often form dominance hierarchies and also sometimes enhance group cohesion through the ostracism of others. As much as we'd like everyone to just get along, in truth, it goes against our animal instincts. We have social categorization and intergroup bias.

In one study, led by Dr. Carsten de Dreu at the University of Leiden, male subjects self-administering oxytocin or placebo were found to be more self-sacrificing under the influence of oxytocin. Aggression also increased, but only defensive aggression, a frame of mind that de Dreu calls "tend and defend" (that's a little neurology joke). The study didn't require subjects to form roving warlike bands—instead it made use of financial games and prisoner's dilemma problems as proxies for altruism and aggression. But the results implicated oxytocin in both.

Another study looked at memories of maternal care under oxytocin. Surprisingly, the addition of oxytocin didn't just make everyone feel all warm and cuddly toward mom. It did for those who had secure attachments, but for those with anxious attachment, the addition of oxytocin increased their negative recollections and made their assessment of their mother's care even worse. Oxytocin seemed to amplify the success or failure of that original attachment bond, suggesting that for those with insecure attachments, the addition of the so-called love hormone might only bring them more vivid memories of that original negative experience.

The lead author of the maternal study, Dr. Jennifer Bartz, points out that oxytocin, contrary to its reputation, can be polarizing, and that its role in life's crucial attachments, and in the memory of attachments in general, should be reassessed with a more nuanced view. Oxytocin, the study suggests, can act to reinforce current beliefs and interpretations, in both a positive and negative direction. Dreu was more direct. "Oxytocin is a double-edged sword," he told the *Daily Telegraph*. "It makes you kinder to your group, but more aggressive to those outside."

Oxytocin doesn't just help you bond with someone; it enables "derogation of the other." If you are loyal to your mate, you will discount the attractiveness of an interloper. It's part of the process of fidelity. And if you're bonded with a group, nothing helps strengthen that unity like having a "them" to unite against.

Which brings us to ostracism and shunning—group strengthening on a whole other level. When a group member breaks the rules and the other members rally around the idea that this rule breaker must be shunned, it's a very strong unifying experience. Having a target or scapegoat helps with group cohesion. That's why so many kids turned their backs on me in eighth grade. It was a solid return on their investment.

In the same manner as individuals, groups can project their unwanted shadow side onto other groups. Often, people in a dyad will not only project onto each other, but they will dig in on what they believe is right. We see this quite a bit in communities, where mores get passed down for generations. People identify very strongly with their beliefs and their ways of doing things. Recent research has shown that we process challenges to our beliefs as if we have been physically threatened. Two areas are active in neuroimaging studies. The area that fires when we're believing things that are important to us is the default mode network, the circuitry that in some ways mirrors our own sense of self, or ego. Even when people read stories that reflect their personal values, this default mode circuitry becomes active. You can think of this self-involved loop as the self-defense machinery of the brain. And the best defense is a good offense. If the self feels threatened, whether physically or mentally, whether to our bodies or just our identities and beliefs, the amygdala (fear center) will fire up. There's a classic film of a black cat having its amygdala stimulated. It arches its back, hisses, and is ready to strike. It's a terrifying thing to watch. I think of that cat a lot when people are triggered and get upset. Interestingly, it's the people who are most resistant to changing their minds, rigid in their beliefs, who show the biggest amygdala threat response. You'll have to help them get back into para if you want to have a rational discussion. (Mirroring, validating, empathizing, anchoring gaze, soothing tone.)

And remember how childhood trauma can have a lasting impact on our perceptions and experiences with others because of this fearful reaction? A history of trauma can lead to an overactive threat response in the amygdala, too. One practical application of this information is that childhood trauma issues can sometimes be played out in office settings between coworkers (in fact, it's worth keeping this in mind when you have interpersonal challenges at work). But even on a much larger scale, as a nation, childhood issues can get acted out. For instance, perhaps you can see how the reality of our nation's earliest days, both with slavery and also the genocide of the native population, function as our nation's version of its own early wounding and childhood trauma. These types of wounds fester if they remain unprocessed, which means they are not yet integrated. As such, they fuel racism and cruelty and inequality. And until we admit and process our transgressions and make reparations, America will never be whole or healed.

Dr. Monnica Williams is an expert on racial trauma and discrepancies of delivery within the medical system. She proposed a study of MDMA-assisted psychotherapy for helping people process trauma associated with racism, and has been focusing on making sure people of color have access to treatment with psychedelic medicines. Currently, a disproportionate percent of research participants are white, a fact that MAPS and other groups are actively addressing. What are desperately needed are more therapists and physicians of color who want to be involved in this type of work. Just like any other community, the psychedelic research community will have to strive for equal representation and integration.

In the Yukon community in Saskatchewan, they practice a particular kind of restorative justice called circles. Here, the offender and offended are contained within a group process. These sentencing, or healing, circles are a way of sharing justice with a larger community. They come together to deal with the harm created by the offender, to heal the victim, and to restore the community. The community is involved in the decision-making process, with everyone affected given a voice in the proceedings, as well as the victim's and the offender's families. The process is designed to bring understanding and healing to all participants. The community is empowered to help decide what is to be done, and also to understand what underlying problems led to the offense in the first place. It's a shining example of how people can come together, across their dividing lines, in order to grow, change, and heal one another.

Connection across social divides is also the key to a growing body of research suggesting that integrating students of different social classes and races can not only improve test scores in children but can also help develop empathy. Other studies show that being part of a diverse community can decrease anxiety. What's clear is that having meaningful relationships with people from different racial or ethnic backgrounds has a positive impact on how we treat others. So does something called loving-kindness (or metta) meditation, which is based on disengaging from the usual level of self-preoccupation in favor of compassion and benevolence for others. This helps to facilitate altruistic behaviors as well as enhance spirituality and a sense of connectedness.

TRIPPING THE SCALES

Rosalind Watts of Imperial College London wanted to do a follow-up with the twenty participants of the college's successful research study, a psilocybin-assisted therapy program for people with treatment-resistant depression. Most of those in the study had been suffering for an average of twenty years from depression so entrenched that no medication or therapy of any sort had offered them relief. Nevertheless, seventeen out of the twenty participants reported substantial benefits from the psilocybin protocol. In follow-up conversations, Watts heard a few consistent themes emerge. The participants tended to describe their depression as "disconnection," and by contrast the healing mechanism of psilocybin, from a psychological standpoint, seemed to arise from feeling more connected—to themselves, others, and the world around them.

Most pinpointed avoidance as one of the identifying features of depression—avoiding people or situations that might trigger negative thoughts and psychic pain in general by indulging in behaviors that helped them push that aside, like watching too much TV, eating, drinking, or shopping. However, their experience with psilocybin helped them go from avoidance to acceptance. Suddenly, they could sit with their negative thoughts and feel resilient enough to be okay with them. "I think that was linked to connection as well," Watts says. "They felt a sense of connection to themselves and others, and that gave them resilience and a connection to love—because connection is love as well. When people feel a sense of connection or love, they're more able to accept the shitty stuff."

In her clinical experience, psilocybin didn't work like other medications, which are generally designed to treat a specific condition or set of symptoms. The medicine seemed helpful for so many populations—people with trauma, depression, terminal illness, and obsessive-compulsive disorder. "So I started to think maybe psilocybin is targeting a deeper level," Watts says. "And that underneath all these presenting problems, all these different pathologies, there is a fundamental disconnection. That disconnection can look like depression or addiction or anorexia. And psilocybin is working on that deep level of disconnection. It helps people feel a strong sense of connection." Watts continues, "And this interconnectedness, this love thing that people feel, is what's helping them to get better."

However, follow-up interviews revealed that after opening to connection, people often closed down again and the symptoms of depression returned. Watts says this is because "in order to stay open, you need the community to keep you open. You open up, you feel this connection to yourself, to others, and the world around you. But that's not the way the world is. Our society is not based on those ideas. It's a Western society based on competition and capitalism and individualism." The experience of psilocybin seemed to make people soften and open, she said. "But if you take someone that's opening and becoming more vulnerable, and you put them back in their hard, achievement-oriented culture, they're going to close up again, because they have to. It's very hard to stay open and soft and vulnerable in a fast-paced, hard-edged culture."

The Imperial College experiment, like many of the other studies we've looked at, was set up to provide maximum support for the person undergoing psilocybin-assisted therapy, with preparatory sessions and integration sessions bookending the psychedelic experience. But even before the study began, Watts realized that the format didn't provide any sense of community in its design. The participants didn't get to sit down together and compare notes or stay in touch. So she and a colleague set up a psychedelic integration group, not just for people in their study but for anybody doing psychedelic work, with the idea that they could come for free and become part of a supportive psychedelic community. When not as many people took advantage of the group as she had hoped, because most of them didn't live in London, they started a WhatsApp group. One of the participants in the study agreed to be the monitor, so whenever anyone reached their six-week follow-up meeting, they received his number. She's now planning an integration weekend in the countryside for people doing psychedelic work and their partners, as an exercise in community building, so people can preserve that sense of openness and oneness they discovered thanks to psilocybin treatments.

Once she discovered how important maximizing and extending the sense of connection was to long-term positive outcomes, it made her go searching for a measure of connectedness. After all, there were a host of other well-established measures, for anger, depression, anxiety, etc. And these measures were often included prominently in the clinical metrics. She had a doctorate in clinical psychology, so she looked through her textbooks to see if there was one she'd missed. But there wasn't a single measure for connectedness that she could find. She decided to come up with one herself by using the qualitative study she'd done of all her follow-up interviews with patients after their experience.

The result was the Watts Connectedness Scale (see below), which is now being validated as part of a massive survey through Imperial College. That survey form includes a battery of measures that thousands of people who have had a psychedelic experience are now filling out. The respondents are coming not just from Imperial College studies, they're also pouring in from individuals doing psychedelic work on their own, at ayahuasca ceremonies and retreats, or at other research centers.

THE WATTS CONNECTEDNESS SCALE

A. 1.   Disconnection
A. 1. 1.   "Trapped in my mind"
A. 1. 2.   Disconnected from senses
A. 1. 3.   Disconnected from self
A. 1. 4.   Disconnected from others
A. 1. 5.   Disconnected from the world
A. 2.   Connection
A. 2. 1.   Mind "rebooted"/"opened up"/"switched on"
A. 2. 2.   Connection to senses
A. 2. 3.   Connection to self
A. 2. 4.   Connection to others
A. 2. 5.   Connection to the world
A. 2. 6.   Connection to a spiritual principle

One of the biggest data streams for the survey comes from Synthesis, a legal truffle retreat in the Netherlands (the world's most powerful psilocybin truffle is native to the country). Watts says that they're sending her "loads and loads" of data. The Synthesis retreats, generally group sessions held at a lighthouse in Zandvoort, thirty minutes outside Amsterdam, are well subscribed and medically supervised. The programs are designed to resemble the clinical setups we have seen in these pages, with preparatory and integration sessions sandwiched around the psilocybin experience, though significantly fewer in number.

Synthesis participants fill out the surveys before and after their psilocybin experience. The surveys track multiple psychological measures, but the one that shows the greatest change is the Watts Connectedness Scale. Those who attend are usually going to Synthesis for their own well-being, so it's a healthy sample of the population and not a clinical slice. Not surprisingly, before-and-after readings of the depression scale show only a 10 percent decrease—granted probably because people with the money and time to travel to the Netherlands for psychedelic retreats are, for the most part, healthy to start. Anxiety also declines to a small degree. Connectedness, on the other hand, increases by roughly 180 percent. "So I think people go in feeling pretty disconnected and alone. And they come out feeling very super-hyper-mega connected," Watts says. "It seems to be the fundamental mechanism." To put it another way, the Watts Connectedness Scale is helping to put hard numbers behind something that was long suspected—that what psychedelics actually "turn on" is our sense of connection, to one another, to nature, to transcendent values.

One experience that really opened Watts's eyes to the importance of community support came in the aftermath of the early morning blaze at Grenfell Tower that killed seventy-two residents, London's deadliest fire since World War II. The tower is close to the Imperial College clinical research unit, in Hammersmith Hospital in North Kensington; staffers can look out the office windows and see the derelict remains of the twenty-four-story residential tower. Grenfell provided a stark contrast, even before the blaze turned the building into a charred ruin; Watts calls it "a pretty deprived community at the heart of a very, very rich area of London."

Watts recalls a hasty decision by the town council to put up cladding on the building's exterior, a move that seemed designed to pacify wealthy neighbors who considered it an eyesore. But the job went to the lowest bidder, and the cladding they put up was cheap and flammable. So, when a small fire from a fourth-floor appliance spread to the flat upstairs, the cladding caught fire, quickly turning into a column of flame that lit up the whole building like a torch. Many of the residents, both those who lived in the tower and managed to escape and those adults and children who lived in tower blocks nearby and watched it burn, suffered from PTSD. However, in the aftermath of the tragedy, there were few mental health initiatives offered to the survivors.

One woman whose PTSD symptoms were linked to the sounds of helicopters turned to kambo, a legal drug derived from the secretions of an Amazonian tree frog that acts on many receptors in the brain and body and has a dramatic purgative effect. She became a practitioner—the frog paste is applied to small burns on the skin—and that led her to explore further, taking a trip to Mexico to be part of an ayahuasca ceremony, and trying other treatments to help her relive and thoroughly process her trauma. Now, Watts says, the woman has recovered, and not just recovered but thrived. Today, she has a warm presence and bright eyes and radiates vibrant health. As a way to address the PTSD in her community, she's applying for funding to provide regular kambo sessions and to start a psychedelic integration group for present and former residents of Grenfell. For those who want to go a step further, she'll take them to Mexico or Peru and guide them to the same people and places that helped her.

Watts says this was all happening at the same time as she was puzzling over how to make a welcoming community for people who have had psychedelic experiences. Grenfell had been the opposite of welcoming: a place that had become toxic and traumatized, where people had been through a horrific experience, losing friends, loved ones, and children, with no sense of community in the aftermath.

Watts has a researcher's gift for organization and is now helping to start a psychedelic integration group in Grenfell, too. "It would be an incredible thing to see happen. That somewhere so deprived and destroyed could, through some self-organizing process, start to revitalize their community with these ancient healing practices," Watts says. "Meditation isn't going to help them. Individual therapy isn't going to help them. But one of the things psychedelics can do is bond a community. And these tools are so good at going toward trauma and supporting people when they revisit the trauma."

One of the tools Watts uses with this integration is a therapy called Acceptance and Commitment Therapy, or ACT. This type of therapy promotes psychological flexibility, and it helps capitalize on the newfound acceptance of trauma that participants in a psilocybin session describe. "I'm very aware of how much work this takes," Watts says. "I love sitting in ceremony and having that connection. But there is also acceptance of the trauma, which is hard because it takes time, resources, and a commitment to doing it. And often that kind of work is really unglamorous. The hard slog of learning from these experiences and trying to conduct relationships differently, that's difficult." She likes to arm people with a visualization, of diving under the surface turbulence of negative thoughts to the still-blue bottom of the ocean, digging up a prickly oyster shell that has a pearl inside it—that's the trauma and the meaning you take from it—and then swimming back up to reemerge where the sea is now calm and the sky is pink. "Whatever you're doing," she says, "remember to accept your feelings, accept the pain. Stay with it and connect to meaning," she says. "As long as you remember that, you're probably on the right track."

THE SURPRISE OF CLARITY

Many years ago, I surmised that the effects of MDMA (in particular, the sense of calm and the desire to connect) might be particularly helpful to people who are "on the spectrum" and have Asperger's syndrome (a label that has since been removed from the DSM). Many studies have shown that at least acutely, MDMA enhances emotional empathy and pro-social behavior.

Alicia Danforth ran one of those studies that aimed to reduce social anxiety in autistic adults through MDMA-assisted psychotherapy. And she says one of the wisest things she did when she began her dissertation on the topic was intentionally avoiding reading the literature by the "so-called experts." Instead, she immersed herself in the writings of autistic adults. "Someone involved in the dissertation process said, 'Oh, this is wonderful. You're giving a voice to the voiceless.' And I said, 'I'm just listening to them. I'm not giving anybody a voice. They're perfectly capable of speaking for themselves.'"

The work Danforth did by herself and on herself—what she describes as "emptying her brain of the biases and stereotypes that weren't accurate"—reminded her that reducing social anxiety is not just an individual project. Connection is a two-way street. "Practicing empathy—it's not just talking about it," she says. Before she began her study, she tried to put herself in the place of her patients, lying on the floor of the empty treatment room and trying to imagine everything that an autistic individual might find annoying in the setup, from the lighting to the temperature to the sound. She went shopping for furniture, choosing smooth textures and soothing colors, and, since so many treatment centers for autism are aimed at children, she made sure it seemed specifically designed for adults. Then when patients came in, she would start by asking if there was anything in the space that was uncomfortable to any of their five senses.

"Autistic individuals are a neurocognitive minority that make up about 1 to 2 percent of the population," she says. "And they often have a history of having their lived experience invalidated. They've often been bullied. And they've often not had anybody in a medical setting willing to slow down and listen to them." She and her co-leader in the study, Dr. Charles Grob, made sure that therapy sessions were a minimum of ninety minutes so that nobody felt the pressure to communicate at the pace that neurotypical people use, so they could feel comfortable taking as long as they needed to express themselves. "The irony is that autistic individuals often have a lifetime of being accused of being the ones who lack empathy. But it's often the people providing services in medical and mental health settings that have the empathy deficit."

Danforth is measured in reporting the results—as in many preliminary studies, she hoped to establish the safety and feasibility of the treatment, and questions of efficacy and effectiveness were secondary in the design. So yes, it was safe. And yes, she did see "significantly marked" reductions in the Liebowitz social anxiety scale, consistent with the remarkable results in many psychedelic studies. Her concern now is to see the results replicated in other labs, in greater numbers, hoping to prove that breakthroughs like this aren't just attributable to test administrators with the "magic touch" or good "interpersonal chemistry."

Still, her own sessions might make you think that she has some of this magic touch. Early in the preparatory stage, she spreads out a deck of cards called Mixed Emotions on the floor, each card showing an illustration of a separate emotion labeled on the card with some synonyms at the bottom. She asks test participants—or clients in her private practice aimed at adults on the spectrum—if they could pick out any card depicting an emotion that they have never felt. They rarely do. Sometimes a younger person will pick grief, because no one close to them has died yet (although grief can come from other losses besides death). Occasionally, someone will pick the "receptive" card, because that's a concept they might not be familiar with. This lets someone new to therapy begin with an experience that's validating, that challenges the stereotype that autistic people do not feel emotion.

Another technique she invented after years of listening to people with autism was giving her patients a token or talisman they could carry with them from one session to the next. The token she chose was a marble that both she and her patient—and the second facilitator present in the sessions of the study—would roll in circles on a table or floor. She didn't want to bring religious iconography into the room—no sitting Buddhas or Mother Marys or Stars of David—because quite a few participants were atheist, and others had experienced "deep religious wounding." So instead she introduced this secular marble ritual in concrete and explicit language that these individuals could appreciate. After all, ritual is a technique that humans have used as long as they've been in tribes cooperating together. It marks the fact that something unusual, something meaningful, something out of the ordinary is happening.

At the beginning and end of sessions, she'd invite the subjects to speak their intentions for the study or for the session that day out loud. Then the two facilitators in the room would each roll the marble, imagining that it was a battery that they could charge with their well wishes. Next the participant would roll it, imagining the marble as a place they could also stow their intentions. And on the day of the MDMA session at Los Angeles County Harbor General Hospital, the support person that the research subject had chosen to stay with them on their overnight before the session (and to take them home after the session, and come back with them for an integration session on the day after) would also say some words of encouragement and hand the marble to the participant.

On top of this ritual significance, the marble worked well as a fidget object. For those subjects who had a tendency to stim, that is, to use stereotypical repetitive hand motions or to rock back and forth, it could serve as an outlet for an overactive nervous system once the amphetamine-like effects of MDMA began to kick in. It was socially acceptable, the way having a cigarette used to be. It also served another purpose as a transitional object, something the participant could take with them; the marble was a tangible reminder, after the sessions were over, of both the progress in the sessions and the encouragement of the therapists. It helped the participant remember the insights they'd had in the MDMA mind state. The marble became a literal touchstone.

Danforth wrote her dissertation on what happens when adults with autism take MDMA and she sums up those findings in a *Wizard of Oz*–themed mnemonic that she calls the five *C*s:

Courage. "It's like the Cowardly Lion. There's a courage to try new things, express things that were difficult to talk about before. There's social courage: I danced for the first time, I could flirt even more, I was able to engage in small talk."

Communication. "I thought of them oiling the Tin Man, so there's this new ability for social ease and flow, to take in what someone else is saying."

Connection. "This is the Tin Man getting his heart: there's an openness that helps reduce social anxiety and allows people to connect."

Communion. "This is a cut above just connecting. It's a connection to a group, a cause bigger than oneself, participating in communication that relies on social inference, like 'It was part of the unspoken vibe' or 'I became one with everyone on the dance floor.' A sense of communion and belonging."

Clarity. "This is the one that surprised me. It's like the moment when Scarecrow gets his brains, that aha moment. The way people described it was, 'The thought loops stopped,' 'There was a calm in my thinking I'd never experienced before,' or 'There was a straightening out of my thoughts.' This was a qualitatively different reaction from the ones you'd hear after an MDMA session from neurotypicals. We're left to speculate that this mental calm and clarity might be related to a reduction in left amygdalar activation. The threat center in the mind calms down. It's like, 'Somebody finally shut the alarm off. I can hear myself think.' And when that goes away, the individual who can relax and be present appears."

Danforth says that the improvements they measured in the study proved durable, with social anxiety scores still well below clinically significant levels six months after the end of the sessions. The other feedback she's got has been anecdotal, from people who just wanted to touch base to say they're still doing well. She has not reached out to any of the participants in her study, except in one case, when she was asked to present an MDMA panel at the American Psychological Association Conference in Chicago this past summer. In most instances she's against what she calls "media intrusion," wary of historical missteps in psychedelic science that could be traced to misrepresentation in the press. Her first reaction, she said, was, "No, no, no, you can't exploit them!"

But then she and Grob reconvened, trying to think if there was anyone who completed the study for whom this kind of public performance could be a positive experience. When they reached out to the person they'd both agreed on, his answer was an immediate, unambiguous yes. He did want to appear on the stage with her.

After her first study on social anxiety for autistic adults, Danforth realized that she loved working with this population and started a private practice, working exclusively with adults whose autism isn't always readily apparent. Thanks to that experience, she says, she's learned how to be supportive without being intrusive or condescending. Throughout the Chicago trip, that was the voice she used, discreetly spinning, gently letting the participant know what was coming next: *We're about to get in line, you're going to have to take off your shoes, we're going to take our laptops out and put them on the conveyor belt*, and so on.

But the night before their joint appearance as they were going over their notes, hashing out what they were going to say, they both began to panic a little. They worried that their original approach felt awkward before both of them decided to practice what Danforth preached. They took the mindfulness techniques that they had worked on in the study, and "harnessed that anxiety to compel us forward."

Public speaking wasn't the only first of the trip. He'd never been on an airplane, or to a convention, never stayed at a fancy hotel with an extravagant breakfast buffet. In a sense, Danforth says, their mutual fascination with the buffet helped them both stumble upon a way of looking at things that put them both at ease onstage. She told her volunteer speaker that she would feel out of place at this convention if she weren't a mental health professional. "'But let me assure you, no one here is going to have anything to share that's more interesting than what you're going to say about your own experience, just as is, with no embellishment. It's a symposium. Everybody coming is interested in MDMA therapy. It's like this buffet.'" She started recalling for his benefit the presenters the two of them had met. "'And Michael will be the scrambled eggs. Perry's the bacon. I'll be the side of fruit.' And since he loved the special jam at the hotel, I said, 'And you're the toast and jam.'

"That clicked. And our anxiety diminished. He realized he was part of the buffet. And when our time came, he was the last one to speak in front of an audience of 350 mental health professionals in a big room. And right as we were getting to start, the author Michael Pollan"—the scrambled eggs in their buffet—"walked into the room. And he knew he was there. It was the two of us on the stage. I just gave him general questions, and he connected with that audience. He had them in the palm of his hand. And he said, 'If you're wondering if I still have social anxiety, I'm here talking to you.' And he laughed."

TREATING A COMMUNITY

Psychedelic medicines (narrowly defined for the moment as psychedelic substances taken as part of a federally approved medical study) are primarily administered in individual sessions. There's some circular thinking here. Individual sessions carefully overseen by medical professionals are the usual setup, not necessarily because it's the best or most medically effective strategy, but because it's the setup that's most likely to win federal approval.

The truth is, getting better when receiving plant medicines in a group setting has a long and well-established history. There are two psychedelics in particular that could help fight the opioid epidemic, and each has a group tradition. Ibogaine, a medicine from the root of the iboga shrub, can reverse opioid dependence. It is traditionally used in ceremonies of the Bwiti tribe in Gabon, Africa. Ayahuasca, a tea brewed from local plants that contain DMT (a short-acting psychedelic that is not active orally) and ß-carboline (an enzyme inhibitor that makes it orally active), is traditionally consumed in groups. The South American tradition involves a shaman guiding any number of participants through a ceremony. There are indigenous psychedelic group rituals that go back hundreds of years. Further, they're part of a lineage of using psychedelic substances that goes back for millennia.

In more recent years, in Switzerland, where Albert Hofmann first synthesized LSD while working as a research chemist at Sandoz Laboratories in 1936, practitioners like Peter Gasser have revived the practice of psychedelic group sessions that first came into vogue in the fifties and sixties. This revival can be traced to discussions that began at celebrations of Hofmann's one hundredth birthday in 2006.

In 2017, when Dr. Brian Anderson, then a psychiatric resident with the BAND Lab at UCSF, was designing a study, he wanted to carry out the research in a group setting. The study was meant for long-term HIV/AIDS survivors, and the hope was that psilocybin-assisted therapy could help relieve their demoralization. It was a small feasibility study—only eighteen men were selected. And although individual treatment was the norm, Anderson believed that for this population, who'd all been diagnosed with AIDS in the eighties or nineties and continued to struggle with a monumental and pervasive sense of loss, coming together as a group could be healing in itself.

The immediate inspiration for the group therapy design came from a talk by Dr. Tony Bossis, who spoke about participants in a psychedelic study he'd been part of at NYU treating depression and anxiety in people with advanced cancer. Even though that had been an individual program, a significant percentage of the participants asked, separately, to be put in touch with others in the study. The same thing happened in another study at the University of Wisconsin, looking into the pharmacokinetics of escalating doses of psilocybin, another small feasibility experiment designed to follow the progress of the drug through the body. There the participants sought one another out on Craigslist because they just wanted to talk with somebody else who'd been through this amazing experience.

There were other reasons for the group format. Even though the HIV/AIDS study took place in San Francisco—where you might expect heightened awareness and a supportive community—the men all suffered from a profound sense of abandonment, beyond what was normal for solitary people in their fifties or sixties. Throughout the Reagan, Bush, and Clinton years, HIV/AIDS had a devastating effect and exacted a tremendous death count, but at least in those years there'd been passion in the struggle. Now, more than twenty years later, nearly all of them felt that history had abandoned them. It was hard to find anybody who still shared the sense of mission that once served as a rallying cry for the community. Anderson thought a group setting might help them overcome their brutal sense of desertion and isolation.

There is a growing consensus among doctors and researchers involved in these studies that group therapy, even group sessions for administering the psychedelic medicine, is likely inevitable—the costs of having one and often two facilitators for every individual six- to eight-hour session is so prohibitively expensive that it threatens to cripple the treatment before it even gains approval. A group setting may even be preferable, providing connectedness and communion and a corrective experience to the alienation that's often at the heart of the conditions these studies take on. Also, having social relationships can dampen the stress response, so it's particularly important for people with PTSD or those who have immune-related diseases to stay connected.

That kind of group session was included in an earlier design for the study, but Anderson was advised that the setup was unlikely to gain official approval. So instead they planned on group sessions for the preparation and integration before and after, but individual sessions for the actual psilocybin treatment. Once that was settled, Anderson and his team (which included Alicia Danforth as lead clinician and Chris Stauffer as co-investigator and study clinician) still had to settle on the right type of group therapy that could work for long-term HIV/AIDS survivors. The BAND Lab—the name stands for Bonding and Attachment in Neuropsychiatric Disorders—is run by Josh Woolley and specializes in studying human connection; they do a lot of studies with oxytocin, intimacy, and social interaction. The setting was perfect for group therapy—but which kind? They needed one that could help them take on the existential despair these men were all too familiar with.

They toyed with a popular style of group therapy called meaning-centered group psychotherapy, which was then being used at Memorial Sloan Kettering for people with advanced cancer. Viktor Frankl, who'd survived four separate concentration camps and had written about the sustaining power of "man's search for meaning," had developed the program. It seemed like a promising setup for processing the anxiety of living with HIV/AIDS. But the structure proved to be too rigorous, with a strict outline of topics to be covered in each successive session. That kind of rigor didn't seem like a good fit for a psilocybin study.

So the team went back to the literature until they came

across supportive-expressive group therapy, a design pioneered by two Stanford psychiatrists, Drs. David Spiegel and Irvin Yalom, for metastatic breast cancer patients in the seventies. This had several appealing points. It had a more flexible structure favoring "here and now" processing in the group and focused on "detoxifying death," encouraging people to speak freely and engage one another on the subject. It also made building social connection a core part of the intervention. People were not only allowed to meet outside of group—often against the rules in other forms of group therapy—but they were also encouraged to do so.

Supportive-expressive group therapy had risen to prominence when the idea of speaking openly and fearlessly about cancer felt revolutionary. That outspokenness made it a prime candidate for revival in the nineties among people dying of HIV/AIDS. It seemed ideal for dealing with isolation and depression.

The study aimed to reduce the demoralization of the long-term AIDS survivors, and while Anderson only recently submitted the final results—the significant improvement from the initial baseline reading to the final measurement at the end of treatment—he did spot-testing throughout the study that told the story in greater detail. He took a reading at the end of the first four prep sessions: a few participants did register improvement just from the group sessions alone, but the communal format hadn't made a real dent across all eighteen participants in demoralization. However, the readings taken right after the first psilocybin and integration sessions showed a sharp drop in demoralization. These low levels persisted not just through the study but all the way to the final measurement, three months after the final session.

The study was set up in three cohorts of six participants each, with varying levels of sociability. The first cohort didn't meet up outside of the actual sessions, while people from the second group liked to grab dinner here and there, and the third group also seemed satisfied with just the time spent together in sessions. Still, steady friendships developed.

Interestingly, after the program, many participants reported seeking out support groups or going to community service agencies to try to meet people and be part of something again. That was a big step. Prior to the study, the losses they'd suffered acted as a disincentive to reaching out. And they'd also gotten to an age where it was harder to go out and make new friends, regardless of their HIV status. "This is not something particular to AIDS survivors," Anderson said, "but it was compounded by what they'd been through." Many had evolved elaborate coping techniques of avoidance, and being part of the study helped them emerge from that social cocoon.

One participant in particular came in talking about how hard it was to connect with others; he'd arranged his life in ways that were designed to keep the world at arm's length. His significant other lived in a city that was hours away, and they saw each other only for short stays. But after the study, this man decided to invite his long-distance partner to move to San Francisco and start a more committed relationship where they could be with each other all the time. He'd made the decision that he wasn't going to be afraid to let someone get close again.

Anderson could see these shifts taking place in the sessions. In one, a large man with a history of trauma—childhood neglect and physical abuse, threats of violence that followed him into adulthood—took a large dose, which is administered based on weight. At that dosage level, most people would have been lying down, having difficulty engaging at all, but instead he sat straight up the whole time with his eyes open, recounting the disturbing incidents as they crossed his mind. "We'd built up a lot of comfort and trust with this participant," Anderson said. "But he was very clear: he wasn't going to put on headphones because that would mean he couldn't hear what was going on in the room around him." The man felt this need to be attentive to everything around him not because the drug was making him paranoid, but because that was who he was at baseline. He later explained that until he'd been through this study, [he] hadn't gone out and eaten in a restaurant in over a decade because he had a debilitating anxiety that somebody would put something in his food. Basically, he said, he didn't spend time with people, except for [doctors'] visits."

Anderson, who was one of the facilitators in the room for this participant's session, worried about him becoming overwhelmed by the volume of trauma he was processing. But the man's torrent of confessions seemed to allow him space to process, and after the session, this person experienced a tremendous improvement in self-confidence and a huge decrease in anxiety. And he started eating in restaurants again.

Another participant in the study, a proud and proper man who'd never taken any kind of psychedelic in his life, also took a very high dose. After the first hour, he complained, saying that he wanted the experience to end. "Please stop this. I don't want this to go on," he said. But he trusted his clinicians, who encouraged him to go with his feelings. At one point, he lay down in the small bed in the room and lost control of his bladder. The normally impeccable figure lay there, unbothered and relaxed, and his experience changed. He wasn't struggling. He described swimming deep in the ocean in beautiful blue light, exploring a sunken pirate ship he'd found. After this experience, he was able to tell his guides what had happened and they helped him out of his clothes, changed the sheets, and he lay there naked under the covers, recounting the loss of his mother, who'd died slowly over the past few years. "It sounds very simple," Anderson said. There he was, "in an apparent regressed state, as a young naked child under the bed sheets, being comforted by two women, processing the loss of his maternal figure."

The participant's turnaround during the experience had been dramatic. He'd started out tense, sweating, walking back and forth to the bathroom repeatedly, frustrated, unable to let go. Then when he did let go, it opened him up, and he was able to experience a flood of memory, which included profound loss.

When the study began, Anderson was a research fellow in the BAND Lab, and now he's an attending psychiatrist at Zuckerberg San Francisco General Hospital. Like many of us, he is looking ahead to a day when psilocybin and MDMA will be approved for treating certain mental health conditions. When that day comes, Anderson would likely be one of the experienced practitioners helping to train the first generation of licensed psychedelic therapists. With an eye to controlling costs, he imagines a practical change, administering psilocybin in group settings, something he was unable to do in this study. Almost immediately, he broadens this vision, calculating "the real benefits that seem to come from people going through experiences like this in a community" and the types of emotional exploration that people can do in a group setting.

In Anderson's first foray into group therapy, there were more than a few who resisted, showing little excitement for the setting. But by the end, he said, "Almost everyone was really happy that it was a group." No one missed a single session, an extremely rare occurrence. He took care to open up the connections beyond the group, recommending that a significant other be the person who came to pick up the participant on the day of the psilocybin session. Often he or one of the other facilitators would dedicate some time, preparing the significant other to engage with their partner after the session was over, helping them feel comfortable. "A couple of times, the significant other, who hadn't gone through the trial, who hadn't just had a high-dose psilocybin experience, would be concerned, saying things like, 'Is he still my partner?' 'Is he going to be changed?' 'Will he still want to be with me?' It took some work to help them feel comfortable with that. And we'd say, 'No, listen. He's still the same person. He's still your partner. But he's going to be looking at things a little differently and maybe talking about things a little differently, at least for now. And this is a chance for you guys to, you know, actually connect. They may feel more open, and they may want to talk to you about more things than they usually do. And they may really need you to be close to them for the next day or so because they're probably going to really desire connecting with you.'"

CHILLS, TINGLES, AND GROUP MIND

What these experiences are doing, primarily, is bringing us back in tune with our need for unity. Psychedelic experiences unlock our natural drive to be unified with something bigger than ourselves. Of course, there are other ways to achieve this transcendent state of oneness, and many of them are easily accessible. Group activities like dancing, drumming, chanting, and singing can all give us a sense of belonging, putting us in a state of para that triggers good chemistry. It's worth noting that these activities, which used to be a mainstay of our tribal living, have long been repressed and deemphasized in our culture. We will need to look to aboriginal and indigenous societies to be reminded of how humans used to live, weaving ritual, rhythm, and repetition in order to induce altered states as a group.

Whether we gather in arenas or house parties, we can hook into that rewarding state of social cohesion. Multiple studies suggest that listening to music is good for your physical and mental health, with reports of higher well-being and life satisfaction scores, lower stress levels, increased social bonds, and decreased levels of pain for those who report they attend musical events or dance with other people. I came across one report that asserted attending live concerts can help overall health, happiness, productivity, and self-esteem, enhance feelings of closeness to others, and increase life expectancy, with the authors going so far as to "prescribe a gig a fortnight, which could pave the way for almost a decade more years of life." (It is worth noting this study was paid for by a group that owns musical venues.) But their heart (and data) is in the right place. People love music, they love to dance (if the lights are low enough!), and they love sharing that experience.

Intensely pleasurable responses to music can trigger activity in the same brain regions that are responsible for reward, motivation, emotion, and arousal. Just how good does music feel? It depends on if you are more or less sensitive or empathic, it seems. In response to intense passages of music, or particularly poignant harmonies, many, myself included, will cry. Some people get chills up and down their spine, goose bumps, their hair stands on end (called "skin-gasms," although I am open to other nomenclature—"piloerection," for example). The chill that accompanies music is known as "frisson." Brain tingles are another matter entirely.

There is a new term made up by Jennifer Allen: "ASMR," which stands for autonomous sensory meridian response. My daughter, Molly, finds certain sounds immensely soothing and will sometimes use them to help her get to sleep. It turns out she's not alone. Some of us can get this particular head tingle that sometimes spreads down the spine, and subsequent positive flow-like states of relaxation and well-being, from these sounds. I hope this helps explain all the videos of people whispering, cleaning ears, brushing hair, chewing, or scratching nubby fabrics that are popping up over the past decade. The intensity of the tingles can be increased by exposure to more triggers, and some people spend a lot of time on these sites.

Dr. Craig Richard, author of *Brain Tingles*, believes that because these tingles are triggered by a range of behaviors that soothe infants or occur between intimates, the ASMR response has something to do with social bonding. We know that affiliative behaviors help a person to feel safe and cared for, and are lubricated by oxytocin. The studies of brain chemistry with ASMR so far are implicating oxytocin, dopamine, and endorphins. (No one has looked at endocannabinoids, but it wouldn't surprise me at all.) Some data reveals that people who engage in ASMR show temporary improvements in symptoms of depression, stress, and chronic pain.

With ASMR, the heart rate lowers; the body relaxes. While the frisson that comes from music may raise or lower the heart rate depending on tempo and emotional factors, and there's usually a strong emotional component to this experience, there is much less emotional arousal with ASMR. The default mode network in people who are able to experience ASMR is less cohesive, or has less functional connectivity than in people who don't have this sensation. Imaging of brain activity during ASMR stimulation showed increased activity in areas involved with empathy, social cognition, and caring for others. Actually, the fMRI activity shows similar patterns when looking at all three: ASMR, musical frisson, and prosocial affiliative behaviors.

Interestingly, people who experience frisson with music score higher on the personality trait called "openness to experience." So do people who experience ASMR. Empathy and openness are necessary prerequisites for experiencing musical frisson. Mirror neurons, the brain cells that help us mimic others or have a theory of mind about them, are highly active during music-mediated empathy. Musicologist Zachary Wallmark conducted an fMRI-based study that found high-empathy people use their social cognitive circuitry to process music. Music can soothe any beast, savage or not, and can act as a "hidden therapist," as Dr. Mendel Kaelen calls it in his paper showing music's central therapeutic function in psychedelic therapy. The nature of subjects' music experience was significantly predictive of reductions in depression one week after their psilocybin experiences, whereas "drug intensity" scores (how intense their entire drug experience was rated) were not.

Speaking of music and group mind, there was a great gathering of singers after the final day of Ramadan in June 2018, where hundreds of Christians, Muslims, and Jews came together at the Tower of David in Jerusalem to sing "One Love" by Bob Marley in three-part harmony and in three languages. The video is beautiful and moving, as these things usually are, but it also clearly shows us that people can come together. They can cooperate and learn a song together for an hour before they roll tape. The organizer of the event, Koolulam, is a social musical initiative, producing mass singing events to promote the idea that musical harmony can inspire harmony in humanity. We do know that music can increase acts of altruism, so it's not such a stretch to consider that large gatherings of musicians or music lovers may help to change the social climate for the better.

Music has been a huge part of my life since I was a toddler. I was singing soon after I could speak, which pleased my mother immensely. (She sang bass in a barbershop chorus.) First with trumpet, and then later with guitar and vocals, I've played in bands since I was in sixth grade. From guitars around summer campfires to leading a soft-rock band—even several not-so-soft-rock bands—I've played it all, through college and into medical school. Once I saw that some of the psychiatric units had a music therapist, I started to rationalize bringing my guitar to the VA hospital every once in a while, to sing with patients. In medical school, my big solo performance occurred in the ER, when I sang James Taylor songs and lullabies to a man I was stitching up for hours. My favorite musical therapy story is from the Bellevue psych ER, where once upon a time a group of patients and I sang "He's Got the Whole World in His Hands." We began to make up various things in his hands, as one does, and we ended with "He's got the Bellevue Hospital in his hands." At this point, as usual, I couldn't sing because I was too choked up. Music is a great equalizer, something that brings us together and enables us to stay tightly connected.

I've had a few other experiences of group mind in my life catalyzed by music. I still remember the ecstatic sense of oneness with the other people on the dance floor, like a murmuration of starlings, back when I used to rave in the nineties. Group mind is a heady experience and it kept me coming back for more, even when I was aging out of the rave scene. I ended up returning to the clubs to do research, giving out a survey to try to ascertain what was pulling people to these gatherings. The ethos of the rave culture was something called PLUR—peace, love, unity, and respect. It's part of what drew me, and while my raving days are behind me, the special unity that comes from sharing the joy of music is one of the reasons I still dance at weddings and get together to jam with my friends.

We also get together for monthly potlucks and to play our instruments. Playing music with others in a group is an exquisite pleasure; there is nothing quite like that feeling of being "in the pocket" of a groove with good friends. In the past few years, some younger friends also began attending these potlucks. They've started to have children, and the combination of good food and conversation, playing music, and holding newborns brings my oxytocin levels up to overflowing. Honestly, holding a newborn gives me such an acute sense of calm, it's better than most drugs I've tried. As I slow my breathing down so that the baby will sense safety, I can feel that soothing synchronization, just like I get with my fellow musicians.

This kind of synchronization probably happens more than we realize. When two people work on a project together, even something as simple as doing a puzzle, their brains can synchronize. There is a unique brain-to-brain coupling that is specific to the experience of shared intentionality. I believe that musicians have this brain-to-brain synchronization in larger groups, though there is no study yet to prove this.

However, there is something called musical entrainment. When people gather to hear music, they clap together, dance together, perhaps sing together. This level of social entrainment is likely reflected in a shared physiology, meaning perhaps their heartbeats synchronize, or their brain waves might. Recent psychological studies have described rhythmic entrainment, among other mechanisms, as an "emotion induction principle." (Meaning that the periodicity in drumming or music can make people happy.) We also know that music can decrease stress by lowering cortisol secretion and increase acts of altruism through regulating the secretion of oxytocin. Many of us know that special vibe at large music festivals, regardless of drug ingestion.

Speaking of that special vibe, social experiments like Burning Man will continue to thrive, as they are more likely to build trust, a sense of safety, connection, and compassion. The cashless system of barter that is inherent in the culture of Burning Man, or simply the communal living experience of other large assemblies, like the Rainbow Gatherings, demonstrate the possibility of people living within a shared ideology, respecting freedoms, and enabling artistic expressions of hope and peace. Cue the Kumbaya soundtrack all you want, but in reality, these are festivals of oxytocin, meaning they will get you high in the best possible way. Here again, oxytocin is enabling neuroplasticity in yet another arena. Participating in these sorts of social experiments where we physically come together can open us up, teaching us new ways and changing minds and lives.

The other reinforcing and rewarding part of these large gatherings is due to the power of ritual. Remember the marble being used to create a sense of safety, to anchor to the event? Whether the context is drug use or religious rites and ceremonies, ritual enhances the pleasure and the meaning of any experience. Many religions incorporate psychedelic use as part of their ritual. Ayahuasca in the Santo Daime church or the União de Vegetal tradition, San Pedro cactus with aboriginal religions of the Americas, and peyote in the Native American Church all use psychedelics as part of a ritualized communal religious experience. In North America, ayahuasca circles are an example of group healing that can occur in altered states accompanied by ritual. In fact, participants in ayahuasca traditions show lower rates of addiction and depression than general populations. For many, that weekend retreat (or a series of them) is a turning point in their lives.

Although the psychedelic experience may be an internal one, the group experience—first of being altered as one and then of processing the epiphanies—can create a strong sense of communion and community. And as usual, our brains will reward this experience with good chemistry.

COMING TOGETHER

Whenever many people come together with a similar goal, amazing things can happen. This includes political activism, whether on a local or national scale. Civic engagement isn't just good for your community, it's also good for you. That's why I often recommend volunteering to my patients; it can be helpful in treating depression. Giving to others can help make your own life more meaningful. Besides tangible health benefits like enhanced longevity, reduced stress levels, and lower blood pressure, there is robust evidence that volunteers are more satisfied with their lives than nonvolunteers, likely due to oxytocin's stress-reducing effects. Helping really is its own reward! Whether charitable giving or simply being kind to others, altruism has neurological, and therefore pharmacological, rewards.

So then what do music, volunteering, and altruism have in common? Connection with others and giving to others in order to receive. There's a science to selflessness, and it requires multiple steps. The first is to abandon the idea of separation, to accept that we are all connected. Becoming less fixated on the self, and its separateness from the rest of the world, will be easier if your default mode network is less engaged and less active. Neuroimaging supports this idea, though the science of selflessness is just beginning to be understood. By imaging people who are expert meditators or who are experiencing psychedelics, it becomes easier to pinpoint when our boundaries begin to blur. In the metta meditators, who focus on compassion and benevolence for all, the default mode network was quieted down significantly. You do have to get out of your own head to be of use to others, and sometimes you have to give a little to get a little.

Unselfish, cooperative behavior has evolved in our genes for millennia. Primarily, it protected us against predators. It also signals to potential mates that you are a good caregiver, so it's selected for in the gene pool. Even if cooperation requires some sacrifice on our parts, we do it because it works for the common good, and because we are pharmacologically rewarded for it.

So we'll assist family because it improves the likelihood of our genes being passed on, but when will we assist community? Do you remember the caregiving system from the last chapter? Research shows that the exact same system is triggered in altruistic behavior. Whether caregiving for family members or showing compassion for non–family members, the underlying neurocircuitry is the same in either case. The insula (intuition) is activated, oxytocin is secreted, and the caregiving system adapts to and learns from the environment. In altruism as in caregiving, the system recognizes a need in another, feels compelled to act, and delivers a helping response. It's worth mentioning here that oxytocin (and not vasopressin) enables both types of altruism, that aimed at family members (parochial) and nonkin (universal). Oxytocin function helps explain the connection between prosocial behavior and health.

Because of oxytocin, compassionate activities and altruism can have an anti-inflammatory effect on our bodies, something we all need more of, to avoid vulnerability to cancer, diabetes, and cardiovascular disease. Psychological well-being founded upon service to others actually outflanks the satisfaction from consumptive pleasures (eating, shopping) when you look at the biomarkers for inflammation.

Altruism also improves long-term happiness scores. Because we're pharmacologically hardwired to be selfless, not selfish, the same areas of the brain that "light up" when we have sex or enjoy eating food also fire when we're being altruistic. Giving feels good and keeps us feeling good.

Studies show that as far as the brain is concerned, when money is exchanged, these three disparate activities provide similar activation in reward processing areas: giving money to yourself, observing a charity getting money, and even giving mandatory tax-like transfers to a charity. And while it is worth remembering that dopamine drives the reward train, there are oxytocin receptors in the engine, the nucleus accumbens. This area is also involved in partner preference and falling in love; it's a key component of the reward circuitry and is implicated in many addictive processes. Many drugs cause a surge of dopamine through this circuit, and the reward from charity is no exception—though social reward requires a coordination of oxytocin and serotonin. So in the case of altruism, that's a good start to some serious feel-good chemistry.

The bottom line is this: giving feels good. It's supposed to. It's good for our bodies, feeds our soul, and helps us to get out of our head and into someone else's experience for a while. With our sense of separateness on the back burner, a feeling of connection fills the void. If we feel like we belong, the brain is happy, and the body follows suit.

To better understand where and how we can practice altruism and inclusion, the social experiments must continue, whether on the internet, "in the field," or in the laboratory. A recent MDMA study using the classic game of the prisoner's dilemma showed that those who were given placebo made decisions out of self-interest more than those who were given MDMA. Participants given MDMA showed more willingness to cooperate for the collective good as long as they deemed other participants trustworthy. Interestingly, MDMA did not affect how trustworthy subjects found one another, but it did lead to greater recovery of cooperation with trustworthy partners following a breach in trust. This means that MDMA can help repair rifts in connection, which helps one understand not only why it can be so helpful in couples' therapy but also perhaps how it may help repair rifts within families or communities.

I found this quote in an MDMA research paper, hinting at the societal implications of this kind of research: "At a time of great hostility and mistrust both nationally in the United States and internationally, what is more important than elucidating the mechanisms in our brains that generate empathy, openness, and the most positive of social experiences?"

THE POLITICS THAT DIVIDE US

The sense of communion with others is powerfully rewarding, particularly pharmacologically, and is likely the main reason why we keep logging on to Facebook. We have an innate drive to be part of a community. It's this drive to belong that keeps us hooked in, scrolling through our feed, whether to like others' posts or to see how many likes we're getting, or to feel the wrench of someone else's horror through "trauma porn." It's not just that the flickering device itself is alluring, but also that the content is addictive. These are digital drugs. And because we are in this mildly altered state of mind when we're on our phones, it's a perfect receptive state for advertising and propaganda. Because of video editing, we can no longer trust our own eyes. And because of our consistent input influencing the algorithms, we're reinforcing our own beliefs. We may go there to feel connected, but of course, being synthetic, it doesn't really do the job. Remember how we can never get enough of something that almost works? For the good chemistry of connection, you need the real thing.

A group called Better Angels is having small face-to-face meetings across America of "reds and blues" for people to cross the divide of their ideologies. The best way to address this schismogenesis of our culture is through education and exposure. It may be true, as Dr. Arthur Janov says in his seminal book *The Biology of Love*, that "ideas cannot change feelings," but the corollary, that feelings can change minds, does have traction. This issue of openness, of being cognitively flexible and able to change our minds, is a key part of social change and progress. If you're trying to convince someone with facts, the best one to remind people of is this: who you are and what you believe are two separate things.

The concept of "identity politics" really hits home when you look at the biology of it. It comes down to the default mode network again, this "us vs. them" mentality, and strengthening our sense of self, which is separate from everything else. Remember that our brains may respond to foreign ideas as if our very bodies are being attacked. Ideological challenges need to happen compassionately, in a safe environment. In one study by Dr. Jonas Kaplan, the participants who were able to change their minds when evaluating counterevidence showed lower signaling coming from the fearful amygdala.

There is a phenomenon called reversal learning, which is widely used as a test of cognitive flexibility. If an animal or person is trained to respond one way, but then subsequently trained to reverse the reward values, this is known as reversal learning. The behavior that was previously rewarded is now punished and vice versa. Psychedelics help to accelerate reversal learning. This can be particularly helpful in treating addictions. Combine that with the traumatic memory reconsolidation that can happen with MDMA-assisted psychotherapy, and you start to see a way out of this mess.

For all of us, changing our minds and being open still comes back to the choice of being in para versus fight or flight. Psychological flexibility is a yin state, relaxed and receiving. It's a better state for learning and growing, because it's in para where oxytocin dominates. If we are in fight or flight, we cannot take in new information or consider changing our ways. This is a big factor in how we arrive at our own political decisions. Do you want to spend your life in a fear-based state, where it is dog-eat-dog and "every man for himself," or do you want to be compassionate and inclusive and connected?

When reviewing research involving liberals and conservatives, the results paint a particular picture. They suggest that conservatives test higher on fear and anxiety, have larger amygdalae and a bias toward paying attention to negative stimuli. They also have a stronger physiological response to startling noises and images. Liberals are quicker to focus on positive images and tend to be more novelty seeking. They both want to and do feel more empathy than conservatives. The research also suggests that liberals express empathy toward larger social circles, with conservatives expressing it toward smaller circles.

The term "bleeding-heart liberal" always bothered me. Why is that such a bad thing? What about the Christian precept to love our neighbors as ourselves? Why are their circles smaller? One thing we know about altruism, or its extreme version, heroism, is that people tend to be more compassionate and see others more inclusively. Heroism reflects a concern for other people in need, even if there is personal risk, and there is no expectation of reward. They see people less as "them" and more as "us."

My friend and colleague Dr. Doug Rushkoff argues that our digital ecosystem is designed to exploit and divide us rather than enhance and unite us. I'm afraid our technology may be making it all worse, and not better. My fear is that because it is easier to find like-minded people, the internet emboldens those who have racist or misogynistic views. Tend and befriend means accepting and integrating others into your life, just as we need to accept and integrate our own selves. My assumption is that the people who are most invested in "othering" certain people, in creating divisions where there needn't be any, may have some deep personal work to do on their own self-divisions and self-hatred. And my advice would be to turn those judgments around on themselves (there is a fair amount of projection happening with politicians) and, importantly, to focus on their own embodiment. As a physician and psychiatrist, I feel I may weigh in on something sensitive but potentially very important. Some of our politicians appear physically unhealthy and out of touch with their own bodies and, I daresay, with their own sexuality. Much of the hate we see fomenting on social media and elsewhere, whether coming from trolls or some politicians, is projected self-hatred. We need to remember this, and hopefully it will allow us some measure of compassion for the "haters." People who traumatize were traumatized.

My patients with a history of sexual trauma are so completely triggered by Trump, from his predatory stance behind Hillary Clinton during a 2016 presidential debate to his routine dismissal of the accusers of his sexual transgressions. When Mitch McConnell said "we're going to plow right through it" in getting Brett Kavanaugh confirmed, despite the credible testimony from Dr. Christine Blasey Ford, it was exquisitely traumatizing for my patients, and for the many women who weren't believed when they were brave enough to stand up and make an accusation. We used to be "one nation, indivisible." But not anymore. Now we are more divided than ever, thanks to the most divisive president in our history.

When I attended the Women's March, I carried a sign. On one side, it said: FORGET SURGEON GENERAL, WE NEED A PSYCHIATRIST! On the other side it said: TRUMP IS A TRAUMATIZER. Jeremy helped me create a rotating button for the two sides to show how trauma begets trauma. We all know that hurt people hurt people. There is also the phenomenon of "identification with the aggressor." Many people want to be on the side that's winning, and so join the bully rather than risk being bullied. One interesting factoid: people who use psilocybin mushrooms are less likely to perpetrate intimate partner violence.

It's a hard cycle to interrupt. The only way in is compassion.

To process what was happening, I attended an ayahuasca circle very soon after Trump was elected. The room was all women and the mood was dour. The curandera leading the circle insisted that Trump needed our compassion. Her suggestion was met with halfhearted grunts.

With ayahuasca, the suffering happens collectively, overnight, with the revelations processed in a group therapy–type format the day after. I imagined Trump there with us, drinking the tea, vomiting and crying, writhing on the floor as the memories came, fast and furious. I imagined him sharing in our circle, coming to terms with his childhood pain and how it's driving his behavior. The psychiatric journals have always reported that narcissism is a tough nut to crack, perhaps even untreatable, but the data on psychedelics being beneficial actually looks very promising.

Whoever chooses to undertake this spiritual work—and it is work—it needs to begin at home for each of us. It's clear we have a long way to go in maintaining healthy relationships within ourselves, and so of course there are issues in our relationships within our communities. But when I log off my devices and head out the door, things seem less dire up close. I had an uplifting chat with a man at the grocery store because I didn't notice his NRA hat. Face-to-face, heart-to-heart, it's easier to connect and find compassion.

After integrating and connecting with the self and tending to our families, it's time to prioritize empathizing with our neighbors and accepting that we are interdependent on one another. Even though we are creating rifts and rivalries that will be hard to bridge, in truth, we all belong on the same team, because we're all traveling together on this planet. And that brings us to the next topic: connecting with our fragile earth.

CHAPTER 5

CONNECTION WITH THE EARTH

If our religion is based on salvation, our chief emotions will be fear and trembling. If our religion is based on wonder, our chief emotion will be gratitude.

—CARL JUNG

There comes a point when you have to face the fact that we're in an abusive relationship with our planet:

- The glaciers are losing an estimated seventy-five billion tons of ice a year.
- The oceans, which absorb more than 90 percent of the excess heat trapped by greenhouse gases, are rapidly warming and acidifying, creating oxygen-starved dead zones and melting the polar ice caps, which in turn (combined with the expansion of the ocean's volume as

it warms) results in rising sea levels that threaten life in coastal zones and low-lying islands.

- The average size of vertebrate populations (mammals, reptiles, fish) has dropped 60 percent between 1972 and 2014.
- One hundred fifty to two hundred species of plant, insect, bird, and mammal are going extinct every twenty-four hours, one thousand times the natural or background rate of extinction.
- The number of floods and heavy rains each year has more than quadrupled since 1980 and doubled since 2004.
- More than forty-six thousand square miles of tropical forest were lost to wildfires and cultivation in 2018 alone, a landmass nearly equivalent to the size of New England.
- Feedback loops—as when the loss of snow- and ice-covered regions, which reflect sunlight back into space and reduce the heat, give way to darker land or masses that absorb the heat instead and warm the planet more—threaten to accelerate the pace of global warming. Not all potential feedback loops are known, but the more the temperatures rise, the more likely we are to trigger them.
- When enough of these feedback loops are triggered, the rate of acceleration will exceed a level where human intervention can turn it back.

I can assure you, when you're dangling off a cliff, your physiological state is not in para. If you're not upset, then you're not paying attention, or are in denial. Some of my patients carry this anxiety with them, and others, not so much. Many of us who are "woke" are in deep despair as the ecocide progresses.

In *Braiding Sweetgrass*, botanist and indigenous author

Robin Wall Kimmerer writes on how plants can teach us, restoring our relationship with the land. She understands the "deep ecological grief" many of us feel currently. "Grief is a measure of how much we love. And so I honor that grief. But then you roll up your sleeves. Out of the love that you have for the world—that's expressed in that grief—then you get to work, the work of restoration."

Problems this huge will require cooperative solutions on a global scale, testing our capacity for interconnectivity. Treaties like the Paris Climate Agreement are a good start, especially if the United States signs back on, but we need popular movements, too, like Extinction Rebellion, with its imaginative acts of civil disobedience. And we need the new generation of heroes inspiring us, people like sixteen-year-old climate-change activist Greta Thunberg, and Autumn Peltier, the fifteen-year-old member of the Wikwemikong First Nation and "water warrior" who confronted Canadian prime minister Justin Trudeau about his pipeline policies.

This isn't the first time we've faced the threat of complete extinction. The Doomsday Clock, an annual warning about how close we're coming to a global catastrophe of our own creation, is now set at two minutes to midnight. These updates have been put out every year since 1947 by the Bulletin of the Atomic Scientists. This is the closest it's come to midnight since 1953, just after the United States tested its first thermonuclear device on the Enewetak Atoll in the North Pacific. For most of my life the clock gauged how close we were getting to nuclear holocaust—that was the kind of apocalypse that the atomic scientists first had in mind. But since 2010, the scientists added the threat that climate change poses to life on Earth. It's been grim news all along, with the greatest relief (from the immediate threat of nuclear war, at least) coming in 1991, after the collapse of the Soviet Union and the end of the Cold War.

Regardless of what time it is, none of this is good. The entire Earth has been in an adrenalized state of fight-or-flight mode for seven decades and counting. It's as bad for the health of the planet as it is for each of us. What can we do? How do we flip an entire planet into para?

In some ways, we have to start where we do with ourselves: with the simple things. The first thing to remember is that when we are out in natural beauty, or even just viewing natural landscapes, we are more likely to be in para. Connection is the key here, too—connection to one another, of course, but above all to the earth.

The Aboriginal people of Australia have a saying: "If the land is sick, you are sick." This is proving all too true right now. In northwest Australia, Aboriginal people have been taken from their land in forced removals, and those who have remained have had to farm land devastated by prolonged and severe drought brought on by climate change. Over the past thirty years, their suicide rates have skyrocketed. But through it all, their tradition of "songlines" (elaborate songs that are geographically connected to landmarks in a blend of map and cosmology, intertwining oral tradition and personal identity) has kept them connected to the earth. The songs mark the plants and animals that are just as tied to the landscape as they are. All of them have suffered in the drought.

We can adapt this Aboriginal wisdom to our own land. In 1984, the biologist E. O. Wilson popularized the concept of "biophilia," the idea that love of the land, the earth, and the systems of nature is inborn, a necessity to us, like language or movement. Wilson believed nature exerts a gravitational pull on the human psyche, and he defined biophilia as the "innate tendency to affiliate with life and lifelike processes." Biophilia has crept into design and architecture, where design places a premium on bringing nature inside, especially in office buildings, by offering sweeping views, incorporating water and plant life into social and working spaces, and using lighting that's responsive to the changing sun outside.

Besides simply appreciating beauty, being in nature enhances the body's ability to cope with stress and recover from injury or illness. Some of this is physical: pine forests, for example, secrete something that kills pathogenic microbes in the air (which means that a pine forest may be a better site to have surgery than a hospital!). The restorative power of nature was demonstrated by medical researchers in 1984 with a study showing that natural views outside the windows of surgery patients had a positive effect on their recovery. Since the body only does its maintenance and repair work when it's in the parasympathetic state—as the release of oxytocin helps wounds heal—it makes sense to use nature as a soothing stimulus to keep a body in that state.

Pleasant nature scenes also activate the reward system, an area rich in opiate receptors. Neuroeconomist Dr. Nik Sawe conducted early fMRI studies showing that when people view iconic natural images, their reward circuitry lights up as if they've eaten food or had sex. Other brain areas that become more active when subjects view nature scenes are the insula (empathy, intuition) and the anterior cingulate (also empathy, and impulse control, emotion, and decision-making). Kids who grow up surrounded by nature become happier adults, with lower risks of psychiatric disorders from adolescence into adulthood.

Urban scenes, in contrast, activate the amygdala, the fear center. No big surprise there. In a study looking at brain activity, city folk had more activity in their amygdalae than country folk. They also showed more anterior cingulate activity after stressful tasks than country folk did. The anterior cingulate is a part of the brain commonly implicated in depression. In an American study, 22 percent of people felt more depressed after walking in a mall, while 92 percent felt less depressed after an outdoor walk. The outdoor walkers also felt less tense, angry, confused, and fatigued. Take urban dwellers out into nature, and they'll show a more positive outlook on life and higher satisfaction.

One study conducted in Scotland found that access to green space—forests, fields, green open spaces, natural landscape—lessened the effect of income inequality on health outcomes. This is a roundabout way of saying that if you can get out in nature, you're going to live longer, maybe as long as or even longer than your wealthier neighbors.

A Canadian study confirmed the Scottish study principle with a focus on cities, finding that how wealthy you are had far less of an impact on how long you lived—if you lived in a greener part of the city. So, get outside, if you want to live longer. Go look at trees, breathe for a while in a forest or the closest thing you've got to one.

LONGING FOR NATURE

In bullfighting, the word "querencia" refers to the spot in the ring that the bull returns to to gather strength. After the painful encounters with the matador, the bull is drawn to this place again and again. Environmental essayist Barry Lopez has taken the word "querencia" and applied it to the feeling of longing for nature. Lopez wanted to load as much meaning as he could into this word. To him, "querencia" included both the sense of nature under threat, but also the homing instinct, that longing to return to the place where we can remember exactly who we are and where we can gather our strength.

Lopez used the concept of querencia to evoke the connection to the land that was lost in the Native genocide during the British conquest of America. In "The Rediscovery of North America," he writes: "The discovery of a *querencia*, I believe, hinges on the perfection of a sense of place. A sense of place must include, at the very least, knowledge of what is inviolate about the relationship between a people and the place they occupy, and certainly, too, how the destruction of this relationship, or the failure to attend to it, wounds people."

Lately, the word has acquired an even broader meaning than Lopez envisioned. For me, querencia is New Hampshire, where I went to summer camp for nine years. For Jeremy, it's Cape Cod, where he's been every summer since he was born. Those are the places that restore us to ourselves.

However, my spot under duress, like the bull, is a bit different. It may seem odd to think of gardening as a centering, healing practice, but it is. Gardening is essentially tending to a very specific place, which is not just a declaration of allegiance, but also a ritual of healing to that bit of land. In fact, several studies by Dr. Mark Detweiler, at the Veterans Affairs Medical Center in Salem, Virginia, have shown the healing powers of gardening. One demonstrated that gardening lowered cortisol levels in veterans with PTSD, which means not just that it can flip you over into para, but also that, as a habit, it can chip away at the kind of long-term hypervigilance that plagues so many veterans. Another one of his studies showed that box gardening reduces stress. Veterans in the study tended to continue to garden for years after the clinical trial was over. A third showed that time spent in a "dementia wander garden," a green space with carefully designed paths, helped stroke patients in recovery. Also keep in mind that bacteria in dirt is often good for your body and your mood, so feel free to forgo the gloves. Techno-clean is unhealthy, increasing the risk of inflammation and autoimmune issues. Immersion in nature is anti-inflammatory.

Actually, I'm going to give you a few other quick suggestions for how to stay healthy and in para. We know from chapter one that we need to feel our feelings and be true to ourselves. When we align with our true nature, when we have emotional integrity, it makes us calmer. And so, if we care about the environment, we need to act like it. This is part of that integrity. Being eco-friendly and eco-conscious means I can feel like I'm helping, not hurting, the environment and my household. This good feeling helps trigger good chemistry as a bonus.

- Wash clothes and dishes in cold water (when hygiene allows). Add a dry towel to your clothes when putting them in the dryer. (They'll dry more quickly and use less energy.)
- Use "light" or "energy saver" settings instead of "normal."
- Eat local produce that is in season. It's healthier for your body and the planet.
- Compost, Recycle, and Go Paperless.
- Reduce your compulsion to buy new things. Donate to

and buy from thrift stores, hold clothing swaps with your friends, or borrow tools from libraries or co-ops.

- If you make a cup of tea, use the extra boiled water for sticky spots on your kitchen counters instead of detergents.
- If you do need household cleaners, make them yourself with diluted vinegar or bleach in mason jars. (No supporting big corporations and no more plastic containers in your house!) Buy from companies who practice "conscious capitalism," with good social policies that put people over profit, like Dr. Bronner's, Patagonia, Ben & Jerry's, TOMS, and LEGO.

These may seem like small things, but many people making little changes can make great things happen. In *Silent Spring*, Rachel Carson said, "In nature, nothing exists alone." In the forest where Jeremy and I live, we see interdependence every time we go outside. The birds warn the other animals of predators; the mushrooms, part of a mycelial network, are connected to the trees to form a "cross-kingdom" partnership. There is a "wood-wide web" of microscopic mycological fibers; the fungal network contributes phosphorus and nitrogen for the trees while getting sugar in return, but more than trafficking in nutrients, the network provides a way for the trees to communicate with one another. Tree experts say they can "form bonds like an old couple, where one looks after the other." This is a beautiful example of how nature cooperates. Another example of the intricacies of nature can be found in the entourage effect, where the sum of a plant's effects is greater than its parts. This is crucial to all of phytomedicine, the practice of using various plants to heal.

When I am in my garden, breaking off what is dead and

brittle to make room for what is young and green, I am reminded to stay flexible and resilient, and that death is a natural part of the life cycle. Gardening, as any gardener can tell you, is therapeutic. Time melts away, and it is easy to find myself in a state of flow. Gardening can lower cortisol levels, helping to put us in para. Studies point to reductions in anxiety and depression symptoms, improvements in cognitive function, physical activity levels, body mass index, and quality of life. Gardening helps to impart a sense of community, and green spaces in cities help to form and solidify local communities. Horticultural therapy is now available in many hospitals, rehabilitation centers, and elder-care facilities.

Gardening also entails being in a relationship with the earth. We pay attention and notice new things about the plants we cultivate, and if we're doing it right, we adapt our behavior to what we've learned. It can be something as simple as "this one needs water," to something more complex like "these plants like being next to each other."

Being outside is also a great time to practice the open hand of meditation; the birds alight, and then they fly. Best not to be too attached to their comings and goings. Garden long enough, and time seems to shift. There is a particular "earth time," which is different from "clock time." Seasons come and go; the light changes. Caterpillars move slowly across a stem, butterflies flit by, mushrooms sprout up overnight. Spend enough time in your garden and you may even find yourself dreaming about it. This is querencia, too.

One property of psychedelics that's useful here: people who have had some experience with them, according to a 2018 study at Imperial College London, report a greater sense of connection to nature and a lower tolerance for authoritarianism, two helpful traits for fighting climate change. One study participant reported, "Before I enjoyed nature, now I feel part of it." We are learning that nature connectedness is a strong predictor of happiness, and that it can help to engender pro-environmental attitudes and behaviors. This would seem to suggest that psychedelic medicine is good for you and the earth. In a paper titled, "From Egoism to Ecoism," researchers showed that the frequency of psychedelic use correlated with nature relatedness at baseline. They also followed their subjects prospectively, showing that nature relatedness significantly increased after psychedelic experiences.

One of the people we'll hear from in this chapter, Dr. David Luke of the University of Greenwich in London, has done a lot of work studying the connections between psychedelics and eco-consciousness. He'll walk us through some of the history of the ecology movement, and how it grew up hand in hand with the human potential movement and sixties-era experimentation with psychedelics.

Luke calls himself a jack-of-all-trades from an academic standpoint—he's done clinical research into psychedelics and parapsychological phenomena and also extensive anthropological fieldwork. He'll explain some of the shamanic practices he observed among the Wixáritari, as they call themselves, or the Huicholes, as they are known outside their homeland in the Sierra Madres of Mexico, and how these practices can be applied elsewhere, helping to create a sense of interconnectedness rooted in the place you live.

Dr. Peter Hendricks came to the study of interconnectedness after working with people who were at the greatest risk of losing it: he volunteered after college at a homeless shelter run by the Russian Orthodox Church. The experience made him decide to study addiction in graduate school, since it was such a common affliction—if not the primary reason for the homelessness he encountered, it was almost always a contributing factor. He felt that, if he could learn more about addiction, he could maybe help address it, even in a small way.

In 2006, when Hendricks first picked up the issue of the *Journal of Psychopharmacology* with his dissertation study, it opened instead to Dr. Roland Griffiths's now landmark study on psilocybin and how it can "occasion mystical-type experiences"—a revelation of an essay that shaped his future. Hendricks now does research using psilocybin to treat substance-use disorders. He believes that the active ingredient and primary agent of psychological change in the psychedelic experience is a sense of awe, of transcendence, the egoless feeling that leads to a deepened sense of interconnectedness.

In some ways, the greatest test of interconnectedness comes when we try to connect with our enemies. We'll talk with Natalie Ginsberg, who has been looking at trauma and conflict on a person-to-person level in Israel and Palestine. Ginsberg, who is working with both Palestinians and Israelis, will speak about the use of psychedelics in this contested land. She is looking at how ayahuasca circles that include both of these ancestral enemies have helped promote a relaxation of the prevailing tensions. These ceremonies have fostered, despite societal incentives that would reinforce their ancient division, a profound connection between people with little opportunity for contact.

On the way out, we'll look back at Earth the way it appears to astronauts, who often speak of the feeling they get when they spot the home planet for the first time out the windows of their rockets. From that perspective, the beauty and fragility of Earth can take them by surprise. This overwhelming sensation of our interconnectedness is so remarkable and identifiable that it has its own name: the Overview Effect. We'll hear from them how that rush of tender emotions affected them in space and long after their return home.

PSYCHEDELIC ECO-CONSCIOUSNESS

Not everyone in the field of psychedelic studies feels comfortable talking about their personal experiences with them—and there are still a few who've never tried them. Many operate in a kind of in-between land, maintaining scientific impartiality in public, but happy to discuss their own experiences off camera. In general, those in the field assume some level of familiarity with colleagues. Nobody objects one way or the other. You can't study the empathogens without acquiring a little empathy of your own. And as the field explodes, I'm hoping there's more than enough room for everybody, including the "underground" therapists who helped get us here.

But, as one of the researchers who declined to speak about personal use did say: "Look, nobody flies to Ibiza to spend all night in a club taking allergy medicine." Which brings us to the other camp, the people who celebrate the use of psychedelics, or at least defend the importance of personal experience to their own research.

There's an honorific for those who've been especially brave in their explorations: psychonaut. David Luke is one of those who's transparent about his CV on this score. As he's said in lectures, "I do research on psychedelics. Sometimes I do research when I'm not on psychedelics as well." Luke has worked on clinical research, directed his own studies, and published broadly. He has even volunteered to take LSD himself, while the neuroscientists at Imperial College wired his brain to their fMRI machines, which looked to him like those big metal hair dryers in a beauty salon. "A cosmic perm," he called it. He has also spent years in the field, investigating what he calls the "nature-based epistemology of indigenous cultures," ethnographic studies that have taken him, among other places, to Mexico to follow the Huichol people on the 250-mile pilgrimage to their ancestral homeland, where they gather the peyote that grows there.

The small cactus, for the Huichol, is what ethnographers call an entheogen—a psychoactive plant whose use is sacred and designed to induce a spiritual experience. "You can't separate their use of peyote from their cosmology," Luke, who has participated in peyote rituals, says. "The two things are completely merged, as is their interaction with nature." This contrasts with the brief history of psychoactive use in the West, he points out. Early experimenters with LSD and psilocybin, like Aldous Huxley and R. Gordon Wasson, took the substances in laboratory conditions, operating on the hypothesis that the substances would be useful adjuncts to psychiatry and psychopharmacology. That slowly began to change in 1960, when Timothy Leary, who set up the Harvard Psilocybin Project (which mostly used LSD from Sandoz labs in Switzerland), switched the settings to more soothing, but still indoor surroundings. Even in those settings, people grew much more connected to nature after their experiences, with more expansive attitudes and, for many, a newfound environmental activism.

The Leary experiments at Harvard came at the beginning

of an era of social change that saw a number of transformative movements explode onto the national scene simultaneously: civil rights, women's liberation, the ecology movement, antiwar activism, the Gay Liberation Front. Leary's advice to "turn on, tune in, drop out" became a motto for the back-to-the-land impulse of the Flower Power era. This made Leary a lightning rod for mainstream criticism. At one point, President Richard Nixon called him "the most dangerous man in America." In 1971, in what seemed like a backlash against the whole slate of countercultural movements, the Nixon administration criminalized LSD and other hallucinogens, reclassifying them as Schedule I narcotics, with no medical use. The prohibition had little impact on popular use, which continued to grow, but it did effectively shut down medical research until near the beginning of this century.

Many who experimented with psychedelics, then and now, spoke of sensing subtle energies under the influence of the plant medicine, such as visions of interconnectedness or even direct communication with plants and animals. These effects were dismissed as "hallucinations" by detractors, or simply packaged under the broader categorization of "mystical experience." However they are categorized, one of the well-documented effects of psychedelics is an increased sense of connection with nature. Luke points to a recent study at Imperial College with before-and-after measurements that showed a marked increase in biophilia after taking psilocybin in the lab. "They became more ecologically connected," Luke said. "I think that's part of how we now frame psychedelics: People become generally nicer people, more open to experience, right? More likely to engage on an ecological level, more concerned and connected with nature. Finally, on a cosmological level, psychedelics give us a sense of the spiritual, or if not the spiritual, a sense of deeper connection with the universe at large, beyond our egocentric perspective."

The alliance between eco-consciousness and psychedelics was never total. "People in the ecological movement are somewhat wary of the idea that psychedelics are the answer," he says. "And there are some in the psychedelic community who are suspicious of climate science. But there's a healthy overlap in the Venn diagram." Beyond opening people up to nature and awakening their biophilia, psychedelics help people overcome the alienation that comes with increasing urbanization, Luke says. It alerts people to the urgency of the climate crisis on a visceral level and makes them more likely to take action.

There's another way that psychedelics can contribute to eco-consciousness, he says: increasingly, it brings people into contact with the shamanic worldview. He points to the case of Gail Bradbrook, a molecular biophysicist and the cofounder of Extinction Rebellion. She'd been involved with a series of environmental groups and protests, for animal rights, against fracking, and against the building of a local incinerator. She'd started a few of these activist groups herself, including an earlier version of Extinction Rebellion, but she wasn't seeing results on the scale she wanted. Then she went to Costa Rica, where she took part in ayahuasca circles. "She basically discovered the solution to her question about how to bring about social change on the ecological front—by taking psychedelics," Luke says. She came back and, with the help of Roger Hallam, fellow Extinction Rebellion cofounder, began the peaceful massive civil disobedience events—shutting down major intersections in London, blocking bridges over the River Thames—that has made Extinction Rebellion a major force for climate action.

In 2019, Bradbrook spoke about her experiences with Dr. Ben Sessa at the biennial Breaking Convention conference on psychedelic consciousness, explicitly tying psychedelics to her own sense of "compassionate rage." She sees the role of psychedelics in social movements as a stimulus to action, largely by helping people, as she puts it, "sort out our shit. But not just any old shit: What's in the way of our contribution?" Bradbrook stresses the importance of intention, of going into the psychedelic experience seeking answers, especially to the question, Where can I act in service? As she told those at Breaking Convention, "I've maybe been that lone voice praying for a rebellion, feeling like a bit of a nutter. In fact, in my tradition, or the path I sit in, we rattle and we sing. And I remember singing, 'Bugger the bankers,' one time, because that was my holy song, you know?"

Luke shares this activist impulse. In the years that he's been following the Huichol, a Canadian mining company, First Majestic Silver, has tried to purchase mining rights to Wirikuta, a sacred mountain in the Huichol tradition. The extraction techniques the Canadians use—open-pit mining and a form of leaching that relies on cyanide—would ruin the land and extract groundwater from an arid terrain. Despite an official international designation that made Wirikuta a sacred site, a move that should have protected the land from any exploitation at all, the government sold mining rights to the mountain. In 2015, further work on the project was suspended until the conclusion of a suit over the mining. But the threat to their sacred land remains. "The desert where they pick their peyote is full of silver and gold," Luke says. "But they have no interest in extracting it. They say, 'It's the heart of the mountain. It belongs in the ground. We have no need for it.'"

Luke sees the shamanic perspective as a crucial one that can help Westerners move beyond the "species-centric view we have with humans on the top of the pile." Among the Huichol, the shamans act as go-betweens for communications between the human and nonhuman communities, negotiating with both sides and keeping things in balance—not just interceding for rain because the plants are drying up but also enforcing taboos, ensuring that certain animals are never eaten and that offerings are made to the land. In the case of the gold and silver buried beneath the mountain, they see to it that people don't take things they don't need. Among the Huichol, Luke says, the shamans are responsible for keeping order among "the parliament of species."

There are groups in the UK who have been adopting neo-shamanic practices informed by the Huicholes. "One thing [the Huicholes] do is a pilgrimage to sacred sites in Mexico where they harvest the peyote. So, we've been adopting not their actual practices but our own practices, informed by their way of life, of reconnecting with the land, going on our own pilgrimages, to our own sacred sites, making offerings, rediscovering our indigenous power plants—mushrooms in our case," Luke notes. In the course of these eco-spiritual quests, people engage in ecological activism, wilderness training, tree-planting, and eco-psychology therapy, based on the idea that mental and ecological health are connected.

"I'm glad psychedelic research is on the table again," Luke says. "Once you start earnestly studying psychedelics, you can't ignore these experiences. Therapists will say, 'Let's just call them mystical experiences and we don't have to explain too much. We can say it's useful for therapeutic outcomes.' I'm not saying everyone has to be a spiritual neo-shamanic mystic. But [psychedelic medicine] opens people up to something beyond themselves, and it gives them more meaning. And it can change one's perspective on our position in the cosmos, on the planet, in relationships, in nature. If it gives people a sense of 'Okay, we are a part of nature, not apart from nature' then that is going to help us survive a lot longer—and all the other species on the planet."

EVERY DOG IS A THERAPY DOG

When I was at Penn, I signed up to be a volunteer in a research project. (There were a lot of opportunities like this throughout college and medical school.) For this study, we were interviewed about our thoughts on ecology in a group, and at some point, a dog came into the room. They made it seem like a happy accident that the investigator's dog had wandered in, but I knew it was part of the experiment. Having a pet, or even just petting someone else's while you fill out surveys, can have an influence on environmental attitudes. But more than that, our relationships with our pets are special and deserve to be recognized as legitimate forms of connection. My patients will often discuss their dogs in particular (although there is research suggesting that cats, too, are capable of attachment behaviors). They sleep with their dogs, even when they interrupt that sleep, and care for them as attentively as many parents do their children. I even have one patient who used a service called Cuddle Clones when she had to put down her dog after its dementia grew too severe. Using the many pictures she sent them, the company created a stuffed animal that she could sleep with. (Try doing that with taxidermy.)

My patient who is battling cancer got a dog because she was told to do so repeatedly at support groups. They assured her that this would make a huge difference in her life and her health.

"Did it?" I ask her.

"It absolutely did," she replied. "That dog gets me out of the house to walk it, and keeps me company, and something else: I take better care of myself when I take care of something else. It rubs off on me."

There is a company I often recommend for CBD products, and they have a great line for pets, called "companion oils" and "companion capsules." Our pets are our companions, and just like caring for others, caring for a pet can help us feel less alone and more connected, and give us a greater sense of purpose. Our pets elicit caregiving behaviors from us, and when we perform these behaviors—especially if they were prompted by a dog's gaze—they increase oxytocin concentrations in their owners as a manifestation of attachment behavior. There is a positive loop that can arise when pet and owner engage in extended eye contact, increasing oxytocin in both gazers. There is one particular levator muscle above the inner eyebrow. It's small, and all dogs have it, but wolves don't. It makes dogs' eyes look sad or soulful, more like the wide eyes of a baby. You remember all the good chemistry those baby's eyes can trigger? These so-called puppy-dog eyes turn their owners into pushovers, and are highly effective at manipulating caregiving behavior. (Perhaps you know some grown men who attempt this?)

Dogs have co-evolved with humans for thousands of years, and it may be that the pleasure a dog experiences in the presence of people, and the ease of triggering it, have been built into their genome. Clinical studies show that by acting as social catalysts, companion animals can help to treat depression, loneliness, bereavement, and even the effects of institutionalization. One study showed that new dog owners felt less lonely and had fewer negative emotions (like nervousness or distress), often within three months of getting a dog. Another study showed that exposure to a dog at any time in childhood reduced the risk of schizophrenia by 24 percent. Other research shows that dogs decrease blood pressure, cortisol levels, and heart rate in stressful situations in their owners, possibly even better than humans do. One scientist put dogs in MRIs to discover that the part of the dog's brain that lights up when they hear their owners' voices is the same part of the human brain that lights up when we are fond of someone, implying that dogs can love people, at least neurologically, as we do. Dog researcher Clive Wynne doesn't think that dogs have a unique ability to understand and communicate with humans, but rather a unique capacity for interspecies love.

There are so many examples of what looks like empathy and caregiving in the animal kingdom. Perhaps it's my history of expanded experiences that has opened me to the idea of communicating with the animals of the forest, but I absolutely do attain a particularly altered state when I have extended eye contact with an eagle or a hawk as I'm paddleboarding out on the lake across from my house. Having intimate contact with animals is, for many of us, a particularly pleasurable form of connection—some would even say mystical.

80 PERCENT CHANCE OF A
MYSTICAL EXPERIENCE

The psychiatrist Dr. Stan Grof, a longtime psychedelic researcher and developer of Holotropic Breathwork (a nonpsychedelic way to alter your consciousness through breath), said in an interview with Dr. Albert Hofmann that psychedelics are spiritual tools. "If they are properly used, they open spiritual awareness. They also engender ecological sensitivity, reverence for life, and a capacity for peaceful cooperation with other people and other species. I think, in the kind of world we have today, resurrection of humanity into this direction might well be our only real hope for survival. It's essential for our planetary future to develop tools that can change the consciousness that has created the crisis we are in." It's a twist on the idea that you can't use the master's tools to dismantle the master's house. Desperate times call for desperate measures, and it may be that mystical experiences, helping us to feel connected to nature and the earth in its entirety, can help get us out of this mess in which we find ourselves.

One person who isn't afraid of taking a closer look into the mystical part of the mystical-type experience is Peter Hendricks, the clinical psychologist and associate professor at the University of Alabama at Birmingham. He first spotted the combination of psychedelics and the mystical-type experience when he read the Johns Hopkins study, "Psilocybin Can Occasion Mystical-Type Experiences, Having Substantial and Sustained Personal Meaning and Spiritual Significance." Hendricks said the paper spoke to him "as a person of faith, that a profoundly meaningful spiritual experience could change behavior in a very profound way." Not too many years later, he was conducting psilocybin-assisted psychotherapy of his own.

He felt the need to explain the psychological mechanism of this experience to the people in his studies. The neurological explanations proposed by Robin Carhart-Harris at Imperial College focused on a decoupling between the default mode network and the medial temporal lobes, an area involved in cognitive and emotional functions, which are normally significantly coupled. But a highly technical explanation like that didn't easily translate outside of neuroscientific circles. "As interesting as that work is, what do I do with that clinically?" he wondered. "If I'm working with someone who's ingesting the substance, how do I understand why they're changing? And how do I explain to them why they might change, recognizing that I can only do that if I understand what's taking place at the psychological level?"

He attended a symposium of the Association for Psychological Science in 2015 devoted to awe, and it struck him how neatly the experiences the speakers described matched descriptions from the psychedelic case reports and from the participants in his studies. When he got home, he did a deep dive on the literature of awe. His paper in the *International Review of Psychiatry*, "Awe: A Putative Mechanism Underlying the Effects of Classic Psychedelic-Assisted Psychotherapy," came out of that research. This hit home for a lot of people, including me, because it made sense intuitively and translated the salient parts of a profound and often ineffable experience into terms that could be readily understood. I added that to the intriguing work done a few years earlier by Dr. Paul Piff, showing that experiencing awe made people feel smaller and less self-important. It reduced self-serving, narcissistic behaviors and also led to increased prosocial behaviors, helpful interactions intended to promote friendship.

In some ways, Hendricks's theory helps translate Carhart-Harris's ideas about the default mode network into laypeople's terms. Awe, which can be experienced in many nonpsychedelic ways—at a cathedral, in a museum, at a concert, out in nature—is an extreme state of openness that is also particularly fertile ground for learning. An experience of awe provides certain recognizable sensations: timelessness, transcendence, a liberating sense of the smallness of the self, and a compensating sense of connection to a cause, an idea, or a collective that's bigger than ourselves. There's a component of awe, Hendricks points out, "that allows us to take the focus off these nagging self-thoughts," a succinct reframing of Carhart-Harris's neurological insight that the default mode network is deemphasized.

In Hendricks's formulation, this sense of awe leads to a cooperative urge, an instinct that's fundamental to our success as a social species. He calls this the Ebenezer Scrooge effect, when a person suddenly thinks not of himself but of how his behavior has affected others. "He realizes, in an epiphanic manner, 'My God, I have made other people miserable in my pursuit of wealth. I have hurt other people. I ruined relationships. And I have potentially even contributed to the poor health of my employee's child. Do I exist only for my own needs or to be a better person to others, to attempt to, in my own way, contribute to the betterment of humankind?'"

Awe is not necessarily a euphoric emotion. Two aspects of awe—the sense of vastness and the need to integrate a new, almost alien experience—can involve fear, disorientation, and ego dissolution. "In the case of psychedelics, we're talking about a profound experience of awe, unlike anything you experience in daily life," he says. "In the case of extraordinarily profound awe, what might that do? I think everybody—whether you meet criteria for a mental health condition or not—could probably benefit from fewer nagging self-referential thoughts. We probably all worry a bit more than we should. We could probably all be encouraged to cooperate with others a bit more. I think we right that balance by seeking awe experiences, including religious observations." (I would like to add that for many of us who are not very religious, being enveloped in any intense natural beauty can be awe-inspiring.)

Like so many others in the field, Hendricks thinks psychedelic experiences could benefit people who don't meet the mental health criteria in current FDA studies. For the healthy population, a profound experience of awe would increase mindfulness and a sense of gratitude (which can combat depressive thinking). And it probably would increase altruistic behavior—all points borne out in Roland Griffiths's psilocybin study with healthy participants. "These individuals say, after these experiences, that they feel kinder, gentler, warmer," Hendricks tells me. "And the people who know them say the same thing. They have an increase in positive emotion. Psychedelics may even be one solution to the global climate-change crisis, because this is an experience that promotes a greater sense of connectedness to nature."

When speaking of the spiritual, Hendricks broadens the emotion from its traditional religious context. "I think ultimately when we talk about the spiritual, we're talking about that which an individual holds to be sacred. And that means that everybody has a sense of the spiritual. Whether you are Jewish, Catholic, Buddhist, or a strict materialist, somebody who sees the universe as all that there is and all that ever will be, you still have a sense of what's sacred. And humans, by virtue of being humans, often feel that ultimately what's sacred is our connection with others." For centuries, the greatest part of the literature on these profound experiences came from religious mystics—which is why they're described as mystical experiences. But, as Hendricks points out, you could fast and meditate your whole life and you might not necessarily have an experience like this. "And yet, with psilocybin and related compounds, we can pretty reliably make this happen at a specific time and place. The likelihood in any given administration might be, let's say, 80 percent. That's pretty darn good. That means four out of every five times you're going to have a pretty intense mystical experience. And if you don't have it the first time, then we can try again."

THE SPECIAL CASE OF WATER

Nature relatedness, or how connected you are to nature, has a direct correlation with happiness. In a study using a smartphone app, Mappiness, researchers mapped over one million responses to "Where are you?" and "How happy are you right now?" among other questions. They showed people were happier outdoors in nature than when in an urban environment. Interestingly, they were the happiest of all if they were near water. Wallace Nichols wrote a book, *Blue Mind*, explaining the mildly meditative state we experience when we're near water or immersed in it.

Double Blind, a magazine devoted to psychedelic culture and science, interviewed Nichols, and this part really spoke to me. He says: "Awe over the natural world is what's needed to disrupt apathy towards climate change." Nichols talks about how to recruit more people into environmental activism. He notes, "If our toolkit is fear, guilt, and shame, they're not going to join our club. You have to have a hell of a lot of beauty and awe and wonder and compassion and love. We've been leaving that part out of our eco-spirituality for a long time." He's responding to a 2018 survey called "Climate Change and the American Mind," which found that 61 percent of Americans are worried about global warming, but only 41 percent think it will harm them personally, and only 36 percent ever discuss the topic.

Nichols suggests we exploit our innate biological connection with water, using our brain's response as an opportunity to galvanize society around ecological protection. He calls it "neuro-conservation." In *Blue Mind*, he reviews neurological data from EEGs and MRIs to show that proximity to water, and even just recalling memories of being in water, can flood the brain with the good chemistry we've been learning about in these pages. Further, water seems to stimulate parts of the brain associated with empathy, encouraging an important shift from selfish to selfless, from "me" to "we."

I have a patient who has sold her house to live on a boat with her partner. She was reporting episodes of feeling dissociated, like she had no beginning or end, and it made her feel anxious and unmoored. She mentioned the word "boundlessness" to me. I explained how there is a component of mystical experiences called "oceanic boundlessness" and that these episodes, if they're happening out on the water, may simply be experiences of awe triggered by the vastness of nature. This explanation floored her; it was a real aha moment, turning something pathological into something natural and even desirable. The more we talked, the more it made sense to her; we began discussing how she was meditating and doing more yoga. Her mind and body were more open to the possibility of experiencing awe, and when it happened, she simply didn't know what to make of it. It was an extreme state of "blue mind."

Whenever I travel to Amsterdam, I notice how the canals that striate the city help to keep everyone calm and connected to nature. (Although one shouldn't discount the effect cannabis may have on the chill vibe there.) I have always loved the water, enjoyed swimming and boating, and still find myself traveling to edges of continents, which not only puts me in proximity to water, but also reminds me that I am on a rock hurtling through space. Being on a coastline puts things in perspective. In fact, last spring, Jeremy and I went to Big Sur for a psychedelic conference at Esalen, which sits on spectacular vertical cliffs overlooking the crashing waves of the Pacific. There were regular soaks in the hot tubs, followed by standing in my favorite shower in the world, with the doors open onto the ocean. Three weeks later, we were in Morocco for a long-planned family vacation, on the western edge of the African continent, with sunsets over the Atlantic this time. Both edges gave me that feeling of smallness and awe.

Morocco was most interesting to me because of how the men behaved with one another. They kissed each other, hugged each other. They'd walk arm in arm down the street, talking with their heads close together. It made me realize how touch-starved the men in my country are. How, except for handshakes and pats on the back (or butt if you're an athlete) or a quick bro-hug, men don't really touch each other. There's no alcohol use in that Muslim country, so they don't have to wait till they're trashed to come out with an "I love you, man." They're able to be loving to each other while sober, and in public. It was the thing I talked about most when I returned. I even saw two fights broken up through kindness, holding, kissing on the head, whispering into the ear. Men treating each other tenderly was a revelation.

WAR, PEACE, AND PSYCHEDELICS

When we look for possible solutions to the climate-change crisis, it seems clear that more spiritualism leads to less consumerism, and breaking free of materialism can lead to a more eco-conscious way of being. Being nonprofit enables more social profit. We can also rein in disaster capitalism: cutting fossil-fuel consumption or curbing overpopulation or rethinking urbanization or protecting the rain forest or preventing mass extinctions. But this kind of catalog overlooks one of the most destructive forces on the planet: war.

Ever since people started banding together in nation-states and those nations started plotting to raid and overthrow other nations, war became a potent force of environmental destruction. The Romans salted the farmland of their enemies so they would not be able to feed their armies. Seafaring countries systematically devastated their timber reserves to make fleets of war vessels. On land, siege strategy relied on laying waste to any land in cultivation.

In recent history, the United States defoliated vast areas of forest and mangrove swamps in Vietnam with Agent Orange. During the Sino-Japanese Wars, Chinese military dynamited a dike on the Yellow River, drowning Japanese soldiers and Chinese farmers, and flooding millions of acres in the process. During the Gulf War, the United States bombed Iraq with missiles containing depleted uranium, leaving radioactive waste. Retreating Iraqi armies set Kuwaiti oil fields on fire. US-backed warlords in Afghanistan engaged in illegal logging, reducing the country's forests by nearly a third.

Civil wars, like the ones in Sudan and Syria, drag on with little oversight from outside forces. During these wars, cash-strapped armies raid protected wilderness areas, as the Sudanese forces have done in Garamba National Park, just over the border in the Democratic Republic of Congo. Conflicts in Africa have led to ivory poaching on a massive scale, devastating elephant and hippopotamus populations. Factions in war exploit natural resources in unsustainable ways—timber in Liberia, diamonds in Sierra Leone—to support the war efforts.

Extended conflicts lead to the diaspora of millions of people, disproportionately women and children, who settle in massive refugee camps or in scattered improvised encampments, where uncertainty and desperation force them to meet immediate needs with little thought to environmental consequences, harvesting trees for firewood, killing wildlife for food, polluting rivers with waste. Many massive camps are located in remote areas where local resources were already depleted before the refugees arrived.

Some wars have gone on so long that it is hard to separate the conflict from the land. This is certainly the case in Israel and Palestine, where the imminent dangers of climate change—principally rising temperatures and diminishing water resources—will only increase the unequal access to natural resources and economic opportunity for Israelis and Palestinians. It would be impossible to take any action to protect the land that did not address this long-standing conflict. Any environmental action has to double as conflict resolution.

Natalie Ginsberg, the policy and advocacy director at MAPS, is aiming to address the conflict through psychedelic medicine, or to put it in more modest terms, she's planning to bring together Israelis and Palestinians in ayahuasca circles, with the hope that the shared experience will begin to sow the seeds of connection, reconciliation, and ultimately peacemaking. Ginsberg has a background in social work and is in some ways part of the next wave of the psychedelic renaissance: she's already making plans for a time when the medicine is legal, when its benefits can be part of broader public health policy and even a legitimate force in politics.

Ginsberg is collaborating on this project with Dr. Leor Roseman, an Israeli neuroscientist who works with Carhart-Harris at Imperial College, and with Antwan Saca, a Palestinian peace activist. The project takes its inspiration from similar ongoing efforts at conflict resolution and restorative justice in Colombia, where the Union of Indigenous Yagé Medics of the Colombian Amazon (UMIYAC) is attempting to address a similar centuries-old conflict that has drawn in indigenous tribes, revolutionary forces, drug cartels, and other strains within Colombia. There, the practitioners of traditional medicine use *"yagé"* (the word for "ayahuasca" in the region) to bring together representatives of the many factions to help them all address the pressures of war and the devastation to their environment using overtly spiritual means, over long nights of rituals, guided by their ancestral medicine.

Roseman is the one with clinical experience, and he'll be designing the protocol for the Israeli/Palestinian experiment, determining the before-and-after measurements, and writing up the study. But medical data may be beside the point. These ayahuasca circles are meant to be an exercise in building awareness and consensus, and Ginsberg is handling that strategy. Because the power differential between the two communities is so stark, there is no neutral territory, which has made it impossible to find a meeting place where both peoples could feel equally relaxed. So Ginsberg has been looking to transport the entire operation to Spain or Portugal, both countries where ayahuasca is decriminalized, just so that everyone can enter the plant-teacher ceremony on equal footing.

The funding for the process has been secured (by this point, you're probably not surprised to learn that there are wealthy patrons of psychedelic research who are also interested in the peace process). While nearly every research project has some element of the political—usually to gain FDA approval and help reverse the classification of psychedelics as a Schedule I drug—this project has explicitly political goals, namely contributing to broader peace efforts, included in its design. To that end, Ginsberg and her team are interviewing directors and assembling a film crew, hoping that the entire process could become part of a documentary that would serve as model for rapprochement between Israelis and Palestinians. Of course, this adds an unprecedented degree of difficulty to an already complicated process, as Ginsberg tacks "film producer" onto her list of duties.

The conflict resolution project is unusual in other ways. For individual psychedelic sessions, therapist-assisted administration is the primary model, but when it comes to group settings, shamanism is the dominant model. The guides that Ginsberg has arranged for the ceremonies have been trained in indigenous practices, which means they'll be incorporating ritual and singing, and processing the experience together the next day. "If you can feel safe in that context," Ginsberg says, "you can go quite deep. So much of our trauma in Israel and Palestine is about disconnection. So being able to be in a healing circle is an opportunity for deeper healing than in an individual setting. In individual therapy, you have an integration session afterward and a lot of follow-up, but in group work you integrate right after your journey. You have a circle and everyone shares, then you continue to meet for potlucks and you talk and you process. Now you have this group of friends, a community. And that feels so much more holistic and effective, especially when you have so much loneliness and disconnection."

Ginsberg points out that many things that might seem like sources of conflict between Palestinians and Israelis can also be viewed as points of connection: both peoples live with trauma as a feature of everyday life—checkpoints, metal detectors in markets, a nearly universal experience of personal involvement in the conflict at some moment; both share a history of dispossession, flight, oppression, and maintaining their culture in a diaspora.

"Also, in my very unscientific sampling, this is a country with the highest per capita use of psychedelics of any place I've ever visited," she says. "And I think a lot of it is because of the widespread trauma and the need to process that."

Other factors contribute: everyone on the Israeli side has to spend a year in military service. A high percentage follow their year of service with a year of travel, doing "really hippie things," according to Ginsberg, like taking psychedelics and backpacking through Thailand and India. This means that despite the background of mutual distrust, there's a level of openness to new experience and familiarity with the psychedelic process.

In fact, in preparation for their study, Ginsberg, Roseman, and Saca first traveled the region speaking to Israelis and Palestinians about their experiences using psychedelics in nightclubs and at ayahuasca ceremonies, raves, and nature parties (rave-like trance events in Galilee or the Negev desert). They followed that with more formal interviews with eighteen Jewish Israelis and thirteen Palestinians, of whom seventeen were men, thirteen were women, and one was gender nonbinary. Of the thirteen Palestinians, seven were Christian and six were Muslim; four lived in the West Bank, and nine lived in Israel with Israeli citizenship.

From the beginning, there was an acknowledgment of the difficulty of the enterprise. One Palestinian man wondered how it would be possible to heal a trauma that's ongoing. "I cannot go to a checkpoint and be like, 'I'm a human being. Let me go through. I'm a spiritual light being!'" he said. But at some point in the ceremonies, the typical features of a psychedelic experience—the sense of oneness and connectedness, the relaxation of fears, the increase of compassion—began to take over participants on both sides. A Palestinian woman said, "There's no 'You are Jewish, Arab, Muslim, Christian.' Everything was stripped. All this nonsense was out and only acceptance and love were present."

For many, the feelings of otherness associated with their supposed enemy dissolved over the hours of the ceremony. As one Jewish woman, a veteran of multiple shared psychedelic experiences, said, "At almost every retreat, there is a moment in which [a small group of Palestinians] are comfortable enough to sing in Arabic. This is always an amazing moment. Suddenly you hear your most hated language, by far, maybe the only language in the world that you really didn't like, and suddenly it sends you to light and love." Another participant, a Palestinian with an extensive record of nonviolent protest, reassessed his own intentions after the experience. "My activism has changed tremendously," he said. "A big part of what I realized was how much this activism, and even nonviolent activism, was motivated by hatred towards the other. My activism of nonviolence meant that I would expose *them* and I would amplify how terrible *they* are. So it was more of a demonizing nonviolence motivated by hatred, not by love and compassion."

Many were preoccupied with how they could move from the unity and connections they had made in the ayahuasca circle to the political reality that surrounded the rest of their lives. One Christian Palestinian man thought that embracing their essential unity was the only way forward: "Then from there we could say, 'How do we honor and celebrate diversity?' not 'How do we create diversity because we are afraid of each other—because the Jews are afraid demographically or the Palestinians are afraid demographically?' It's the foundation of the issue for me. And so in a sense we could only accept the two-state solution if we fully embrace the one-state solution first."

The psychedelic experience also provided visceral representations of what the other lived with. A Christian Palestinian man said he suddenly "had this weird experience of being in the body of an Israeli soldier. It was like seconds. The whole experience was the eye looking down to shoot as the trigger is pulled. And that's it, there was no seeing after. But I could feel him after. This is painful, this is not an easy life after."

A Jewish Israeli man also remembered a forceful insight that took shape thanks to the ayahuasca:

> There was one session that a group came from the occupied territories, if I'm not mistaken, about six Palestinians— Palestinian Palestinians, not Israeli Arabs. And someone began to cry. I heard the accent of the weeping somehow, I recognized it. And the minute I heard him cry—they were all sitting together—suddenly the ayahuasca showed me them as a separate unit within us. And another one of them began to cry, and it took me automatically to the madness of the pain of a whole people. I could see it. It was clear to me that they weren't weeping because they remembered a dead aunt. They were weeping for the pain of their people. And I am connected to that pain. I caused the pain of their people. I began to break, I couldn't stand to hear them crying and she [the ayahuasca] began showing me so much, I can't describe it visually, just this crazy pain and hate and crying for the evil they experienced.

Ginsberg is right to make a movie out of these experiences. The stakes are high and the pain is deep, so the shift in perspective, when it comes, is dramatic.

There's trauma on all sides, and as so many have said, psychedelics seem to have a way of finding trauma and animating it, making it available as an opportunity for healing. The hard work comes in the integration. But the process, at least from the point of view of the participants, seems to provide a reason for hope. As one Palestinian Muslim man said, "I can tell you that one of the illusions that I understood is that the Arab-Jewish conflict as it is now, that we think is the conflict of a century, is an eternal conflict, that will go on till the last drop of life. What ayahuasca taught me about this conflict, one more time, I'll say is that it gave me the choice to belong to these conflicts or not, to look for what's common, not what's different."

EARTH FROM ABOVE

It's hard to live to adulthood without facing the fact that life is fragile. Maybe, at some point, you've also sensed how connected we all are—the people we love, the strangers we meet, the trees and rivers in the landscape we're moving through, the clouds overhead and the light and the heat and the pulse of life everywhere. Maybe, sometimes, the beauty of it all fills you with awe.

The simultaneous perception of these three feelings—our fragility, interconnectedness, the sensation of beauty and awe—is a common experience for astronauts. It wasn't something that NASA planned for. In fact, the first crews traveling beyond Earth's atmosphere weren't expecting it. They were focused on their checklists, their equipment, their timetables—nearly every minute of their time in space choreographed and coordinated.

So it took them by surprise, in the middle of all the mission-specific duties, to float over to the window and look back at the blue planet hanging in space against the backdrop of the sun and the infinity of stars. They weren't prepared for how overwhelming and beautiful it was—the colors of the oceans, the long shadows of the mountains at sunset, the lightning moving through the clouds like a fireworks show, the lights of cities and towns as their orbital path crossed to the night side of the planet. Even later in the space race, after so many of them had come back and described the feeling and the feeling got a name, the Overview Effect, it still didn't prepare astronauts for the moment they saw it themselves.

From that perspective, that vision of Earth—the beauty of the planet against the immensity of space—inspires a protective, caregiving impulse. From space, Earth's atmosphere, the only place in the universe known to support life, looks paper-thin. "It looks like a living breathing organism," Ron Garan, a shuttle astronaut, said. "But it also, at the same time, looks extremely fragile." Politics and national boundaries disappear; there is an immediate sense of unity, a oneness of self and the world. As Neil Armstrong, the first man to walk on the moon, said, "I put up my thumb and shut one eye, and my thumb blotted out the planet Earth. I didn't feel like a giant. I felt very, very small."

"We have this connection to the earth," Nicole Stott, the first person to live-tweet from space, said. "I mean, it's our home. And I don't know how you can come back and not, you know, in some way be changed."

These are all firsthand accounts from NASA engineers. It's safe to say that none of them came to this experience through psychedelics. However, the Overview Effect seems to create a profound and lasting cognitive shift through many of the same psychological mechanisms as the "mystic-type experiences" described in these pages—awe, vastness, interconnectedness, a sense of belonging to a collective far greater than the self.

So now I ask you: Who's to say which trip—to space or deeper into your own mind—is better for the planet?

CHAPTER 6

CONNECTION WITH THE COSMOS

The first half of life is devoted to forming a healthy ego, the second half is going inward and letting go of it.

—CARL JUNG

We've spent this whole book connecting. We're social creatures. It's how we're happiest. It's what we're built to do. And we're rewarded for making contact with each other in a cascade of good chemistry that can reshape us, rewire our neural networks, renew our thinking, reframe our entire outlook, and—hopefully sooner rather than later—restore our planet.

Now our progress has brought us to the cosmos, the infinite. During every step so far, we've tried to find the simple strides to make that connection: breathing, floating, hugging, dancing, singing, getting naked, getting our hands dirty, digging into the earth. But how do we connect with the cosmos, with the infinite?

It turns out there are some simple answers here, too.

We die. We all do it. Maybe it's not easy, although there's no rule that says it has to be hard. We've even had a little practice by now, at least in letting go of our egos, when we tame our default mode network. Knowing how to set aside our preoccupations with ourselves to connect with others is good preparation for laying it all down forever (or, if we take it one breath at a time, just this once). Humans may be the only animal aware of the temporariness of existence. Knowing life will end helps to keep it precious. Many people are in complete denial about their impending impermanence, of course, but that, to me, is not fully living. Pema Chödrön, a Buddhist nun and teacher, says that embracing the entirety of your human experience, and that includes your death, is a sacred journey.

Let's remember the Overview Effect—that mystical yet grounding experience of the astronauts looking back at Earth from a distance. Along with our planet, the view includes the space above and below Earth—the infinite cosmos every way they looked. That, too, is our home. We seem to avoid talking about that vast expanse of nothingness the same way we avoid talking about death. But that is not all they have in common.

When my grandfather lay dying, his last words to me were, "Help me get away from myself." I was glad I was there for him then, and that I could reassure him, because I knew exactly what he meant. I'd been there. Ego disintegration can be terrifying and challenging for many, causing what some would label "bad trips." There can be a void, terrifying and vast, a black space much like the cosmos, that offers nothing. The silence and solitude are stultifying. But the best part comes next. Like dessert once you eat your vegetables, after the void comes the light, and merging with it brings intense comforting bliss—oceanic, boundless joy.

Psychedelic medicines can help us understand this vast boundlessness. They can help us prepare for death, not only helping us let go gently when we near the end, but more crucially letting us live all the life we have left. We'll talk with psychiatrist Dr. Jeff Guss, the director of Psychedelic Psychotherapy Training for the NYU Psilocybin Cancer Anxiety Study. "I don't think that the fear of death is as inconsolable as you think," he says. "The people in the cancer anxiety study are actually having an adjustment reaction to some really, really, really bad news. They're being called upon to face something we all have to face, which is our own mortality. And there's an antidote to that, which is love: loving people around you, loving life, loving yourself, caring, connecting, being present. That's the antidote, and that's the medicine. It's loving every minute you have and not dying before you die. And honestly, a lot of people get that from psychedelics. They realize, 'OK, I've gotta wake up and love my family, love every glass of orange juice that I have, and look at the trees, and take in the beauty of life every minute.'"

We'll talk with Dr. Katherine MacLean, who began her research career working with Roland Griffiths and Mary Cosimano at the Johns Hopkins Center for Psychedelic & Consciousness Research. While there, she published a key study showing that psilocybin-induced mystical experiences led to significant measurable increases in openness, one of the five broad personality domains (neuroticism, extroversion, openness, agreeableness, and conscientiousness). This was significant because before her study, these traits had been assumed to be relatively unchanging after the age of thirty. Then, after her sister died too young and too fast, MacLean began speaking about the experience of sitting with the dying, incorporating elements of her research on meditation, mindfulness, and psychedelics. This combination of disciplines and personal experience has led her to view death as a sacrament. She spoke about the recent death of her father and how death, she says, "keeps inviting me into this ongoing psychedelic, expansive growth experience."

In different ways, both Guss and MacLean see death and the influence it exerts on life as an existential opportunity. Both, in different ways, view the role of psychedelics as preparation. "One of the things that a spiritual experience helps people do is accept the inevitability of death," Guss says. "It helps you look at your life in retrospect and find meaning. And it helps you find what you want to do with the rest of your life." This perspective is not new. It has been a principle of basic palliative care for the past thirty or forty years. So how is it different today? "With psychedelics?" Guss asks. "It works better."

This is because psychedelics help to "reset" the brain. They are growth promoters and life shifters, in part because they're meaning makers. The resetting is part of a resettling. First, the default mode network is quieted, then there is a hyperconnection of nearly every other area of the brain. After all these areas communicate, things are never quite the same. The brain may have been "shaken up" a bit, and old ruts and trenches may have been smoothed over in the process. The most impressive resetting occurs with some of the strongest psychedelics. The anti-addictive ibogaine is highly effective in opioid detoxification, reducing withdrawal and craving. Is this part of the brain unlearning and relearning? It's not just that ibogaine is active at the opioid-receptor level, helping to reset the tolerance and dependence. It's also that this ultra–long-acting psychedelic provides a marathon of meaningful insights, helping to solidify changes in behavior.

How do psychedelics make things so meaningful? They activate semantic networks (which provide meaning to words) and secondary association areas (which provide context for whatever your brain is processing) via massive stimulation of one receptor in particular, the 5HT2A receptor. This is a particular kind of serotonin receptor being activated during the use of most every psychedelic you can name—LSD, psilocybin, ayahuasca, and other DMT-containing compounds. Further, the reason psychedelics can have an effect on reversal learning is because of this receptor. Some people call it the psychedelic receptor, and it's worth noting here that one of the reasons I consider cannabis to be a psychedelic is that high enough doses of THC will trigger the 5HT2A receptor. Certainly, cannabis is a meaning maker.

When examined through the lens of positive psychology, the study of healthy human functioning, we see that psychedelics have acute and long-term effects on many of the parameters that enrich our lives: mood, cognitive flexibility, prosocial behaviors, empathy, openness, nature relatedness, mindfulness, well-being, creativity, spirituality, and self-transcendence. And stimulating the psychedelic receptor is anti-inflammatory, which means it is pro-health. But the part that I still can't fully explain is this: Where does the oxytocin fit in? The psychedelic experience can't be fully understood via serotonin and nothing else, because how do you explain the neuroplasticity, and also the oneness?

So often the psychedelic experience peaks with a sense of connection with everything, that everything is connected. I kept looking for a connection between serotonin and oxytocin that could explain the peak oneness experience, and I finally found it in the months leading up to my talk at Esalen. On the morning I was to speak, pharmacology researcher Dr. Harriet Schellekens, away from work on maternity leave with her third child, emailed me a rough draft of the abstract for her new paper. In it, she describes a never-before-reported phenomenon: a dimerization of the serotonin receptor with the oxytocin receptor. This means that when 5HT2A receptors get stimulated enough with a psychedelic, they can form a union with the oxytocin receptors. This new receptor compound, the dimer, has a different shape altogether, and has different downstream effects from either receptor alone. These dimers, or "heteroreceptor complexes" (meaning they're made up of two different types of receptors), were seen in key areas in the brain associated with emotion, cognition, and social behaviors.

This sort of chemical cross talk—one neurotransmitter system interacting with another—is neither the norm nor the exception in the brain. With all our talk of "this neurotransmitter does this" and "that hormone does that," it's really more of a complicated soup. First of all, many of the compounds we've been learning about—oxytocin, vasopressin, serotonin, and dopamine—act as both neurotransmitters (within the brain) and hormones (between the brain and body). Second, all these different pharmacological systems interact, and third, even the receptors themselves are binding to one another and creating new docking sites with different conformations. Not only do oxytocin and the 5HT2A receptor create a dimer but the cannabinoid receptor CB1 also dimerizes with 5HT2A. Clearly, we can no longer match one brain chemical to one feeling or diagnosis.

PSYCHOANALYST OR SHAMAN?

As a psychotherapist, Jeff Guss brings an infectious level of enthusiasm to matching a presenting condition to a proven psychological approach. End-of-life anxiety in a cancer patient? Existential psychotherapy, he says, helps people face the two scariest aspects of life (death and freedom). Depression? Acceptance and commitment therapy, or ACT, which is designed to foster psychological flexibility and help people lead a values-driven life. So, it's not surprising that when he began to be interested in the clinical uses of psychedelic medicine in 2006, he headed straight to Switzerland with a few colleagues to celebrate the centennial of Albert Hofmann, the Swiss chemist who first synthesized (and later first ingested) LSD.

That mass gathering of psychedelic academia is remembered as the first convention to foreshadow the explosion of interest in the field that soon followed. There, Guss spoke at length with Charles Grob from UCLA, one of the first people to do research treating cancer-related anxiety with psilocybin-assisted psychotherapy. When Guss returned to NYU, he started a reading group that quickly morphed into a research group on psilocybin-assisted therapy, with the goal of launching a study. The principal investigator asked him to be the director of psychedelic training, even though Guss had never done any himself.

The proposed design called for participants to have two therapists present when the psilocybin medicine was administered, so Guss developed a dyad training program that would help the two therapists get in tune, if not in agreement, on existential issues, such as facing death and illness, and where they stood on questions of heaven, hell, and afterlife. "When someone is tripping on psilocybin, they are highly attuned and sensitive to things that are going on around them. We try to get them to turn inward, by using eyeshades and headphones, if they want it to be an inward journey. But they're also being watched over by two therapists, three feet away, for six hours. There's pressure to trust and be connected. In traditional psychotherapy, it might take months to work through basic trust. But in psychedelic therapy, we only have three sessions before the first dosing."

Guss also believes that the therapist (or therapy team) makes significant contributions to the psychedelic experience. There are some who think that therapists are there to act as nonspecific support people while the medicine does all the work, like "Florence Nightingale, a fluttering presence of kindness in the background." Guss finds this notion ridiculous and impossible.

Instead, Guss compares the role of the therapist in the psychedelic experience to that of the shaman; both are part of a three-way relationship established between the seeker, the medicine, and the guide. In some ways, for Westerners, the psychoanalyst may prove to be a more suitable match than a shaman, who often doesn't share a language with the typical psychedelic adventurer showing up in South America for a ceremony. On top of the language barrier, there's also the question of worldview: a shaman believes in concrete spirits. "They have a cosmology about jaguars and anacondas and literally seeing visions. We use a different language. We don't say, 'I became an antelope' or 'my grandmother appeared before me,' we say, 'I thought about my grandmother' or 'I felt like an animal.'"

Guss points out that the psychoanalyst, like the shaman, is trained in detecting the unseen, hidden, and unconscious realms, and both can help you reach into unknown, forbidden, put-away spaces and bring them into consciousness. On top of that, the psychoanalyst speaks in an idiom that Westerners can understand. "One of the beefs I have with the contemporary academic psychedelic research project is that it's somewhat anti-psychological." Currently, he says, the goal is evoking a mystical experience that, in controlled research conditions with carefully screened participants, is very effective at producing the kind of results that "the FDA says we want, in order to reschedule and make these medicines legal. So it's almost like the FDA is driving the conceptualization of psychedelics."

In this scenario, psychedelics have been reduced to medicines that evoke a mystical experience and make depression scores go down. I've heard these plant medicines referred to as "mysticogenic medicines," by my friend and colleague Charles Grob. I understand the reasoning. The mystical experience is really where science and spirituality interface. The spiritual epiphany correlates with the behavioral changes seen in the response to the experience. The larger and more intense the mystical experience, the greater its impact. But my assumption is that this name, "mysticogenic," isn't going to stick any better than entheogens, entactogens, empathogens, plasticogens (because: neuroplasticity), or any of the other names we've made up over the years to replace "psychedelic." And it's not going to matter much longer anyway, once the corporate cat is out of the bag.

Guss also gives expression to an anxiety that's common in the field—that in the race for FDA approval, we might be boxing ourselves in, ignoring broader applications of medicine that might be prohibited in the FDA's final Risk Evaluation and Mitigation Strategies, which is essentially a rule book for approved applications that might constrain a doctor's ability to prescribe. Compare the narrow view, Guss says, "to what the medicines really do in my opinion, which is a lot of things. They shatter your ego so you can build it back together again. They make you see the world in a fresh, new, dishabituated way. They increase your sense of connection to other human beings. They reduce your tight grip on your identity, which allows all of the things you think you are and all of the things you think you need to do to fall away, so you can discover a more transcendent self that is abiding and is always present. There are a lot of things that psychedelics do that we could talk about in human psychological language."

There's a broad range of psychological transformations that can happen with psychedelic medicines that Guss believes are being overlooked, simply because they're not directly useful in the race to reschedule the drug. "I think one of the things we're going to discover is that psychedelic therapy helps people get more out of a variety of therapies. There isn't one treatment that's best. Whatever kind of therapy you're involved in, a psychedelic experience may be valuable in helping you feel it more deeply, retain it more deeply, and change your brain—because psychedelics stimulate neuroplasticity."

Guss is a bracing presence in the psychedelic world, strict and delightful at the same time. "One of the things I dislike about psychedelics is that it has become a magnet for all kinds of half-baked hodgepodge of religious tropes from all over the place, from yoga and chakras to crystals and herbology. Any old alternative thing, people like to bring that into psychedelics. People think I'm stuffy, but I think we're working in psychology and psychiatry. If people want to be Hindu psychedelic workers, that's a religious use. Mine is a Western psychiatric, psychoanalytic humanistic approach that believes that even deep spirituality and mystical states can be humanist. They're based in the natural world and don't require the existence of a supernatural power. I'm much more of a 'they reveal the things that are in you' kind of person." Guss changes when describing the sessions themselves. He seems to set aside his skepticism and critical eye and lead with his empathy. "Most, not all, but most of my psychedelic sessions have been peaceful and beautiful experiences," he says. By design, both the clinicians and the participants do not know whether the dosage is a placebo or an active drug. Still, Guss says he's able to feel whether the person is tripping or napping. "If they're very quiet, you can imagine what they're feeling. Sometimes they have a big smile on their face. Sometimes they have tears of joy—not sobbing, or painful, but tears of joy coming out of their eyes. And I feel that I'm just the luckiest person in the world to be able to be part of this." And he's not thrown on the rare occasions when someone is in distress. "I'm very familiar with people being in distress in intense therapy situations," he says. "No therapist in the world is going to get very far if they can't tolerate people being upset."

He can recall only a single case when he was actually afraid for someone on the medicine. It happened in the cancer anxiety study with a heavy woman, over three hundred pounds. In every case, the dosage is based on weight—so many milligrams of psilocybin per kilo. Ideally, at this ratio, any trauma or psycho-spiritual distress that surfaces comes at a therapeutic rate, so the patient is able to talk and process it "like an old-fashioned Freudian concept of catharsis," Guss says, "leading to relief." Though this woman got a large dose because of her weight, she had no more blood circulating in her brain than a woman who weighed a hundred and fifty pounds. With that much psilocybin, the woman "lost contact with us and we lost contact with her." She became nonresponsive to stimuli. She was moving around, obviously agitated and uncomfortable, groaning and moaning, making the noises of someone in pain. She was bald from her cancer, and the wig on her head had become cockeyed, so she looked even more disturbed. Guss and his cotherapist both worried that they had overdosed her. "She came down, later than we thought. Normally, people finish around 3:00 or 3:30 and by [4:00] you're talking and eating a snack. At 5:00, they're going home. But she was still out of it at 6:30. She didn't start to become connected until 7:00. And the amazing thing was that when she started coming out of it, she said it was beautiful. It was so profound and wonderful. She said, 'I could tell you were upset, Jeff. I could tell you were worried about me. I couldn't speak, but I could feel that you were upset. I wanted to reassure you, but I just couldn't.' And that helped me trust in the medicine even more."

The problem that cancer patients face, Guss says, is they lose touch with what gave their life meaning and become nothing more than a cancer patient, a body riddled with irregular cells and fear. Everything is lost except tumor markers, when their next blood work or CAT scan is, what medications they're on, the next time they're going to throw up. "What we tried to do was help people get back in touch with what really matters to them. And the other thing people have to do is accept that they're going to die. And one of the things that a spiritual experience helps people do is accept the inevitability of death."

THE LAST RETORT

Like Guss, Katherine MacLean (she'll always be KMac to me) is looking beyond the push for approval to the challenges of the next phase of psychedelic medicine. One of the drawbacks of the medical approach, she says, is the current emphasis on the "initiatory experience" and the therapeutically useful effects of the mystical experience. Her focus now has shifted to how to integrate that experience meaningfully into a daily practice. "To me, it matters less and less what happens when you're taking the psychedelic, and it matters more and more what you're doing with those experiences in your ordinary life."

MacLean cofounded and was the first director of the Psychedelic Education and Continuing Care Program in New

York City, where she led training workshops and monthly integration groups focused on increasing awareness and reducing the risks of psychedelic use. The push to integrate the lessons has led her to work with community-based groups like Psychedelic Sangha in New York City, and Tam Integration in Oakland, California, which are providing safe spaces for meditation, using roughly the same quiet, supportive, inward-looking settings as in the medical model, but designed for groups.

The Oakland group was aided by the fact that in June 2019, the city decriminalized psychoactive mushroom use—the actual ordinance referred to "entheogenic plants" in general. In fact, they were the second city to do so after Denver in May of that year. This trending shift in legal status allowed for a more or less open forum for the group psychedelic experience to take place. She considers this model a viable alternative to "the only other thing that's being talked about, which is having one person in a room with one or two doctors" a lengthy and labor-intensive structure whose only parallel in the medical system is chemotherapy. Many in the field are coming to view the accepted two-on-one research design as expensive and impractical in the long run once it's introduced into wider use. She says, "I don't see people coming in for psychedelic infusions in the same way they go in for chemotherapy."

Her advocacy for the community approach—a more practical and, in the long-term, perhaps more meaningful method for the administration of a medicine that promotes connection—is not the only major shift in thinking that she has undergone lately. MacLean has changed her own work from clinical research to private practice. This is in part due to the death of her sister Rebecca in January 2013, at the age of twenty-nine, from aggressively metastatic breast cancer. She took a sabbatical from Johns Hopkins soon after that, and left for good when the sabbatical ended. Over that time, she thought a lot about death and her sister's last days.

MacLean had stayed with Rebecca for much of that time, holding her hand, talking with her, providing whatever comfort she could. "The thing that's nicer about the psychedelic work," she said, "is that it's time limited. No matter what happens, it's going to be resolved in eight hours. It can be a safer feeling as a facilitator, because there's an arc and the person will return to some sense of their normal self and then they can do the integration. I think sitting with real death, in those last days, is more intense because it's so unknown. You don't know how long it's going to be or what's going to happen."

Something she felt with the dying that she never experienced as a psychedelic facilitator was extrasensory perception. "When my dad and sister were dying, I felt like there was a way of communicating that was not of the ordinary senses. I felt—and this gets more and more powerful after death—that there are ways that they communicate with me that don't make sense scientifically." That experience has led her to consider traditions that have emphasized death "as a birth into something new." Buddhism talks about enlightenment, Christianity talks about life as preparation for the final moment, "the ultimate letting go of everything you know, and opening up into something that no one has ever told you about."

The thinking she did after Rebecca's death helped her to reframe the psychedelic experience as "one thing that helps us prepare for the thing there's no preparing for." From a harm-reduction standpoint, embarking on a psychedelic experience didn't seem appropriate when you're in the process of dying, since it could run the risk of bringing up traumatic experiences that you'd have no time to integrate. But the opposite situation may be the more serious problem: too often people undergo an "initiatory experience" without addressing what they should be doing over a lifetime in light of that experience. "If an eighteen-year-old has a mystical experience, how does that help them die sixty years later? Psychedelics can be a helpful medicine for death, but not necessarily as an experience proximate to death itself. I'd love to see people have lifetime integration. Have your experience, then integrate it over your life. That's what's going to help you die peacefully."

Psychedelics, she warns, are not a cure. They're not like going in for surgery, where you get the operation, do a little rehab, and then you're good to go. "You're really opening up someone to a lifetime of engaging directly with their own experience, which can certainly be joyful and amazing and a better way of life than prior to the psychedelic experience."

When people ask her about taking psychedelics, she has a list of simple things that she encourages people to do first. At this point in the book, her list should sound very familiar.

- Assess the things in your life that you can change without psychedelics: conversations you need to have, relationships that need to be addressed. Then address them.
- Start a simple ten-minute meditation practice. It doesn't have to be a religious practice; just sit still, notice how you feel, and watch your thoughts.

- Spend time outside in nature. If you live in the city, find a park. Connect to something outside of your head. Find a tree and sit with your back against it.

It's better to have these practices in place before you consider psychedelics, because, she says, "psychedelics are like a beautiful storm. And right after the storm, there can be debris. You're kind of figuring out, 'What is this new landscape?' So if you have these healthy practices in place, then even as you're picking your way through the aftermath of the storm, you keep doing those practices." She warns about one thing that doesn't often appear in the medical literature: how, in the weeks following the mystical experience, people begin to question everything. They'll suddenly say, "I'm going to quit my job" or "I'm going to get a divorce." But it's not a good idea to make big changes right away. MacLean counsels them in that situation to keep sitting with the experience, keep going outside in nature. "I always say, 'Wait a couple of weeks, then after a couple of weeks, wait six more months.'"

And your integration has to work on every level, she says. "You don't just integrate the self and assume that your family relations are going to be good or that you have the community piece in place. I think community is going to end up being the key to all of it," she says. "I urge people to be cautious about psychedelics. But for most people, if they have a strong community, it ends up being a safe choice. I feel more cautious about a medical clinic, because there's no community there. You're just an individual going into a clinic, but then you're an individual coming back to what?"

She can envision a happy marriage between the two camps, where you'd have an individual experience covered by insurance, a clinical process to see that you have a safe reaction and to make sure you're not one of those people who'd have an unexpected bad trip. And after that it would be safe to continue the experiences in the community. She's not proposing a screening process, with some authority deciding whether it's okay for you. It would simply be the recommended practice, especially for people with psychiatric conditions who are at greater risk for an adverse response. "But psychedelics aren't even remotely the most dangerous thing we let people do in our society," she says. "We have to remember that the bar for entry shouldn't be safety. It should be education and informed consent."

MacLean is less interested now in these gateway protocols than in how psychedelics can inform an individual practice. "The psychedelic experience teaches you about how to live your life. I get excited about people finding their personal religion," she says. "That thing that will sustain you at all the difficult points of your life. And that's actually the most radical thing about psychedelics—they give every single individual the empowerment to access the divine in themselves. There's no intermediary. That's also the scariest aspect. It scares the medical doctors. I think it rightfully scares governments. It's a lot of power that you're reminding individuals that they have."

This power is also a responsibility. MacLean cites a friend, Bett Williams, who went to Mexico to participate in a traditional mushroom ceremony. When she asked them, "How can I do this when I get back home?" they told her, "Well, don't do what we've done. You have to take the mushrooms and ask the mushrooms what you do, and then do that. It has to be a living practice."

MacLean has quietly put together her own observances with small personal rituals that began when she started with scattering her sister's ashes, first on the farm where she lived, and then on flowers. That turned into planting a garden, which helped her bury a lot of difficult emotions and grief. Seeing the flowers that grew out of that, she says, was a psychedelic experience in itself. "It was like death was the beginning of the teaching, but I hadn't translated that into creation." Now she has a personal altar, a kind of ancestor worship, with items of personal meaning.

"Maybe it's possible to experience death in a very ordinary way," she says. "But for me, every time I go through it, it's like a mystical experience." Her father, like her sister, was not interested in taking psychedelics at the door of death. He'd come of age when acid was popular, and he'd followed the Grateful Dead. But he'd set all that aside to become a corporate attorney, and taking psychedelics now, at the end of life, felt like a Pandora's box he didn't want to open.

MacLean is often asked questions along this line, about death and psychedelics. "I tell this to everyone who says, 'Should I offer my dying loved one psychedelics?' I say, 'See what happens when you take the psychedelics and just be with them, because a lot of what we want for others, we actually want for ourselves.' For many people, death takes care of itself. It's already an altered state. It's psychedelic in and of itself. But psychedelics can help the people who are watching and witnessing. That's where the current emphasis on the medical approach kind of has it backwards. Maybe the loved ones and the caregivers and doctors need the psychedelics and the dying people are fine. They're already going through this amazing process. We just need to stop trying to cure them or treat them."

She didn't have any startling experiences with her father when he was on his deathbed. Instead, she said, there were a lot of sweet, ordinary moments and a lot of the kind of intimacy that she'd never had with him back when he was still tough and in control. But once he couldn't walk or talk, it was a lot easier for the two of them to relate. The armor was gone.

After he died, at home, MacLean did sit vigil with her father. The hospice nurse signed off on the death certificate. She and a few family members moved her father from the hospital bed to his own bed in his own room. They cranked up the AC to keep the room colder. And she spent that night with him. She was the first person in the funeral director's career who'd ever asked to keep the body overnight. She told him that it was important, that she was doing these rituals, like the Irish do at a wake, or Orthodox Jews do with a body until burial. They keep it company. She was a Buddhist, and this was her ritual.

The funeral director said that typically, people don't want to keep the body around. MacLean later learned that there are laws in every state in the country that allow you to keep a loved one's body for three days after death. In Buddhism, she says, they believe that it takes three days to complete the dying process, which continues well after the breath has left the body. There are subtle energies that take longer to complete. She remembers thinking, *If this is my dad's chance, I don't want to screw it up.* "My brother and I sensed a lot of movement and energy in my dad's body. I don't know. Is that a hallucination? But by the next day, I felt like whatever it was that had to be completed was complete. And that's when the funeral director came."

"I don't know if I would have done any of that if I hadn't had my psychedelic experiences to teach me that his body wasn't just a dead body and there was something to learn there," she said. In some way, she felt that her experience with psychedelics had given her the confidence to make that demand to keep the body. "It's such a weird thing to ask. But psychedelics are so weird that it's taught me that it's okay to do weird things, to do the thing that's not ordinary." The hospice nurse clearly thought the request was unusual but signed off on it anyway. "I feel like the experiences I had first with my sister in the hospital and then with my dad at home were informed by my psychedelic experiences. It's hard to pinpoint. It's not psychedelic itself: it's not flashy, there are no visions. But it felt psychedelic."

As a former clinical researcher, MacLean is careful to frame the lessons she's drawn from death and psychedelics, especially the communications she says she still gets from her sister and father, in a way that leaves room for skepticism. "The extreme materialist interpretation is, I am now more open to interpreting the things I see in the world as meaningful, and giving them a meaningful connection to my sister or my dad. There may not be anything supernatural going on."

But, she says, "my experience of it is that it is not my imagination." The day her dad was cremated, she felt it was important to attend the cremation. Again, not a typical request. The folks who run the crematorium are not in the business of dealing with living people. They don't provide psychological support. They aren't equipped to deal with family members sitting in the waiting room for the two hours or more that it takes to reduce a body to ashes. The funeral director was there, coaching her. He told her, "Your dad will be in a cardboard box. You won't be able to check one more time to see that it's him. You'll have to trust me that it's his body." She went in to say a final prayer and a thick metal door rose up and they slid the box into the retort.

"They gave me the choice to press the button to start it. And I chose to," she says. "The whole time, I'm keeping in mind the Buddhist understanding that my dad is still present and that it's my job to help him move on without traumatizing him. So actually in my mind I'm talking to him and saying, 'Your body is going in this thing. You are not your body. This is your body that's being burned. You are not your body. This is you letting go of who you were in this life. But you are not that person.' I'm doing this in a very focused frame of mind. While all this is happening, I feel fine, I feel ordinary. I say goodbye to the funeral director. I get in the car.

"As soon as I start driving, I can't even describe what happened. It was like these rushes of energy. It felt like the experience of fire going through my body but without burning—a huge release of energy and emotions. I was laughing and crying. And I was like, I shouldn't be driving. This is so unsafe." So she pulled over and googled a place where she could just sit and have a cup of coffee. A "Leo's Diner" popped up, but she couldn't find it, so she pulled over again, and sat listening to the same music she listened to during her dad's vigil two nights before.

"I was in a very altered state. But finally I got clear enough that I could figure out where this diner was. And the weird thing was, it was in a town I knew well. I'd driven past this place a thousand times and never even knew the diner was there. That made me pay attention. Now this is where you'll either laugh and be like this lady is crazy, or you'll get it.

"I walk into the diner and there's a little sign that says 'Today's Special: Hakuna Matata Tea.' I'm going to cry when I tell you this. I was like, You've got to be kidding me. My dad, it was our joke that his motto was 'Hakuna Matata.' Like, 'No Worries.'"

MacLean is a popular figure, and her TED Talk, "Open Wide and Say 'Awe,'" in which she talks about her own death—a profoundly dissociative experience she had on a plane trip to Vegas that appears to have been something like a drug-free, open-eyed ego death—is riveting to listen to. The content is incredible, but so is MacLean's style of speaking. She's calm and scientific in her descriptions of the most unusual occurrences. She also speaks at a meditative pace, collected and amused, with inviting silences that make the stories even more charged, as it helps you imagine yourself in the scenes she describes.

"What the hell is Hakuna Matata tea?" MacLean says. "That's not a thing. It doesn't exist. I've never seen it anywhere. No one has ever said to me 'Hakuna Matata tea.' I've never seen it on a menu. It's not a meme. It's not in this world. This sign is basically my dad saying, 'Don't worry, it's fine.' And I was just like, 'My god, it is going to be okay.' And I sat down and got that stupid tea and it was like iced tea with Italian ice, those frozen iced lemon things right in the iced tea.

"It was like the universe just made it up this moment. This thing that has never been served before. This could only be my dad: as soon as he was released from his body, he was able to communicate with me in this completely irrational way. But I knew he was saying, 'Don't worry.' And: 'This is me. I don't want you to mistake this for a coincidence. The only way I can get you to pay attention is for it to be so unbelievable but so personal.' And you know, really skeptical people will hear that story and think it's just a cute little thing that my mind conjured up. But my direct experience was that it was a real communication.

"Maybe it's my personality type that made me first get interested in psychedelics. But I certainly think that psychedelics have made me more open to things like that over the years. So I'm thankful. If these are the ways I can now draw meaning beyond my five senses, like, bring it on. It helps me feel connected. I guess that's my wish for others, too. That they get beyond psychedelic elementary school, and they move beyond the place where you are temporarily healed from the things that you think are your problems, and that they actually get to experience the truly wild, unexplained landscape of what it means to be here as a human being in this universe."

Kmac and I, and countless other psychedelic researchers and partakers around the world, agree. These plant medicines are good for the soul. And there's no branch of medicine yet that deals with the soul, although I would argue that psychiatry's been doing it for years and just not calling it that. I do know that antidepressants and tranquilizers aren't going to get at the root cause of all of our symptoms. They can't spackle over the cracks in our deep spiritual disconnection, and they can't provide meaning to our journey. The psychedelic medicines, by dispelling the illusion of separation and offering deeply meaningful lessons, help to make us feel more whole.

If fear is closed, then love is open. Open is when the growth, repair, and rewiring happen. But these medicines aren't the only things that can help to open us up. Awe can do that, and the restorative power of nature, and belonging, and being held, believed, and seen.

If we can only stay awake and stay present, fully here and now, that is enlightenment. If we don't abandon the present moment, or ourselves, our partners, children, community, or our planet, then we needn't abandon our destiny. For unity, for community, for peace, the answer is simple. Separateness is the enemy. Be one.

EPILOGUE:
CHASING THE MIST

Until you make the unconscious conscious, it will
direct your life and you will call it fate.

—CARL JUNG

We bike the short ride to the lake in the predawn chill, stash-
ing the bikes next to a stone wall away from the road, and
hike the steep path down to the dock. I take baby steps,
avoiding anything that might roll, like a stone or horizontal
stick. Dirt provides the most traction. Falling is a bitch. I hate
that adrenaline drop-off after the initial rush; it's like bad
speed.

The sun is just peeking up over the hills, and swaths of the
sky are the same shade of faded salmon that rich people wear
to lawn parties in July. There are streaks of crimson accented
with pink and yellow, a magical display of nature performed
every morning for those who rise at dawn.

We stand on the dock, admiring the view. As the summer
wanes and autumn commandeers the aesthetic, cooler nights
and warmer water create a ballet of air made visible. Sunlight
streams through choruses of air currents, impregnated with
microdroplets. Where it is wispier, clouds of mist hover a

foot above the lake, loitering, coalescing and disintegrating, forming and reforming, moving gracefully from nothing, into nothing.

We get on our paddleboards and head out toward the rope swing on the eastern side of the lake. There are no homes there, only an abandoned railroad spur, so the shoreline is forest, the leaves beginning to turn ocher and auburn.

There is no mist right around the dock, but it is thick toward the edges of the lake, in the distance. I want to be where the mist is, I want it to envelop me so that I can disappear. I paddle toward it.

It is off in the distance, just ahead of me, if I just paddle a bit more, I can see it farther on. But the closer I get, the more it seems to keep disappearing. I can see it ahead of me, but not around me. It's like I'm dispelling it away from me as I move into it. I keep paddling, but it always seems to be just out of reach, just up ahead of me, but not around me.

I stop and very carefully turn the board around. I get a look at where I've just paddled. From the dock to here, there is a thick layer of mist. Ahead of me, behind me, off in the distance in every direction, there is mist.

But not where I am.

As my paddling changes the lighting, the mist collapses into shadow. I can feel the cool, moist air clinging to my legs, so I know it's still there. It feels like mist, but I can't see it.

It's only when the light is right that I can see it at all, and around me, the angle is all wrong.

Boy, if that's not a metaphor for life in America, I don't know what is. We're so focused on the horizon, on what's next, on striving to get where we think we need to be, that we don't realize we're already there. What we want, we already have; we just can't see it because of our perspective. Like the dust motes in the living room air, momentarily visible in afternoon light, they're always there whether we see them or not.

Too often, when we finally get the thing we thought we wanted, it's not quite enough. We're not satisfied, not satiated, not even relieved by the acquisition. Is that all there is? This is known as the dialectic of desire, and it drives much of our behavior. Set a goal, accomplish the thing, and then realize it doesn't really feed your soul, as you set another goal.

Whatever we're chasing, it is all around us whether we see it or not. Happiness is there for the taking; opportunity surrounds us, invisible. We are hamster-wheeling, swiping left, not stopping to appreciate what we have, how far we've already come, to see that heaven isn't what's promised after we die; we're knee-deep in it now.

I saw that what we were paddling through had a quality of animation, of aliveness—a spirit. Mists are like the breath of the earth, the visible exhale of a lake on a frosty morning.

Breathing deeply and consciously is an instant way to become embodied, and coordinating breathing with a partner can help to put both of you in para. (Conspiracy means breathing together. Consider your partner to be a coconspirator.) But what do we call it when we're breathing in synchrony with the earth?

The word "spirit" comes from the root word for "breathing." And this lake, on this morning, is a spiritual experience, seeing this breath of nature and feeling a connection with it.

If we could see this complex, flowing spirit we're bathing in all the time, it would be beautiful, distracting, and ultimately profound, a trip without psychedelics, like living in a Van Gogh painting.

We know now that connecting with natural beauty can induce awe, and that awe can reduce narcissism, helping us to feel small. We also know that psychedelics can tamp down that narcissism by temporarily quieting the default mode network. Psychedelics can help us to unlearn (remember reversal learning), to become a little less neurotic and a lot more open. These medicines can help us to rediscover parts of ourselves that we've buried or simply lost touch with. And as a society, they can help us cure our "planetary PTSD."

Right now, as I type this, Australia is on fire. Once again, we're on the brink of war (today it's Iran). Rates of suicide, diseases of despair, and loneliness continue to rise. On any given day, things can seem dire, terrifying, and hopeless.

But also right now, people are taking to the streets to protest war or bring awareness to the climate crisis. More states are rolling out medical cannabis programs or legalization to combat the opioid crisis, and after a four-year nosedive, life expectancy statistics are just starting to improve. Activists in cities and counties all over the United States are working toward decriminalizing mushrooms and other psychedelic plants. Social media campaigns like #ThankYouPlantMedicine are destigmatizing their use, allowing people to "come out" and come together. People with histories of trauma, addiction, depression, eating disorders, and autism are sharing their stories of healing, growth, and change with cannabis, psilocybin, ayahuasca, or ibogaine. More people are experimenting with microdosing mushrooms or LSD, and also with anti-addictive medicines that are typically given in "flood doses," like ibogaine and ayahuasca. We are understanding more and more every day how neuroplasticity enables new behavior.

New psychedelic research sites are springing up at major institutions like Massachusetts General Hospital and Columbia University Medical Center. All over the world, a new "green rush" is coming, with nonprofit companies like Usona and for-profit companies like Compass developing psilocybin to treat depression. MedMind is one company developing a derivative of ibogaine to treat opioid dependence, and I imagine there will be more. MAPS, a public benefit corporation, continues to fund the development of MDMA in its promise to treat PTSD. MDMA is also being studied to treat alcoholism, just as LSD was so many decades ago. More studies are under way to understand the ability of psilocybin or LSD to combat the existential suffering around death, and we continue to explore just how psychedelics can unleash creativity.

If we ever needed less suffering and more creativity, it is now. We need outside-the-box solutions to our current psychospiritual problems.

The creativity enabled by psychedelics stems from increased connectivity in the brain, between areas that don't usually communicate. The same thing can happen on a personal level. We can connect with parts of ourselves that seemed lost, or we can open up new avenues of discussion with our partners. We can also choose to connect more fully with our families, or to other people outside our usual circles. All these ways of connecting more deeply lead to a deep healing, to cinching up the ties that bind.

I tried an experiment recently, talking to the disc in my living room.

"Alexa, I'm lonely."

"I'm sorry to hear that. Talking to a friend, listening to music, or taking a walk may help. I hope you feel better soon."

Empathy. Connection. Music. Go outside. Hope with me. What more could you wish for? It's almost enough.

ACKNOWLEDGMENTS

My mother always tells people how my first few words were "I do myself." I was always pushing others away to prove how independent and self-sufficient I was. I want to thank my parents for encouraging my go-it-alone tendencies. They got me very far. However, this book has been a humbling project, in that I simply could not do it alone and had to ask for help. But in being vulnerable, I created more connections. Many people helped to shape and form this project. As always, the earliest ideas were fanned into flames by my partner, artist and writer Jeremy Wolff. I went around in circles on this book more than any other, and he was right there with me, helping me to track down the truth.

Thank you to everyone at WME: Andrea Blatt, Lauren Szurgot, Elizabeth Wachtel, and especially my agent, Suzanne Gluck, who gave me the space I needed and put up with nine iterations of book proposals before we hit on something that felt right. My publisher, Karen Rinaldi, was such a ballbuster you wouldn't believe, but I love her for the lessons she imparted, and I am in awe of her mastery. (This openness of awe created an opportunity for deep learning.) At Harper Wave, I'd like to thank Rebecca Raskin, assistant editor, for coordinating us all, and editor Haley Swanson for her expert eye and probing questions. Thank you, Bonni Leon-Berman, for your beautiful book design, and Janet Rosenberg, for your meticulous copyediting, reinforcing the fact that I never seem to know when to use "that" versus "which," and neither does Kevin Conley, who helped me put this whole thing together top to bottom, inside and out.

Many people were interviewed for this book and most are included by name. But there are others who have informed my thinking that need to be added, like Andrew Tatarsky, harm reduction guru; Bia Labate, ayahuasca anthropologist agitator; and Andrew Weil, alternative medicine founder. Others provided key information for *Moody Bitches* that remains crucial to *Good Chemistry*, like Gábor Maté (don't ask why the addiction; ask why the pain), Harville Hendrix and Helen Hunt (couples concepts), Charles Nichols (psychedelics as anti-inflammatory), and Charles Raison (isolation as pro-inflammatory and anti-learning). Joe Dolce, Gary Greenberg, David Luz, David Presti, and Doug Rushkoff all helped me "think out loud," working out my attempts at a unified theory of connection, and I appreciate their time and encouragement. Michael Pollan was kind enough to indulge me in my concerns of redundancy between our books, and so entertained emails about oxytocin, orgasms, and neuroplasticity.

I wish to thank the patients in my practice. I learn so much about human nature, and my own humanity, while caring for others. I have also seen firsthand the limits of prescription psychiatric medicines and the promise of psychedelics for people with a history of trauma and substance-use problems. I'm so glad we have more options now for true, deep healing.

Many thanks to my family, for putting up with my distant stares while I worked out my preoccupations, and my locking myself away for hours at a time instead of being with you. Lastly, Jeremy and I are so supremely grateful for our circle of friends, artists, musicians, farmers, and healers. The music playing, hikes, potlucks, and saunas nourish our souls. Thank you, Jay Erickson, for talking with me one morning on the train about tribes and rituals, providing an important piece to the puzzle of unity, and for being the great connector that you are. And to Gabrielle Semel, my friend and yoga instructor, who often offered the exact dharma talk I needed to keep me headed in the right direction.

We teach best what we need to learn most. I am still trying, every day, to practice what I preach, to walk the talk. I thank all the people in my life, especially my children, Molly and Joe, who help to keep me honest and enable my emotional integrity.

GLOSSARY

5HT2A receptor: the site in brain cells where many serotonergic psychedelics dock and exert their effects

Adrenaline: a chemical released from the adrenal glands that helps to raise heart rate and blood pressure, preparing the body to fight or flee; often accompanied by cortisol

Alexithymia: the inability to recognize or describe one's emotions

Amygdala: the fear center of the brain; associated also with aggression and anger (the plural is amygdalae)

Anandamide: the main internal cannabis molecule, or endocannabinoid, that enhances pleasure and appetite, helps to tamp down the stress response, and is metabolized by FAAH

Anterior cingulate cortex: a part of the brain where attention, emotion, and memory interact; responsible for emotional regulation and processing; felt to be overactive in depressive disorders

Awe: an altered state of extreme openness conducive to learning

Ayahuasca: a psychedelic tea brewed from two ingredients, *Banisteriopsis caapi* (the ayahuasca vine, a source of harmine that inhibits the enzyme that would break down DMT) and *Psychotria viridis*, a shrub often called "chacruna," which contains DMT—this combination allows DMT to be orally active

BDNF: brain-derived neurotrophic factor, a chemical secreted by brain cells that fosters growth of neurons, driving neuroplasticity

Cannabinoid: any cannabis-like molecule that stimulates the endocannabinoid system, often by binding to cannabinoid receptors

Cannabis: the medical name for marijuana

CB1: the cannabinoid receptors found in the brain

CB2: the cannabinoid receptors found everywhere else in the body, including the white blood cells, skeleton, muscles, liver, spleen, bladder, and uterus

CBD: cannabidiol, a noneuphoric component of the cannabis plant

Cortisol: a stress hormone released from the adrenal glands that acutely suppresses immune function and raises blood sugar levels; often released with adrenaline

DMN: default mode network, a circuit of interacting brain areas that are active when the brain is at rest, not focusing on outside stimuli

DMT: dimethyltryptamine, a short-acting psychedelic that is usually smoked; it can be made orally active by the addition of an enzyme inhibitor called MAOI (mono-amine-oxidase inhibitor)

Dopamine: the neurotransmitter that underlies salience, motivation, and reward

Endocannabinoid: internal cannabis-like molecules like anandamide and 2AG (2-Arachidonoylglycerol)

Endocannabinoid system (ECS or ECB): a body-wide system to fight inflammation, maintain metabolism, and enhance resilience

Endorphin: an internal opiate-like chemical that activates the opiate receptor, causing pain relief or pleasure

fMRI: an imaging technique for measuring and mapping brain activity

Hippocampus: the brain's memory center, it is also involved with emotional regulation

Hypothalamus: the part of the brain involved in balancing temperature and appetite regulation, circadian rhythms, sexual desire, and other functions via hormone release

Integration: either a uniting of the various parts of the self, or the practice of weaving the lessons learned in the psychedelic session into your day-to-day life

Interoception: awareness of inner bodily sensations

Insula: the part of the brain that helps integrate bodily sensations and emotional experiences, facilitating self-awareness

Limbic system: a circuit of brain structures involved with motivation and emotion

LSD: lysergic acid diethylamide, a longer-acting psychedelic

Macrodose: the more typical, full dosage of a psychedelic

Major histocompatibility complex (MHC): molecules on the surface of cells that help to dictate immune responses and compatibility, as in organ transplants

MDMA: methylenedioxymethamphetamine (i.e., Ecstasy, X, or Molly), a stimulant that increases oxytocin and serotonin activity, with heart-opening properties

Microdose: a smaller dose of a psychedelic, or any medicine; typically around one-tenth of the usual dosage, sometimes taken every third day (Fadiman protocol) or five days on, two days off (Stamets protocol)

Mirror neurons: brain cells that fire both during action and during the perception of that action in another

Neuron: brain cell

Norepinephrine: an activating neurotransmitter involved in anxiety and vigilance

Neuroplasticity: the growth of brain cells; new connections being made

Neurotransmitter: a chemical in the brain that allows two neurons, or brain cells, to communicate

Nucleus accumbens: part of the reward circuitry, thought to be involved with motivation

Opioid: any chemical that mimics opium in acting on the opioid receptors

Oxytocin: a hormone secreted in massive amounts during childbirth and orgasm, which often acts, in other moments, as an agent of intimacy, empathy, connection, driving a cascade of chemicals that affect receptors in the body's internal opiate and cannabis systems, enabling social learning and moderating fear

Parasympathetic: the nervous system responsible for "rest, digest, and repair"

Phenylethylamine (PEA): an amphetamine-like neurotransmitter thought to be present during orgasm and love at first sight.

Polymorphism: different versions of inherited genes

Prisoner's dilemma: a situation sometimes used in psychological testing, in which two research subjects each have two options whose outcome depends crucially on the simultaneous choice made by the other; two people acting in their own self-interest won't yield the best outcome

Proceptive behavior: the extent to which a female initiates mating

Proprioception: knowing where your body is in space

Psilocybin: the active ingredient in hallucinogenic mushrooms

Psychonaut: one who explores altered states or "inner voyages"

PTSD: post-traumatic stress disorder, a cluster of symptoms among survivors of trauma

Receptor: a site on a nerve cell where a neurotransmitter docks

Salience: a neurological term for importance, or standing out; crucial for attention

Serotonin: a neurotransmitter involved in mood, social behavior, memory, and appetite, derived from tryptophan (an amino acid); its chemical name is 5-hydroxytryptamine

SSRI: selective serotonin reuptake inhibitor; antidepressant medicines like Prozac, Zoloft, Lexapro and others, which block the recycling of serotonin into the "sending" neuron, allowing more serotonin to get across to the "receiving" neuron

Sympathetic: the nervous system responsible for the fight-or-flight response

Synaptogenesis: a type of neuroplasticity; the growth of new synapses (spaces between nerve cells)

THC: tetrahydrocannabinol, the main psychoactive ingredient in cannabis

SELECTED BIBLIOGRAPHY

For the full version of notes and references, please go to drholland.com/good-chemistry.html.

Books

Allione, T. *Feeding Your Demons: Ancient Wisdom for Resolving Inner Conflict*. New York: Little, Brown and Company, 2008.

Alter, A. *Irresistible: The Rise of Addictive Technology and the Business of Keeping Us Hooked*. New York: Penguin Press, 2017.

Amen, D. G. *Change Your Brain, Change Your Body: Use Your Brain to Get and Keep the Body You Have Always Wanted*. New York: Harmony Books, 2010.

Becker, E. *The Denial of Death*. New York: Simon & Schuster, 2007.

Brown, B. *Braving the Wilderness: The Quest for True Belonging and the Courage to Stand Alone*. New York: Random House, 2017.

Cacioppo, J. T., and W. Patrick. *Loneliness: Human Nature and the Need for Social Connection*. New York: W. W. Norton & Company, 2008.

Carr, N. *The Shallows: What the Internet Is Doing to Our Brains*. New York: W. W. Norton & Company, 2011.

Churchland, P. S. *Braintrust: What Neuroscience Tells Us about Morality*. Princeton, NJ: Princeton University Press, 2018.

Dispenza, J. *Evolve Your Brain: The Science of Changing Your Mind*. Deerfield Beach, FL: Health Communications, Inc., 2008.

Doidge, N. *The Brain's Way of Healing: Remarkable Discoveries and Recoveries from the Frontiers of Neuroplasticity*. New York: Penguin Books, 2016.

Duhigg, C. *The Power of Habit: Why We Do What We Do in Life and Business*. New York: Random House, 2012.

Elkind, D. *The Power of Play: How Spontaneous, Imaginative Activities Lead to Happier, Healthier Children*. New York: Da Capo Lifelong Books, 2007.

Epstein, M. *The Trauma of Everyday Life*. New York: Penguin Books, 2013.

Faber, A., and E. Mazlish. *How to Talk So Kids Will Listen & Listen So Kids Will Talk*. New York: Simon & Schuster, 2012.

Gawande, A. *Being Mortal: Medicine and What Matters in the End*. New York: Metropolitan Books, 2014.

Gazzaley, A., and L. D. Rosen. *The Distracted Mind*. Boston: PBS Distribution, 2013.

Hari, J. *Lost Connections: Uncovering the Real Causes of Depression—and the Unexpected Solutions*. New York: Bloomsbury USA, 2019.

Harpignies, J. P., ed. *Visionary Plant Consciousness: The Shamanic Teachings of the Plant World*. New York: Simon & Schuster, 2007.

Hendrix, H. *Getting the Love You Want*. New York: Henry Holt and Company, 1988.

Holland, J., ed. *The Pot Book: A Complete Guide to Cannabis*. New York: Simon & Schuster, 2010.

———. *Moody Bitches: The Truth about the Drugs You're Taking, the Sleep You're Missing, the Sex You're Not Having, and What's Really Making You Crazy*. New York: Penguin Press, 2015.

Horgan, J. *Rational Mysticism: Spirituality Meets Science in the Search for Enlightenment*. Boston: Houghton Mifflin Harcourt, 2004.

Janov, A. *The Biology of Love*. Buffalo, NY: Prometheus Books, 2010.

Junger, S. *Tribe: On Homecoming and Belonging*. New York: Twelve, 2016.

Kohn, A. *Unconditional Parenting: Moving from Rewards and Punishments to Love and Reason*. New York: Simon & Schuster, 2006.

Labate, B. C., and C. Cavnar, eds. *The Therapeutic Use of Ayahuasca*. New York: Springer, 2013.

Levine, S., and O. Levine. *Who Dies?: An Investigation of Conscious Living and Conscious Dying*. New York: Anchor Books, 2012.

Levine, P. A. *In an Unspoken Voice: How the Body Releases Trauma and Restores Goodness*. Berkeley, CA: North Atlantic Books, 2010.

Levine, P. A., and M. Kline. *Trauma-Proofing Your Kids: A Parents' Guide for Instilling Confidence, Joy and Resilience*. Berkeley, CA: North Atlantic Books, 2014.

Levine, P. A., and A. Frederick. *Waking the Tiger: Healing Trauma: The Innate Capacity to Transform Overwhelming Experiences*. Berkeley, CA: North Atlantic Books, 1997.

Lewis, T., F. Amini, and R. Lannon. *A General Theory of Love*. New York: Vintage Books, 2001.

Luke, D. *Otherworlds: Psychedelics and Exceptional Human Experience*. London, UK: Muswell Hill Press, 2017.

Mate, G. *In the Realm of Hungry Ghosts*. Berkeley, CA: North Atlantic Books, 2010.

Metzner, R. *Green Psychology: Transforming Our Relationship to the Earth*. New York: Simon & Schuster, 1999.

Miller, W. R., and J. C'de Baca. *Quantum Change: When Epiphanies and Sudden Insights Transform Ordinary Lives*. New York: Guilford Press, 2001.

Nichols, W. J. *Blue Mind: The Surprising Science That Shows How Being Near, In, On, or Under Water Can Make You Happier, Healthier, More Connected, and Better at What You Do*. New York: Little, Brown and Company, 2014.

Pieper, M. H., and W. J. Pieper. *Smart Love*. Charlotte Hall, MD: Recorded Books, 1999.

Pollan, M. *How to Change Your Mind: What the New Science of Psychedelics Teaches Us About Consciousness, Dying, Addiction, Depression, and Transcendence*. New York: Penguin Books, 2019.

Porges, S. W. *The Polyvagal Theory: Neurophysiological Foundations of Emotions, Attachment, Communication, and Self-Regulation*. New York: W. W. Norton & Company, 2011.

Richards, W. A. *Sacred Knowledge: Psychedelics and Religious Experiences*. New York: Columbia University Press, 2015.

Roszak, T. E., M. E. Gomes, and A. D. Kanner. *Ecopsychology: Restoring the Earth, Healing the Mind.* San Francisco: Sierra Club Books, 1995.

Rushkoff, D. *Team Human.* New York: W. W. Norton & Company, 2019.

Stoller, K. *Oxytocin: The Hormone of Healing and Hope.* Scotts Valley, CA: CreateSpace, 2012.

Turkle, S. *Alone Together: Why We Expect More from Technology and Less from Each Other.* New York: Basic Books, 2011.

Van der Kolk, B. A. *The Body Keeps the Score: Brain, Mind, and Body in the Healing of Trauma.* New York: Penguin Books, 2015.

Zak, P. J. *The Moral Molecule: Vampire Economics and the New Science of Good and Evil.* London, UK: Transworld Digital, 2012.

Selected Articles

Bowen, M. T., and I. D. Neumann. "Rebalancing the Addicted Brain: Oxytocin Interference with the Neural Substrates of Addiction." *Trends in Neurosciences* 40 no. 12: 691–708.

dos Santos, R. G., and J. E. C. Hallak. "Therapeutic Use of Serotonergic Hallucinogens: A Review of the Evidence and of the Biological and Psychological Mechanisms." *Neuroscience & Biobehavioral Reviews* 108 (January 2020): 423–34. https://www.sciencedirect.com/science/article/pii/S0149763419309649.

Feduccia, A. A., and M. C. Mithoefer. "MDMA-Assisted Psychotherapy for PTSD: Are Memory Reconsolidation and Fear Extinction Underlying Mechanisms?" *Progress in Neuro-Psychopharmacology & Biological Psychiatry* 84 (2018): 221–28.

Griffiths, R. R., W. A. Richards, U. McCann, and R. Jesse. (2006). Psilocybin Can Occasion Mystical-Type Experiences Having Substantial and Sustained Personal Meaning and Spiritual Significance. *Psychopharmacology* 187, no. 3 (2006): 268–83.

Hendricks, P. S. Awe: A Putative Mechanism Underlying the Effects of Classic Psychedelic-Assisted Psychotherapy. *International Review of Psychiatry* 30, no. 4 (2018): 331–42.

Holt-Lunstad, J., T. B. Smith, M. Baker, T. Harris, and D. Stephenson. "Loneliness and Social Isolation as Risk Factors for Mortality: A Meta-Analytic Review." *Perspectives on Psychological Science* 10, no. 2 (2015): 227–37.

Hysek, C. M., Y. Schmid, L. D. Simmler, G. Domes, M. Heinrichs, C. Eisenegger, . . . and M. E. Liechti. "MDMA Enhances Emotional Empathy and Prosocial Behavior." *Social Cognitive and Affective Neuroscience* 9, no. 11 (2013): 1645–52. https:// academic.oup.com/scan/article/9/11/1645/1681238.

Iacoboni, M. "Imitation, Empathy, and Mirror Neurons." *Annual Review of Psychology* 60 (2009): 653–70. https://www .annualreviews.org/doi/abs/10.1146/annurev.psych.60 .110707.163604.

Kettner, H., S. Gandy, E. C. Haijen, and R. L. Carhart-Harris. "From Egoism to Ecoism: Psychedelics Increase Nature Relatedness in a State-Mediated and Context-Dependent Manner." *International Journal of Environmental Research and Public Health* 16, no. 24 (2019): 5147. https://www.mdpi.com/1660–4601/16/24/5147.

Lebedev, A. V., M. Kaelen, M. Lövdén, J. Nilsson, A. Feilding, D. J. Nutt, and R. L. Carhart-Harris. "LSD-Induced Entropic Brain Activity Predicts Subsequent Personality Change." *Human Brain Mapping* 37, no. 9 (2016): 3203–13. https://www .semanticscholar.org/paper/LSD-induced-entropic-brain- activity-predicts-Lebedev-Kaelen/590f892cb4582738e836b22 5a293e2692f8552e0.

MacLean, K. A., M. W. Johnson, and R. R. Griffiths. "Mystical Experiences Occasioned by the Hallucinogen Psilocybin Lead to Increases in the Personality Domain of Openness." *Journal of Psychopharmacology* 25, no. 11 (2011): 1453–61. https://www .ncbi.nlm.nih.gov/pmc/articles/PMC3537171/.

McGregor, I. S., and M. T. Bowen. "Breaking the Loop: Oxytocin as a Potential Treatment for Drug Addiction." *Hormones and Behavior* 61, no. 3 (2012): 331–39. http://ivmedicalcenter.com/wp-content/uploads/2018/10/Breaking-the-loop-Oxytocin-as-a-potential-treatment-for-drug-addiction.pdf.

Mithoefer, M. C., A. T. Mithoefer, A. A. Feduccia, L. Jerome, M. Wagner, J. Wymer, J. Holland, and R. Doblin. "3, 4-methylenedioxymethamphetamine (MDMA)-Assisted Psychotherapy for Post-Traumatic Stress Disorder in Military Veterans, Firefighters, and Police Officers: A Randomised, Double-Blind, Dose-Response, Phase 2 Clinical Trial." *The Lancet Psychiatry* 5, no. 6 (2018): 486–97. http://www.prati.org.il/wp-content/uploads/2019/01/23.pdf.

Mithoefer, M. C., C. S. Grob, and T. D. Brewerton. "Novel Psychopharmacological Therapies for Psychiatric Disorders: Psilocybin and MDMA." *The Lancet Psychiatry* 3, no. 5 (2016): 481–88.

Nardou, R., E. M. Lewis, R. Rothhaas, R. Xu, A. Yang, E. Boyden, and G. Dölen. "Oxytocin-Dependent Reopening of a Social Reward Learning Critical Period with MDMA." *Nature* 569 (2019): 116–120.

Panksepp, J., B. Herman, R. Conner, P. Bishop, and J. P. Scott. "The Biology of Social Attachments: Opiates Alleviate Separation Distress." *Biological Psychiatry* (1978).

Piff, P. K., P. Dietze, M. Feinberg, D. M. Stancato, and D. Keltner. "Awe, the Small Self, and Prosocial Behavior." *Journal of Personality and Social Psychology* 108, no. 6 (2015): 883. https://www.apa.org/pubs/journals/releases/psp-pspi0000018.pdf.

Sales, A. J., M. V. Fogaça, A. G. Sartim, V. S. Pereira, G. Wegener, F. S. Guimarães, and S. R. Joca. "Cannabidiol Induces Rapid and Sustained Antidepressant-Like Effects through Increased BDNF Signaling and Synaptogenesis in the Prefrontal Cortex." *Molecular Neurobiology* 56, no. 2 (2019): 1070–81. https://

www.drperlmutter.com/wp-content/uploads/2018/12/CBD-BDNF.pdf.

Twenge, J. M., T. E. Joiner, M. L. Rogers, and G. N. Martin. "Increases in Depressive Symptoms, Suicide-Related Outcomes, and Suicide Rates Among U.S. Adolescents After 2010 and Links to Increased New Media Screen Time." *Clinical Psychological Science* 6, no. 1 (2018): 3–17. https://journals.sagepub.com/doi/full/10.1177/2167702617723376.

Zelenski, J. M., and E. K. Nisbet. "Happiness and Feeling Connected: The Distinct Role of Nature Relatedness." *Environment and Behavior* 46, no. 1 (2014): 3–23. http://shinrin-yokusweden.se/wp-content/uploads/2016/08/happiness_and_feeling_connected-2014-zelenski-3–23.pdf.

INDEX

ABOUT THE AUTHOR

JULIE HOLLAND is a psychiatrist specializing in psychopharmacology. Her private practice in New York City was established in 1995, while she worked weekends at Bellevue Hospital's psychiatric emergency room. Holland is a medical monitor for many MAPS-supported studies utilizing MDMA-assisted psychotherapy or testing strains of cannabis with varying CBD/THC ratios in veterans with PTSD. On several scientific advisory boards for cannabis, she consults frequently on various drug-related documentaries and assists in forensic cases where drugs are involved. Holland has been involved for decades in US drug-policy reform based on harm-reduction principles. She lives among friends and nature in New York's Harlem Valley with her husband and their two children. You can learn more at NaturalMood.com.